W9-BKF-141

PRAISE FOR A PREVIOUS EDITION OF

Washington, D.C.
Off the Beaten Path®

"These well-researched, straightforward guides take travelers to
popular spots as well as more obscure corners."
—*National Geographic Traveler*

Help Us Keep This Guide Up to Date

Every effort has been made by the author and editors to make this guide as accurate and useful as possible. However, many changes can occur after a guide is published—establishments close, phone numbers change, hiking trails are rerouted, facilities come under new management, etc.

We would love to hear from you concerning your experiences with this guide and how you feel it could be improved and be kept up to date. While we may not be able to respond to all comments and suggestions, we'll take them to heart, and we'll make certain to share them with the author. Please send your comments and suggestions to the following address:

The Globe Pequot Press
Reader Response/Editorial Department
P.O. Box 480
Guilford, CT 06437

Or you may e-mail us at: editorial@GlobePequot.com

Thanks for your input, and happy travels!

INSIDERS' GUIDE®

OFF THE BEATEN PATH® SERIES

Off the
Beaten Path®

FOURTH EDITION

washington, d.c.

A GUIDE TO UNIQUE PLACES

WILLIAM B. WHITMAN

INSIDERS' GUIDE®

GUILFORD, CONNECTICUT
AN IMPRINT OF THE GLOBE PEQUOT PRESS

The prices, rates, and hours listed in this guidebook
were confirmed at press time. We recommend,
however, that you call establishments to obtain
current information before traveling.

To buy books in quantity for corporate use
or incentives, call **(800) 962–0973**
or e-mail **premiums@GlobePequot.com**.

INSIDERS' GUIDE®

Copyright © 2001, 2003, 2005, 2007 by Morris Book Publishing, LLC

Text design by Linda Loiewski
Maps by Equator Graphics © Morris Book Publishing, LLC
Illustrations by Carole Drong
Spot photography throughout © Jon Feingersh/Masterfile

ISSN 1541-5201
ISBN-13: 978-0-7627-4217-2
ISBN-10: 0-7627-4217-8

Manufactured in the United States of America
Fourth Edition/First Printing

D.C.'s one and only area code is 202. When calling from outside the District, all of the phone numbers in this book (unless otherwise noted) can
be reached by using the 202 area code.

To Cameron, my patient wife, editorial assistant,
and boon companion from the District
to Dubrovnik and lots of places in-between.

Contents

Acknowledgments

I'd like to thank my editors at The Globe Pequot Press, Laura Strom, Shelley Wolf, and Hrissi Haldezos for their skillful help, sympathetic support, and occasional forbearance in making this guide a reality. Thanks also to friends who told me about their favorite off-the-beaten-path places and to the Washington, D.C. Convention and Visitors Association, which provided valuable advice and information. And last but by no means least, let's not forget Cultural Tourism D.C., which, through its activities and its fascinating book, *Capital Assets,* is helping the District rediscover and rebuild the hidden places that contribute so much to its rich cultural fabric.

Introduction

As world capitals go, Washington is small and compact, but the settlement on the Potomac that became America's capital has traditionally packed a planetary political punch as the capital of the world's sole superpower. But, closer to home, Washington is also experiencing an urban renaissance. The benefits of better government, including a plunging crime rate, have restored the city's sense of pride and powered investments downtown, where the construction crane has seemingly replaced the Washington Monument as the city's symbol.

And it's more than just real estate. The excitement also extends to the District's lively cultural and arts scene where internationally renowned institutions like the Kennedy Center, the Shakespeare Theatre, and the National Gallery of Art are being joined by small experimental theaters and flocks of new and imaginative art galleries. And, as you're about to find out, Washington's renaissance also includes seemingly nonstop openings of exciting new restaurants and hotels. Although President Kennedy once quipped that Washington is a town of "southern efficiency and northern charm," it's certain that today he'd want to, as they say on Capitol Hill, "amend his remarks."

All of this is very good news for travelers, who have an extraordinary and expanding variety of visit choices. Most tourists often follow well-worn paths to wander through Official Washington, which lines Pennsylvania Avenue from the White House to Capitol Hill, and, of course, Monumental Washington, the marble palaces of government and megamuseums that line the Mall from the Capitol to the Lincoln Memorial. And it's only right that tourists and first-time visitors see the great symbols of our nation's heritage and democracy. But, as Cultural Tourism D.C., which promotes visitor travel to Washington's vibrant neighborhoods, points out, "these sites are overcrowded; tourists are seeing only a fraction of what there is to see."

Tourists become travelers when they move off the Mall to explore Washington's historic neighborhoods to see great history, art, and culture without the crowds and packaging. This guide is aimed at taking you and other urban adventurers to Washington's secret places, where you'll visit often overlooked spots (some even in downtown Washington) that most visitors miss and most other guidebooks don't even mention. That's why you won't find the Capitol, the great Mall Museums, including the Holocaust Museum and the National Gallery, and other much-visited attractions in this guide. What you will find are the city's hidden corners where you can explore art galleries, great architecture, world-class house museums, cultural landmarks, restaurants, and even shops that are indeed "Off the Beaten Path."

History

As you might have guessed, Washington became our capital as part of a political deal, in this case a 1790 trade-off of Southern congressional support for funding Northern state debts in exchange for moving the capital from Philadelphia to a southern location. George Washington determined that the new capital should be at the confluence of the Potomac and Anacostia Rivers, between the thriving ports of Georgetown, Maryland, and Alexandria, Virginia. Washington hired a young Frenchman, Pierre-Charles L'Enfant, who had been one of his staff officers at Valley Forge, to design the new capital. Peering down from the hill that now holds Arlington Cemetery and Lee House at a rural valley of woods and marshlands, L'Enfant saw instead a monumental city—the "Territory of Columbia"—a dream capital with parks, canals, fountains, grand public buildings, and an orderly grid of north-south and east-west streets overlaid by broad diagonal boulevards.

The Grid

Although some of L'Enfant's original plans may have faded away, that combination of a street grid and diagonal avenues, which now bear the names of all fifty states, remains today, sometimes to the confusion of visiting motorists trying to navigate the traffic circles at many of the places where grid and diagonal intersect.

The grid itself is pretty simple: North-south streets are numbered; east-west streets are lettered, starting with A, but there is no J, X, Y, or Z Street. When the east-west grid runs out of single letters, it continues in alphabetical order with two-syllable streets (Adams, Belmont, Channing, and so on), until it reaches Windom or Yuma, after which it resumes in alphabetical order with three-syllable names (Appleton, Brandywine, and so on).

Washington is divided into four quadrants—Northeast (NE), Northwest (NW), Southeast (SE), and Southwest (SW)—which converge at the dome of the U.S. Capitol, the geographic center of Washington. The dividing lines of those quadrants—North Capitol Street, East Capitol Street, South Capitol Street, and the National Mall—radiate out from the Capitol. For example, an address with NW in its street name means the street is north of the Mall and west of North Capitol Street. Pay careful attention to the quadrant abbreviation that follows the street name; seemingly identical addresses can occur in all four quadrants, and you don't want to learn the hard way that the corner of 17th Street and Pennsylvania Avenue NW is a long, long way from that of 17th Street and Pennsylvania Avenue SE.

Getting in from the Airport

A taxi from Dulles Airport costs around $60.00 and the 26-mile ride takes about forty-five minutes. Dulles to downtown bus service is available only via the West Falls Church Metro stop; the bus-Metro connection takes about an hour and costs $8.00 one-way for the Washington Flyer bus, the Metro Trip will run another $2.65. A cab from Reagan National Airport to your hotel should run around $15.00 and take twenty minutes. You can also take a blue or yellow line Metrorail from National Airport to downtown Washington for $1.65.

Both Dulles and National are served by the "Super Shuttle," which will take you and other passengers to and from your hotels. Call 296–6662 to book a seat, or look for the blue van in the taxi area; rates to downtown Washington are around $22.00 from Dulles and $10.00 from National; www.supershuttle.com.

Although Dulles has no direct rail or Metrorail connections with downtown Washington, here's a tip about a bus service known only to District Denizens. You can avoid an expensive 26-mile cab ride to and from Dulles by taking Metrobus line 5A, which connects Dulles with the Metro station at L'Enfant Plaza, conveniently located on the yellow, green, orange, and blue lines. The trip takes fifty-five minutes and will cost you only $3.00 from Dulles Airport. Buses run hourly seven days a week from 5:30 A.M. to 11:35 P.M. For exact times visit www.wmata.com/timetables.

Washington's third airport is Thurgood Marshall Airport a.k.a. Baltimore-Washington International, always referred to as BWI (www.bwiairport.com), and located much nearer Baltimore than D.C. A taxi from BWI to the center of Washington will run you anywhere from $55.00 to $70.00 and take about an hour. However, for a much cheaper and more satisfactory trip, take the free shuttle bus (marked "BWI Rail") from your arrival area about a mile to the airport's rail station, then take either a MARC commuter train or Amtrak to Union Station, where you can grab a Metro ride to your destination. Another option is to take the BWI Express Metro bus (Route B-30) service that connects the airport with the Greenbelt Metro station; buses leave every forty minutes and cost $3.15. For more information about rail connections, call the BWI Rail Station, (410) 672–6167; Amtrak, (800) USA–RAIL; or MARC, (800) 325–RAIL. Super Shuttle vans also service BWI and cost $26.00 to $32.00 each way; reserve by phoning (800) 258–3826; www.supershuttle.com.

Getting Around

If you enjoy dense traffic, dueling over nonexistent parking spots, and negotiating diabolically difficult traffic circles, you'll love driving in the District. Otherwise, give your jalopy a rest and take advantage of the fact that Washington is compact and a great walking town. Washington is also blessed with an excellent, modern subway system called Metrorail, which starts service at 5:00 A.M. weekdays and 7:00 A.M. weekends. It closes at midnight, except on Friday and Saturday, when the witching hour is 3:00 A.M. Metrorail stations are marked by tall columns that bear a big "M," along with the colors of the lines that serve that station.

Metro fares range from $1.35 to $3.90 depending on the length of the ride and the time of day (rush hour fares are more expensive). You can also buy one-day passes for unlimited travel for $6.50 and there's also a seven-day pass for $32.50.

Because Metro is fast, reliable, and safe, it is usually the best way to get around the city, and the places in this guide are often, but not always, keyed to Metro travel and the name of the nearest stop. When Metrorail is not feasible, there's a good chance that the city's excellent Metrobus system will get you there, and the appropriate route will be given. Metrobus fares run from $1.25 to $3.00 depending on the route; since drivers don't carry money, you'll need exact change when boarding. For more information about Washington's public transit system, go to www.wmata.com or phone 637–7000.

Washington has an excellent alternative to Metrobus service in the *"D.C. Circulator,"* a fleet of twenty-nine snazzy, big-windowed buses that operates two express routes that criss-cross the city at the bargain rate of $1.00 per trip (50 cents for seniors). One route runs east-west from Union Station to Georgetown via the Washington Convention Center and K Street. The other is a north-south line from the Convention Center through Chinatown and the Mall to the Southwest waterfront.

A third route makes a continuous loop around the Mall from 9:30 A.M. to 6:00 P.M., stopping at each of the Smithsonian museums and the National Gallery of Art. This is clearly a route designed to spare tourists a case of the dreaded "museum feet." The Mall line will connect with both the east-west and north-south lines, making for a seamless bus service for visitors. To find the nearest stop on any route and start circulating, just look for the spiffy red and silver CIRCULATOR sign. 962–1423; www.dccirculator.com.

Although many Washington taxis are vintage items that belong in the Smithsonian and not in front of it, they are plentiful, relatively inexpensive, and handy for getting around in unfamiliar or edgy neighborhoods. Keep in mind that, unlike most U.S. cities, Washington's taxis do not use meters, relying instead on a zone system so arcane that it can be fully fathomed only by experienced readers of the *Congressional Record*. Minimum fare: $6.50.

Shady Grove
Rockville
Twin Brook
White Flint
Grosvenor
Medical Center
Bethesda
Friendship Heights

Washington D.C.

Glenmont
Wheaton
Forest Glen
Silver Spring

Takoma

Greenbelt
College Park-U of Maryland
Prince George's Plaza
West Hyattsville

Maryland

Tenleytown-AU
Van Ness-UDC
Cleveland Park

Georgia Ave–
Petworth
Fort Totten

Woodley Park-Zoo
Dupont Circle
Farragut North

Columbia
Heights
Shaw-Howard
Univ.

U-Street
Cardozo

Brookland-CUA

Rhode Island Avenue

New Carrollton
Landover
Cheverly
Deanwood
Minnesota Avenue

Rosslyn

Foggy Bottom-GWU
Farragut West

McPherson
Square

Metro Center

Federal Triangle

Mt. Vernon Sq.-UDC
Convention Center

Union Station

Gallery Place
Chinatown

Judiciary Sq.

Archives-
Navy Memorial

Smithsonian

L'Enfant Plaza

Federal Center SW
Capitol South
Eastern Market
Potomac Avenue
Stadium-Armory
Benning Road
Capitol Heights
Addison Road-
Seat Pleasant

Vienna/Fairfax-GMU
Dunn Loring/Merrifield
West Falls Church-VT/UVA
East Falls Church
Ballston-MU
Virginia Square-GMU
Clarendon
Courthouse

Arlington Cemetery

Pentagon
Pentagon City
Crystal City

Water-Front-SEU
Navy Yard
Anacostia

Virginia

National Airport
Braddock Road
King Street
Eisenhower Avenue
Huntington

Van Dorn Street

Franconia–
Springfield

Metro System Legend

= Red Line–Glenmont to Shady Grove

= Orange Line–New Carrollton to Vienna

= Blue Line–Addison Road to Franconia

= Green Line–Anacostia to Greenbelt

= Yellow Line–Huntington to Mt. Vernon Square

Transfer Station

Station Stop

Fees, Prices, and Rates

The good news is that most of Washington's great attractions, both on and off the beaten path, are free. In fact, sightseeing in the nation's capital is a free-loader's dream. Unless this guide mentions an admission fee, you can assume that there isn't one.

Restaurants and lodgings are another matter. Washington consistently ranks as one of America's most expensive cities. This guide will give you an indication of what you can expect to pay for meals: under $15 is considered inexpensive, $15 to $35 is moderate, and $35 and up is expensive.

When it comes to lodgings (a standard double, excluding the District's 13 percent room tax), $125 and under is considered inexpensive, $125 to $225 is moderate, and $225 and up is expensive.

Sources of Info

After you arrive, you'll have several excellent sources for news of what's happening while you're in Washington:

The *Washington Post* (www.washingtonpost.com) is a great national newspaper, but it also pays close attention to its home town. The daily Metro and Style sections are prime sources of news about what's going on, while the Friday Weekend magazine always carries an extensive listing of cultural and other events of the moment.

Washington City Paper (www.washingtoncitypaper.com), widely distributed everywhere (and free!), carries an exhaustive compilation of tours, concerts, and museum happenings, along with highly professional exposés about what's really going on in D.C. Even if you're just hanging out and not thinking much about culture, *City Paper* is for you.

The *Washingtonian* (www.washingtonian.com), the city's local magazine, is very strong on gallery schedules, details about what's happening at local museums, and superb restaurant coverage. Pick one up for both operational information and a good feel for what Washington is all about.

capitalquote

"Wherever else an American citizen may be a stranger, he should be at home in his nation's capital."

—Frederick Douglass, 1877

If you've arrived by air, you've surely seen *Washington Flyer* (www.fly 2dc.com), which is widely circulated at Dulles and National airports. Unlike the usual airport freebie publications, *Flyer* is a magazine with heft and content that will help you get around very nicely, from its front-of-the-book articles on local attractions to its listings of Washington sights, museum happenings, and restaurants. Best of all, *Washington Flyer* regularly covers off-the-beaten-path places like the ones you're going to see.

Washington contains some of the most distinctive and historic residential architecture found in any American city, from the rarified Federal precincts of Georgetown and the opulent Beaux Arts mansions of Embassy Row to the brownstones and bay fronts of many less exalted neighborhoods. If you'd like to know more about the architects and designs you're seeing, be sure to arm yourself with the *American Institute of Architects (AIA) Guide to the Architecture of Washington, D.C.*

Visitor information and hotel reservations are available from the Washington Convention and Tourism Corporation, 901 Seventh Street NW (789–7000, www.washington.org) and the D.C. Chamber of Commerce Visitor Information Center, Ronald Reagan Building, 1300 Pennsylvania Avenue NW (first floor, east side); 328–4748; www.dcvisit.com. Open spring and summer Monday to Friday 8:30 A.M. to 5:30 P.M. and Saturday 9:00 A.M. to 4:00 P.M. Closed Sunday. In fall and winter the center is open Monday to Friday 9:00 A.M. to 4:30 P.M., but closed Saturday and Sunday.

One of the most valuable sources of tourist information on culture and history is Cultural Tourism D.C., a 160-member organization dedicated to promoting the city's cultural life and the tourist potential of Washington's historic neighborhoods. You'll find their Web site, www.culturaltourismdc.org, to be an indispensable source of information about what's going on while you're in town, including a calendar of events, walks through historic neighborhoods, and general information about the District (661–7581).

Washington now has a radio station dedicated to giving visitors the latest news about visiting hours and other information about the city's parks, monuments, and memorials. The station, which is operated by the National Park Service and transmits on 1670 kilocycles AM, can be heard within a 3-mile radius of the National Mall. It will also give you information about some of the places covered in this book on a program called (and this is surely not just a coincidence) *Off the Beaten Path*.

Tour Groups and Organizers

Although there's no shortage of trolley and bus tours to take you to the usual sites, off-the-beaten-path exploration requires more specific and close-up help, ideally a walking or bus tour with a knowledgeable guide. Here are a few to consider, along with a specialized possibility or two:

Anecdotal History Tours. Most Sundays from 11:00 A.M. to 1:00 P.M., tour guide Anthony Pitch takes a group to some of D.C.'s hidden corners. The rotating list includes Georgetown, Around the White House, White House to the Capitol, and Adams Morgan. For a schedule, call (301) 294–9514 or go to www.dcsightseeing.com. Cost is $15 per person. Groups by appointment.

Bike the Sites. Daily three-hour guided bike tours follow paths and trails to visit a number of sites in the District, including Capitol Hill and Georgetown. The $40 price per person includes bike rental, entrance fees, and snack. Tours can be arranged for small groups, so think about family touring. Visit www.bikethe sites.com online or call 842–2453.

City Scooter Tours. If you'd like to explore some of the city's main monuments and either prefer not to hoof it or need mobility assistance, think about an electric scooter tour. Guided tours of the National Mall and Tidal Basin cost $75, last three hours, and cover 6 miles of historic real estate. Walk-up rentals are also available on an hourly and daily basis, starting at $35 for the first two hours. Tours leave from the Bike the Sites kiosk in the Old Post Office Pavilion at 1100 Pennsylvania Avenue, NW, Wednesday and Sunday from 10:00 A.M. to 1:00 P.M. and on Friday 7:00 to 10:00 P.M. Call (888) 441–7575 or visit www .cityscootertours.com.

City Segway Tours. Sightseeing on a Segway, those futuristic two-wheeled electric scooters, is lots of fun and will also take you to zip around to see the monuments. Four-hour tours (including a driver training session) are held at 10:00 A.M., rain or shine. Tours are given daily from April to October and cost $70 per person. Phone (877) 734–8687 or visit www.citysegwaytours.com. It's a good idea to reserve ahead.

D.C. Ducks will take you on a ninety-minute tour of Washington's streets aboard a World War II amphibious troop carrier, after which you'll splash into the Potomac for a short cruise. The charge is $27.00 for adults and $13.50 for kids four to twelve. Call 832–9800 or peek at www.dcducks.com.

Spy Drive. Since Washington is said to be the world's spy capital, it's only natural that someone has organized a tour of the city's espionage attractions. In this case "someone" means a group of former (they say) CIA, KGB, and FBI operatives, who will show you all the top secret sites. No security clearance necessary, just call (866) 779–3748 or check out www.spytrek.com. Private groups of up to 50 only.

Symbols of America. OK, if you still can't resist taking a peek at the well-beaten path, a unique way to visit the Mall and surroundings is this cell phone tour narrated by Larry King. Just dial a local number on your phone at each of the tour's fifteen stops and Larry will give you an earful about what you're seeing. The tour costs $5.95, and you can sign up at 396–8687 or online at www.talkingstreet.com.

Washington Photo Safari. Instead of depending on trite and corny postcards as reminders of your Washington visit, think about making some personal travel statements with your own photographs. On Wednesday and Saturday veteran photographer E. David Luria offers tours of the city's neighborhoods, monuments, and memorials. Along the way you'll receive professional advice about finding just the right perspective, lens, or exposure to capture your own D.C. memories. Walking safaris take three hours. Bring your own camera. Half-day tours, $69; full day, $119. Call (877) 512–5969 or 537–0937; the Web site is www.washingtonphotosafari.com.

Tour D.C. Local writer-historian Mary Kay Ricks offers highly knowledgeable ninety-minute walking tours of Georgetown and Dupont Circle, and other neighborhoods. Call (301) 588–8999 or visit www.tourdc.com for details. Price: $15 for individuals, $350 for groups.

Washington Walks has a wide selection of walks to visit a number of places in this book, plus a "Capital Hauntings" tour to some of the city's ghostly places. Each walk starts at a Metro station, lasts two hours, and costs $10.00 per person; $5.00 for kids under twelve. For details, call 484–1565 or check out www.washingtonwalks.com. Tours are given April through October. No reservation needed.

Art on Call

In the days before 911 and cell phones became the way to report emergencies, D.C.'s metropolitan policemen, while pounding their beat, used street corner call boxes to phone and check in with their local stationhouse. After 1976, when the 911 system made them obsolete, these boxes were slated for removal. However the District's tourist authorities stepped in and rescued them from oblivion by launching "Art on Call," a program for artists to turn these boxes into community icons with tiny sculptures and paintings depicting important historical facts about their neighborhood. That's why, on your walks through Washington you'll see a number of these clever little boxes, each of them brightly repainted and highly informative for visitors like you. This guide will point out a number of them on its wanderings through Washington.

Annual Events

Washington has literally hundreds of special events every year, but listed here are a few of the city's leading festivals, shows, and special tours. Because the dates for many of these occasions vary from year to year, for most events, you'll also find a phone number or Web site where you can find exact dates and more information. The *Washington Post* and *City Paper* are also excellent sources for the latest about these and other major events.

JANUARY

Martin Luther King Jr. Birthday Celebration. Performances, exhibits, and readings all over the city commemorate the life and legacy of the human rights leader (http://godc.about.com).

FEBRUARY

Black History Month at the Smithsonian. Monthlong exhibitions and activities reflecting African-American history and culture (633–4820; www.smithsonian education.org/heritage_month).

Chinese Lunar New Year Parade. Chinatown parade along H Street NW plus fireworks, dragon dancers, and lion dancers (508–5438 or 638–1041).

Washington Boat Show. Hundreds of boats ranging from dinghies to motor yachts (703–823–7960; www.washingtonboatshow.com).

Abraham Lincoln Birthday Celebration. Reading of the Gettysburg Address at the Lincoln Memorial on February 12 (619–7222).

Frederick Douglass Birthday. Frederick Douglass National Historic Site on February 14 (426–5961).

MARCH

St. Patrick's Day Parade. Thousands cheer along Constitution Avenue as the Irish march, the dancers dance, and the bagpipes play (637–2474; www.dcstpats parade.com).

Smithsonian's Annual Kite Festival. Held the last Saturday in March at the Washington Monument (357–3030; http://kitefestival.org).

LATE MARCH OR EARLY APRIL

Cherry Blossom Parade and Festival. Thousands of cherry blossoms, a parade, and a Festival Queen to boot. For details call the Festival Committee at 661–7584 or visit www.nationalcherryblossomfestival.org.

Washington Home and Garden Show. Display gardens with thousands of flowers and trees that are all in full bloom in the Washington Convention Center (703–823–7960).

APRIL

White House Spring Garden Tour. See the great White House gardens while military bands serenade. Get your tickets at the visitor pavilion on the Ellipse (456–2200; www.whitehouse.gov/news).

Annual White House Easter Egg Roll. Children ages three to six gather on the White House South Lawn; older children roll their eggs on the Ellipse. Eggs and live entertainment are provided and, just maybe, an appearance by the president. Call 208–1631 or 456–2121 for into about tickets; www.white house.gov/easter.

Smithsonian Craft Show. More than 100 leading American artisans display and sell their textiles, ceramics, wood, metal, and glass. Held at the National Building Museum (357–4000; www.smithsoniancraftshow.org).

Georgetown House Tour. One weekend each spring some of Georgetown's grandest private homes are open to the public (338–2287; tickets and more details at www.georgetownhousetour.com).

MAY

Georgetown Garden Day. A self-guided walking tour of dozens of beautiful gardens (965–1950; www.georgetowngardentour.com).

The National Cathedral Flower Mart. Flower booths, crafts, and demonstrations, held the first weekend in May (537–3185; www.cathedral.org).

Annual Candlelight Vigil Ceremony. National Law Enforcement Officers Memorial (737–3400; www.nlemf.com/calendar).

Memorial Day Weekend Concerts. The National Symphony Orchestra performs on the West Lawn of the Capitol (619–7222; www.pbs.org/memorialday concert).

Memorial Day Ceremonies. Arlington National Cemetery. (703–607–8585), Vietnam Veterans Memorial (634–1568), and the U.S. Navy Memorial (737–2300). And don't forget the Memorial Day parade down Independence Avenue, starting at 11:00 A.M.

MAY–AUGUST

Twilight Tattoo. At 7:00 P.M. every Wednesday in May and June the U.S. Army Military District of Washington stages a stirring sunset parade on the Ellipse, south of the White House. The U.S. Army Band plays and the army's precision drill team performs. Seating in the bleachers or on the lawn is first come, first served (685–2888; www.usarmyband.com).

Outdoor Sculpture

Washington is supercharged with grandiose outdoor sculpture, much of it decorating federal buildings or paying official tribute to American leaders. But there's a parallel world of unconventional work in D.C. that's sure to revive your interest just when you're sated with the usual tourist fare. Local art maven and sculptor Vlad Lehovich shares his offbeat favorites.

PENNSYLVANIA QUARTER AND CHINATOWN

Viewed from the north, **Guns into Plowshares** (1997) looks just like a giant, 14-foot-high plow, but view it from the south and you'll see exciting metal texture. And close up you'll find that it's made from innumerable confiscated handguns, welded together. This virtuoso piece by Esther and Michael Augsberger is in an area filled with sculpture related to law enforcement. The title is from Isaiah 2:4. *Judiciary Square, Fourth Street between D and E.*

DOWNTOWN

In perhaps the most bizarre work in town, the **Boy Scout Memorial** (1964), an 8-foot tall scout in full uniform strides doggedly toward the Mall, which was the site of the first national Boy Scout jamboree in Washington in 1937. But why is he accompanied by his enormous, naked parents? Good grief! Sculptor Donald DeLue maintained that they represent American manhood and womanhood—you judge! *The Ellipse, near 15th and E Streets NW.*

Two blocks west of the White House, **Don Quixote** (1981) cuts an extraordinary figure in Miles Rolph's tour de force of welded steel. Note how the Don's horse, Rosinante, snarls in anger as her master prepares for another hopeless foray. *1776 G Street NW, in courtyard between F and G and 17th and 18th Streets.*

GEORGETOWN

Four imposing bronze **Dumbarton Buffaloes** (1914) guard the bridge across Rock Creek to eastern Georgetown, splendid despite the ravages of weathering. Locals love these evocative tributes by sculptor Alex Phimester Proctor and call the bridge "Buffalo Bridge." *Dumbarton Bridge at Q Street NW.*

UPPER NORTHWEST

One of D.C.'s noblest pieces of stainless steel, the giant **Behrend Menorah** (1984) by Saunders Schultz and William Severson is a spiritual statement and a gleaming work of art. See it on a sunny day to catch reflections of nearby trees and bushes. Washington Hebrew Congregation, *3935 Macomb Street NW, off Massachusetts Avenue.*

Nudes on the central doorway arch of the National Cathedral? They've been controversial ever since designs were chosen for the central section of **Ex Nihilo** (Out of Nothing), Frederick Hart's interpretation of the Creation. Some find his vision edifying; others recall *Playboy*'s legendary Marilyn Monroe centerfold and other air-brushed females. Hart's smaller lucite and bronze figures are a staple at upscale malls. Completed 1990. *Massachusetts and Wisconsin Avenues NW.*

Methodist leader John Wesley, who said, "I look on the world as my parish," bows wearily over his equally tired horse as he rides westward into the New World. Instead of a sword, he brandishes an open Bible; instead of being heroic, he is slightly smaller than life. Arthur Walker's sensitive 1961 sculpture is at *Wesley Theological Seminary, 4500 Massachusetts Avenue at Tilden Street NW.*

DUPONT CIRCLE

Shirtless, with steel-rimmed glasses and staff, **Mohandas Gandhi** (2000) is a forceful presence on Massachusetts Avenue as he strides forward, seemingly leading a protest march. Calcutta sculptor Gautam Pal's tall bronze blends well with elegant surroundings on a picturesque traffic island opposite the Indian Embassy. *Massachusetts Avenue between Q and 21st Streets NW.*

Saint Jerome the Priest (1954) sits on the curb off bustling Massachusetts Avenue in front of the Croatian Embassy. Oblivious to nearby traffic, the surreal curvature and power of his body obscure the upturned Bible he reads. Croat sculptor Ivan Mestrovic's lugubrious interpretation of the fourth-century hermit and scholar is one of D.C.'s finest grotesques. *2343 Massachusetts Avenue NW.*

THE WATERFRONT AND ANACOSTIA

The **Big Chair** has long become part of the neighborhood in Anacostia. Visitors gape while locals hardly notice. Built in 1959 as a furniture store display, this 19-foot mahogany Duncan Phyfe-style chair has weathered well and packs one of the biggest visual wallops in town. Unpretentious, it is an interesting challenge to culturally correct pop art like Oldenburg's giant eraser off Constitution Avenue. *Martin Luther King Jr. Avenue and V Street SE.*

JUNE

Dupont-Kalorama Museum Walk Weekend. On the first weekend in June, visit ten neighborhood museums and historic houses (387–4062, ext. 12; www.dkmuseums.com).

Shakespeare Theatre Free for All. Carter Barron Amphitheatre. An annual festival put on by the Shakespeare Theatre in Rock Creek Park's Carter Barron Amphitheatre (547–1122; www.shakespearetheatre.org/about/free).

Smithsonian Folklife Festival. This spectacular annual festival of food, crafts, music, and dance, held on the National Mall, begins in late June and runs until July 4. Hours: 11:00 A.M. to 9:00 P.M. (633–9884; www.folk life.si.edu).

JUNE–AUGUST

Summer concerts at the Capitol. Free military band concerts are held on the west steps at 8:00 P.M., June through August. Monday and Thursday you'll hear the Navy Band (433–2525). Wednesday it's the Marine Band (433–4301; www.marineband.usmc.mil), while the Army Band performs Tuesday and Friday (696–3399; www.usarmyband.mil).

JULY

National Independence Day Celebration. Daylong concerts, a morning parade, and the famed National Symphony Orchestra Concert on the National Mall (619–7222; www.july4thparade.com).

Soap Box Derby. Independence day race on Constitution Avenue (216–733–8723; www.228.pair.com/mccary/sbd).

Bastille Day. Always ready for a party, Washington celebrates French Independence Day on July 14 with live entertainment and a race to the U.S. Capitol and back by tray-bearing waiters and waitresses (296–7200).

SEPTEMBER

National Symphony Orchestra's Labor Day Concert. West Lawn of the U.S. Capitol (619–7222).

Black Family Reunion Celebration. The annual celebration of the African-American family features live entertainment, food, and pavilions (383–9130; www.ncnw.org/blackfamily.htm).

Kennedy Center Open House. Free concerts and performances (467–4600).

National Cathedral Open House. Cathedral-related music, tours, tower climbs, and entertainment (537–6200; www.cathedral.org).

SEPTEMBER–OCTOBER

Hispanic Heritage Month. The Smithsonian hosts a month of arts, entertainment, and educational activities celebrating Hispanic culture and traditions (633–1000; www.si.edu).

OCTOBER

Marine Corps Marathon. Thousands run in this annual marathon from the Iwo Jima Memorial in Arlington to the Capitol and back. Applications available February 1 (703–432–1169; www.marinemarathon.com).

Washington International Horse Show. One of the East's premier shows, where hunting and jumping horses compete for prizes at the D.C. Armory (397–SEAT; www.wihs.org).

NOVEMBER

American Indian Heritage Month. The Smithsonian's Museum of the American Indian celebrates with special programs and exhibitions (357–2700; www.smithsonianeducation.org/heritage_month).

Veterans Day Ceremonies. Arlington National Cemetery (703–607–8585), the Vietnam Veterans Memorial (619–7222), and Navy Memorial (737–2300).

DECEMBER

Kennedy Center Holiday Festival. Free performances and holiday concerts all month (467–4600; www.kennedy-center.org).

National Cathedral Christmas Services. A month of pageants, carols, and choruses (537–6200; www.catherdral.org).

National Christmas Tree Lighting and Pageant of Peace. The president lights the nation's Christmas tree on the Ellipse behind the White House, to begin a month-long Pageant of Peace. Events include nightly choral performances, a Nativity scene, and the Pathway of Peace. A collection of smaller, decoratively lit Christmas trees represents each of the nation's fifty-six states and territories (208–1631; www.pageantofpeace.org).

The Washington Ballet's The Nutcracker. A Washington holiday tradition (362–3606; www.washingtonballet.org).

Downtown

Like the rings of a great tree, Washington's buildings and public spaces trace the American past, from the outer layers of Watergate and the Vietnam Memorial down to the innermost bands of pre-Revolutionary Georgetown and the Marine Barracks. But the city's core has always been the White House, more modest by far than the mansions occupied by heads of state in many less affluent or powerful countries, but for more than 200 years the symbol of America all over the planet. Thousands of tourists pour through the Executive Mansion every year before following well-worn paths to the next attraction. More inquisitive travelers with historic perspectives think of the White House in its original role as the center of an old Washington neighborhood. Start exploring the president's neighborhood in *Lafayette Square,* which was the Pierce family farm, orchard, and burial ground when L'Enfant's plan projected it as the President's Park, where the chief executive could relax and seek relief from the capital's sizzling summers.

It may have been named for the Revolutionary War hero the Marquis de Lafayette, but the Square really belongs to Andrew Jackson, starting with the Spanish cannon captured by Old Hickory at Pensacola to the statue of Jackson on a capering horse, as Henry James put it, "as archaic as a Ninevite king,

DOWNTOWN

N

0   1/4 mi

0   1/4 km

RHODE ISLAND AVE

SCOTT CIRCLE

N ST

11TH ST

THOMAS CIRCLE

M ST

DESALES ST

18TH ST

CONNECTICUT AVE

15TH ST

VERMONT AVE

MASSACHUSETTS AVE

10TH ST

17TH ST

L ST

K ST

17TH ST

16TH ST

14TH ST

12TH ST

K ST

Farragut Square

McPherson Square

Franklin Square

I ST

I ST

17TH ST

H ST

NEW YORK AVE

H ST

Nat. Mus. of Women in the Arts

Lafayette Square

13TH ST

G ST

White House

Old Exec. Office Bldg.

Treasury Dept.

F ST

11TH ST

10TH ST

14TH ST

E ST

15TH ST

Pershing Park

Freedom Plaza

PENNSYLVANIA AVE

Zero Milestone

National Aquarium

Old Post Office Pavillion

The Ellipse

Dept. of Commerce

Ronald Reagan Building

IRS

CONSTITUTION AVE

prancing and rocking through the ages." Jackson's statue looks down on the scene of his notorious 1829 inaugural, when tubs of whiskey and high-octane orange punch were rolled into the square to lure the drunken, coonskin-capped crowds out of the White House, touching off a wild melee that prompted the Chief Justice to sniff that "the reign of King Mob seemed triumphant."

The Square has also seen military service, when soldiers bivouacked there, first during the War of 1812 and again during the Civil War, turning it both times into a muddy swamp. President Grant later used it as his private zoo until the aroma of the presidential prairie dogs became intolerable.

But the Square's most distinctive and enduring role was as the social headquarters of antebellum Washington, a time when, as Square-dweller Henry Adams recalled, "beyond the square the country began." President and Mrs. Kennedy rescued many of the Square's elegant town houses from demolition in the 1960s, when the so-called planners saw this as the place for a government office complex.

On your stroll along the east side of the Square you'll pass the *Tayloe House* at number 721 Madison Place, a Federal beauty with an ironwork balcony that was known as "The Little White House" when it was the home of Mark Hanna, President McKinley's éminence grise. The widowed Dolley Madison lived in the Madison-Cutts House, where the Square meets H Street, until her death in 1849. During the Civil War the house belonged to General George McClellan, who, one night in November 1862, deliberately snubbed Abraham Lincoln. After waiting an hour in the parlor to see the absent general, the president was told that McClellan had in the meantime returned but had gone to bed.

At the top of the square stands St. John's Episcopal Church, "the church of the presidents," where every president since Madison has worshiped in pew 54. The parish house next door is Ashburton House, which was the British legation in the 1840s.

TOP ATTRACTIONS DOWNTOWN

Treasury Building

National Geographic Society

Old Executive Office Building

Renwick Gallery

Decatur House

National Museum of Women in the Arts

National Theatre

B'nai B'rith Klutnick National Jewish Museum

Old Post Office Pavilion Observation Deck

At the corner of H Street and Jackson Place visitors get a crash course on the history of Washington social life. Capital insiders have gathered for almost two centuries at *Decatur House,* built in 1819 by Commodore Stephen Decatur, the swashbuckling hero of the War of 1812, with prize money earned from his naval victories. Decatur's architect was the equally distinguished Benjamin Henry Latrobe, known as the "father of American architecture." Decatur's exquisite Federal town house soon became one of the young capital's social and power centers, but not for long; a year later Decatur was mortally wounded in a duel. His house later became the residence of three secretaries of state—Martin Van Buren, Edward Livingston, and Henry Clay, who bragged (correctly) that he was "living in the best home of the city."

In the house's downstairs rooms you'd swear that the Decaturs had just stepped out, perhaps to pay a call on President Monroe just across the park. In the front parlor a gleaming eighteenth-century writing desk and secretary await the commodore's return while a vintage sewing kit reminds us that his wife Susan took an interest in what guys back in 1819 used to call "women's pastimes." On the wall you'll see a painting on glass of the 1812 naval battle where Decatur seized the British warship *Macedonian,* and in doing so made the money to pay for this glorious house. In the stately dining room a table set with Chinese export porcelain awaits the Decaturs' return. On the ground floor you'll also see the kitchen, which is being painstakingly restored with the help of a combination of original drawings and historical sleuthing.

As of mid-2006 visitors to the second floor enter a time warp and fast-forward to the end of the nineteenth-century and the grand Victorian living room of the socially prominent Beale family, who lived in Decatur House from 1871 to 1957. The Beales entertained here in late nineteenth-century grandeur amid an eclectic collection of furnishings, ranging from delicate Japanese screens to ornate Belter-style American furniture of rosewood and red velvet. In the center of the dining room floor the Beales placed a seal of California inlaid in rare woods to remind them of the source of the family's ranching fortune.

In Decatur's time these upstairs rooms were the scene of numerous "crushes" and "squeezes"—the 1820 ancestors of the infamous Washington cocktail party. But some things never change—prominent Washingtonians still gather here for twenty-first-century crushes, a.k.a. fund-raisers.

Don't miss the house's permanent exhibit space and its nifty gift shop, where first ladies Nancy Reagan and Laura Bush have shopped for books and Christmas ornaments.

Decatur House, at 748 Jackson Place NW (entrance at 1610 H Street); 842–0920; www.decaturhouse.org. Both the museum and its shop are open 10:00 A.M. to 5:00 P.M. Tuesday through Saturday and noon to 4:00 P.M. Sunday.

Suggested donation $5.00. This is the only Lafayette Square home open to the public. Metro: Farragut West (orange and blue lines) and Farragut North (red line).

Tucked away in one of those wonderful Jackson Place town houses is one of the city's top gift shops, the **White House Historical Association.** Here you'll find a marvelous collection of books and other items that commemorate "The President's House," including splendid photographic studies of the White House and its public rooms, along with histories and official portraits of the presidents. For the kids, the shop offers educational games, coloring books, and guides to the White House. If you visit in November and December, you'll be able to take away distinctive tree ornaments from many different administrations (check out Teddy Roosevelt's 1902 ornament in Bohemian glass), greeting cards, and notepaper. The White House Historical Association, at 740 Jackson Place NW, is open from 9:00 A.M. to 4:00 P.M. Monday through Friday; 737–8292; www.whitehousehistory.org/shop. The Association operates another gift shop in the White House Visitor Center at 1450 Pennsylvania Avenue NW. Store hours are 7:30 A.M. to 4 P.M. daily.

Before you leave the Square be sure to visit each corner to inspect the statues of foreign heroes of the Revolution: de Rochambeau, Kosciusko, von Steuben, and Lafayette himself at the southeast corner.

Near the corner where Lafayette Square meets Pennsylvania Avenue, you'll find **Blair House,** one of Washington's most historic mansions and now the president's guest house, where visiting heads of state and royalty spend their official days in Washington. The patrician Blair family of Maryland built the original Blair House in 1824, which is the white Federal mansion at 1653 Pennsylvania, while the **Lee House** next door belonged to the aristocratic Lees of Virginia. These two elegant homes lived separate and stately lives until World War II, when Eleanor Roosevelt, wearied of having houseguest Winston Churchill padding around the White House in his Doctor Dentons, a brandy glass in hand, looking for FDR (so would you), used the merged houses to put up visiting dignitaries. In 1950, when Harry and Bess Truman were using Blair House as a temporary White House while 1600 was being rebuilt, Puerto Rican nationalists stormed the buildings in an assassination attempt. A plaque on the Blair House fence honors the bravery of Secret Service agent Leslie Coffelt, who was shot and killed defending the president. In 1969 Blair

capitalquote

"Washington talks about herself, and about almost nothing else. It is about herself as the City of Conversation that she incessantly converses."

—Henry James

House was again expanded to include two adjoining 1860s row houses around the corner on Jackson Place, facing Lafayette Park. These additions turned the original Blair House into a 70,000-square-foot, four-house complex that's larger by far than the White House itself.

Although Blair House is not open to the public, suffice it to say that as a special and small hotel for America's most important foreign guests, it is a treasure trove of the best in American art, interior design, and furnishings. And, of course, of American history. Just behind the deceptively plain front door are the spacious parlors where Andrew Jackson called his cronies together in the original "kitchen cabinet" and where, in wartime, Abraham Lincoln frequently conferred with his friend and confidant, Postmaster General Montgomery Blair after a short stroll across Pennsylvania Avenue. Metro: Farragut West (orange and blue lines).

Next door to Blair House, the **Renwick Gallery** exhibits the best in American arts, crafts, and design. Its gingerbread building was designed by James Renwick (also the architect of the Smithsonian "castle" on the National Mall) to hold the art collection of local banker William Corcoran. Alas, Mr. Corcoran's new toy was completed in 1861, just in time to be seized by the government and used as a warehouse for Army uniforms; when it reopened in 1869 it became Washington's first art museum. When the Corcoran collection moved down 17th Street (see the Foggy Bottom chapter) in 1897, this became the U.S. Court of Claims building until 1964, when it was transferred to the Smithsonian.

After ascending the Renwick's imposing staircase, just as President Grant did at the gala ball that reopened Corcoran's collection, you'll find the gallery's

Renwick Gallery

Monumental Messages

Although the Washington Monument is definitely on the beaten path, almost no one, including most Washingtonians, know that its aluminum cap bears a number of 5 inch-high inscriptions that are completely invisible to the tourist hordes that climb the obelisk every year. The dedication on the north face, looking toward the White House, bears the name of President Chester A. Arthur and other members of the 1876 commission that set the capstone. The west face inscription notes the date that the Monument cornerstone was laid (July 4, 1848) and the date that the capstone was actually set (December 6, 1884), while the south face lists the Monument's chief engineer and architect and his assistants. The east face bears the inscription *Laus Deo,* which in Latin means "Praise be to God."

permanent exhibits of furniture, glassware, and textiles, a nice combination of the traditional and contemporary.

But prepare to be astonished by the sumptuous "Grand Salon" at the top of the stairs. It's always the Gilded Age in this grand, almost overwhelming room, where dozens of great paintings from every era of American history are beautifully hung, salon-style, on high silk-covered walls. Among the most memorable are the George Catlins, with fabulous scenes of the West in the 1830s and portraits of great warrior chiefs in full war dress. The Salon also has some rare pieces by California artist Hugo Ballin, and two Albert Henderson Thayer portraits of his children and family. The Renwick Gallery, at Pennsylvania Avenue and 17th Street (357–2531; www.americanart.si.edu), is open from 10:00 A.M. to 5:30 P.M. every day. Metro: Farragut West (blue and orange lines) and Farragut North (red line).

Across Pennsylvania Avenue looms the ***Eisenhower Executive Office Building,*** another ornate Victorian that somehow manages to be both highly visible and rarely visited. Tourists and Washingtonians hurrying along Pennsylvania Avenue never fail to gaze in wonderment at this massive granite ziggurat next door to the White House. But few realize that behind that operatic facade bristling with columns, pilasters, and porticoes lies a bygone world where graceful stairways, exquisite architectural details, and elegant rooms exude both refinement and power.

As of mid-2006, tours of this Washington landmark had been suspended for security reasons but would be renewed "as soon as possible." To find out if they're being given during your visit, phone 395–5895 between 8:00 A.M. and 5:00 P.M. Monday through Friday. To get a preview visit www.whitehouse.gov/history/eeobtour/.

Eisenhower Executive
Office Building

If you go, you'll see why a visit to what was formerly called the Old Executive Office Building, and still the OEOB to its friends, is a must for anyone interested in American design, politics, and history. This Victorian dowager has been the ground zero of American strength and decision-making since the day it opened in 1875, when it accommodated three entire government departments—State, War, and Navy. Several presidents, including both Roosevelts, Eisenhower, and Taft, worked here before moving next door to 1600 Pennsylvania, while twenty-five secretaries of state have had their offices in the south wing overlooking the Ellipse. The west wing, which once housed the War Department, has its own memories of George C. Marshall, Douglas MacArthur, and Major Dwight D. Eisenhower. Although the three original agencies left long ago, OEOB is still the home of the powerful, whose list of tenants includes the vice president and the chairmen of the Council of Economic Advisors and the National Security Council, where Ollie North and his sidekick Fawn Hall shredded the Iran-Contra documents.

Members of the regular Saturday morning tour of OEOB follow high-ceilinged hallways to explore hidden treasures like the Indian Treaty Room, a jewel box of brightly tiled floors and wrought-iron balconies where presidents since Harry Truman have held press conferences. Another visitor favorite is room 274, once the office of Franklin Roosevelt and other secretaries of the navy and now the ceremonial office of the vice president, where marble fireplaces, gleaming marquetry floors, and gold-framed mirrors epitomize Victorian elegance. Other stops include the former State Department library, with three stories of lacy white and gold railings, a ceiling of filigreed glass, and a floor of antique Minton tile. You'll be impressed by the wealth of architectural craftsmanship on the tour, from grand staircases that swoop up to coffered domes and stained glass rotundas, down to details such as intricately cast door-knobs and trash chutes.

Although security considerations rule out casual strolls around the OEOB, look for some special places in a building where every office has a history. In room 208, on the morning of December 7, 1941, Secretary of State Cordell Hull received, then ejected, Japan's emissaries. Room 488 was once the top secret "black room," where American cryptographers broke enemy codes. Metro: Farragut West (blue and orange lines) and Farragut North (red line).

Yes Virginia, there were coffee houses and bars in Washington long before Starbucks. Just off 17th Street, across from the OEOB, you'll find a classic coffee house at 1702 G Street NW that will warp you back into the days of yore when Woodrow Wilson was president and "latte" was Italian for milk. *M.E. Swing Coffee Roasters* has been a local institution since 1916, and it shows in the mahogany fixtures, mirrored walls, marble bar, and the vintage burr grinder that will pulverize your espresso beans. If your taste runs to other types, there's a wide assortment of freshly roasted beans from everywhere from Ethiopia to South America. Open: Monday through Friday 7:00 A.M. to 6:00 P.M. 628–7601; www.swingscoffee.com.

You'll find one of D.C.'s best-kept secrets at 1500 Pennsylvania Avenue, a.k.a.

macarthur's flowerpower

Displaying his hitherto unseen and unsuspected feminine side, General of the Army Douglas MacArthur designed the flower planters that flank the main entrance to the Eisenhower Executive Office Building.

the *Treasury Department.* Security considerations since September 11 have caused Treasury to suspend the regular Saturday morning tour. Call 622–0896 or visit www.ustreasury.gov to see if tours have been reinstated when you're in town. If they have, you'll walk directly from a busy twentieth-century street into the Treasury Department of 1842. The austerity of these Tyler administration corridors of power, with their cast-iron columns and graceful stairways, seems to embody the spartan tastes of a young, egalitarian republic, that is, until your guide takes you behind those louvered office doors into the suite used by Treasury Secretary Salmon P. Chase during the Civil War, where the simple gives way to the sumptuous.

Everything in these handsome offices—the decoratively stenciled ceilings with allegorical themes, the fireplace with its mammoth over-mantel mirror,

AUTHOR'S FAVORITES IN DOWNTOWN

Eisenhower Executive Office Building	Treasury Department
Lafayette Square and Decatur House	The Palm

and the glossy leather furniture—has been meticulously restored to reflect the days when Lincoln ambled over from the White House to anguish with Chase about finding ways to finance the war effort. Don't let this spoil your tour, but these splendid rooms are the birthplace of the income tax, first levied in 1862 to raise money for the Union cause.

mayflowermadam

Dressed in basic black (no pearls), FBI Director J. Edgar Hoover lunched at the same table at the Mayflower Hotel every day for twenty years.

Just after Lincoln's assassination, the Andrew Johnson Suite down the hall was turned into Johnson's Oval Office, where, as vintage prints show, the new president conducted his first cabinet meetings and received foreign funeral delegations. In the office next door, which once belonged to the secretary of the treasury and is now used by a senior department official, computers and printers coexist nicely with the massive conference tables, richly upholstered chairs, and thick drapes of 1875.

Treasury architect Alfred Mullett wanted the building's Cash Room to be "emblematic of the dignity of the nation and the stability of its credit," so he designed it as an Italian palazzo, its two-story walls covered with colored marble and ringed by a balcony with exquisitely wrought bronze railings. Immense gaslight chandeliers look down on the banking floor where tellers once sold bonds, cashed government checks, and redeemed banknotes with silver and gold hauled from the currency and bullion vaults just below. Although it was called "the most expensive room in the world" when it opened, the Cash Room started off with a social calamity: At Grant's 1869 inaugural reception, hungry guests stampeded the kitchen, women fainted in the crush, and the search for coats went on all night. Be glad you weren't invited.

thezeromilestone

All distances within the United States to Washington are measured from that oblong milestone on the Ellipse directly behind the White House. As you'll see from the inscription, the milestone marks the starting point for the first and second transcontinental automobile convoys of military vehicles across the United States in 1919 to1920.

If you're looking for a map to chart your hike across New Guinea, a guide for your next safari along Namibia's Skeleton Coast, or a bicycle tour of Des Moines, **ADC Map and Travel Center** is just the place for you. ADC offers a huge collection of guides and maps covering the planet and, if you're planning a really long trip, charts of the solar system. ADC is located at 1636 I Street NW, and is open Monday through Thursday from 9:00 A.M. to 6:30 P.M., Friday 9:00 A.M. to 5:30 P.M., and

Saturday 11:00 A.M. to 5:00 P.M. Closed Sunday. Metro: ADC is atop the Farragut West station (orange and blue lines).

The *National Museum of Women in the Arts* is probably the only museum anywhere dedicated to the achievements of women in every area of the arts. Its large and thoughtfully assembled permanent collection showcases women's achievements over five centuries, beginning with rare portraits by two of the few women painters of the Italian Renaissance, Sofonisba Anguissola and Lavinia Fontana. The exhibit continues chronologically through Mary Cassatt right down to the vibrant oils of contemporary artists; the museum also regularly hosts special traveling exhibits. Oddly enough, the museum is located in what was once one of the ultimate boys' clubs, a handsome Renaissance Revival building erected in 1908 as Washington's Masonic Temple. The knockout entrance hall exhibit area dates from its later days as a 1930s movie palace. Adding to the abundance, the fine museum shop is dedicated to books, images, and posters by women artists and photographers. The museum, at 1250 New

Red Meat Department

Washington opened the twenty-first century with a stampede of New York steak houses. The venerable Palm, always a White House–media clubhouse and hangout for local movers and shakers, was joined by fellow New Yorkers Smith and Wollensky and Bobby Van's Steakhouse. So for a thick steak or mammoth lobster, here's what you need to know; just don't tell your cardiologist:

The Palm
1225 19th Street NW
293–9091
www.thepalm.com
Open Monday through Friday 11:45 A.M. to 10:30 P.M., Saturday and Sunday 5:30 to 10:30 P.M. Expensive. Located downtown.

Smith and Wollensky
1112 19th Street NW
466–1100
www.smithandwollensky.com
Open Monday through Friday 11:30 A.M. to 11:30 P.M., Saturday and Sunday 5:00 to 11:00 P.M. Upstairs grill room open 11:30 A.M. to 2:00 A.M. every day. Expensive. Located downtown.

Bobby Van's Steakhouse
809 15th Street NW
589–0060
www.bobbyvans.com
Open Monday through Friday 11:30 A.M. to 10:30 P.M., Saturday 5:00 to 10:30 P.M. Closed Sunday. Expensive. Located downtown.

York Avenue NW, is open Monday through Saturday 10:00 A.M. to 5:00 P.M. and Sunday from noon to 5:00 P.M. Admission: $8.00 for adults, $6.00 for seniors and students. Call 783–5000 or (800) 222–7270, fax 393–3234, or visit www.nmwa.org. Metro: Metro Center (red, blue, and orange lines).

The *National Theatre,* where greats like Helen Hayes, John Barrymore, and Sarah Bernhardt once performed, has been part of America's theatrical tradition since 1835. On a nonperfoming level, Shirley MacLaine and her brother, Warren Beatty, worked as usher and stage doorman, respectively, in the 1950s.

The current theater, at 1321 Pennsylvania Avenue NW, is the fifth edition of the National on this site. Like the Paris Opera, the National also has its very own phantom, the occasionally spotted ghost of John McCullough, a prominent actor of the 1880s who was murdered precisely where the present-day stage is located.

The National is still very much a prominent part of Washington's cultural scene and regularly hosts many pre- and post-Broadway performances, but three much less publicized (and free) presentations are also on the National's regular schedule. Every Monday at 6:00 and 7:30 P.M. from September to May, "Monday Night at the National" features mainly local performers in plays, readings, and performances of dance and music. "Saturday Morning at the National," a children's program that often includes storytellers and puppets, is presented each Saturday from September to May at 9:30 and 11:00 A.M. Every Monday at 6:30 P.M. from June through August, the National hosts a "Summer Cinema Program" of classic films.

Right on the Money

If you want to watch the sun set over some of the nation's most hallowed places, including the Jefferson Memorial and Arlington Cemetery across the Potomac, then head for the *Sky Terrace* on the roof of the Washington Hotel at 515 15th Street NW. While you're up there you'll also have a bird's-eye view of those equally famous buildings that appear on our $5, $10, and $20 bills—the White House, the Treasury, and the Lincoln Memorial. The eleventh-floor Terrace serves cocktails, sandwiches, salads, and cold platters every day from 11:30 A.M. to 1:30 A.M. from the end of April until the end of October. No reservations. While Sky Terrace prices are moderate, the panorama is anything but.

More formal dinners are available atop the Washington in the *Sky Room,* with a memorable view south to the memorials and the Pentagon. The Sky Room, open for dinner only from 6:00 to 10:00 P.M., is also a good choice for dining before performances at the National Theatre. Reserve by calling 347–4499 or at www.hotelwashington.com.

Tokyo on the Potomac

If you're in Washington for the National Cherry Blossom Festival, don't forget to visit the *Sakura Matsuri Japanese Street Festival,* which is held every year in tandem with its better-known cousin. When Sakura Matsuri time rolls around, Pennsylvania Avenue becomes the Ginza, with a Japanese street festival and shopping on 12th Street NW, music and dancing in Freedom Plaza at Pennsylvania and 13th, and exhibits of Japanese woodworking and other arts and crafts. There's even a demonstration of Japanese martial arts and sumo wrestling competitions. The festival is sponsored by the Japan-America Society of Washington. For information about dates and event schedules, phone 833–2210 or visit www.us-japan.org/dc/events/matsuriindex.html.

Although these events are free, you'll still need tickets to get in. To get them, on a first-come first-served basis, turn up at the box office at least thirty minutes prior to the performance. For information about these and any other performances (or if you run into Mr. McCullough), call 628–6161; www.national theatre.org. Metro: Federal Triangle (orange and blue lines).

When it opened in 1997, the ***Ronald Reagan Building and International Trade Center,*** named for the president who strongly favored a massive rollback in the bureaucracy, became the second largest federal office building in the United States, surpassed in floor space only by the Pentagon. The ultimate paradox? Two of its major tenants are agencies The Gipper had sworn to eliminate. Anyway, just because it's full of feds, don't pass up a chance to peer inside this massive structure at the corner of 13th Street and Pennsylvania Avenue NW. Once beyond that ostentatious facade, visitors gaze out over a stunning atrium used for special occasions and regular art exhibits. Free guided tours of the Ronald Reagan Building and International Trade Center start from the concierge desk at the 14th Street entrance on Monday, Wednesday, and Friday at 11:00 A.M. Self-guided walking tours are also available; see the concierge at each entrance for details.

The Reagan building also contains the well-stocked D.C. Visitor Information Center (328–4748) with interactive tours of the city and tickets for real tours. In spring and summer the Center is open Monday through Friday 8:30 A.M. to 5:30 P.M., Saturday 9:00 A.M. to 4:00 P.M.; fall and winter the Center hours are Monday through Friday 9:00 A.M. to 4:30 P.M. but it is closed on weekends; www.dcvisit.com. If it's lunchtime, the building also has a major-league food court that is open Monday through Friday from 7:00 A.M. to 7:00 P.M., Saturday 11:00 A.M. to 6:00 P.M., and on Sunday between March 1 and August 31 from noon to 5:00 P.M.

Stop the Presses!!

Well, they don't really yell that anymore, as you'll see if you take the Monday tour of the *Washington Post*. This is your chance to see how one of America's great newspapers is put together, as the tour winds through an exhibit of the newspaper's history, then moves on to visit the newsroom and the editorial offices. You'll also look in on the paper's graphics and photography departments. Tours are given only for organized groups of ten to thirty on Mondays at 10:00 and 11:00 A.M. and 1:00, 2:00, and 3:00 P.M. Tours leave from the Post's main lobby at 1150 15th Street NW. Reservations are essential, and, for security reasons, well before your intended date you'll have to send the name of your group and the names of all participating members, preferred dates, and other information to the *Post* by fax (202–334–4963) or by mail (*The Washington Post*, Tours, 1150 15th Street NW, Washington, DC 20071). For more information call 334–7969 or check out http://washpost.com/community/you/tours. No children under eleven. Metro: McPherson Square (orange and blue lines).

See vicious sharks dining on the lower end of the food chain! Thrill to razor-toothed piranha fighting for their seafood dinner! Are we somewhere along the Amazon or on a Pacific reef? Not at all; we're in the basement of an utterly prosaic government building, where most of the infighting goes on upstairs in offices and not downstairs in fish tanks. The *National Aquarium,* on the lower level of the Commerce Department Building at 14th Street and Constitution Avenue NW, has seventy tanks teeming with every form of aquatic life, including sea turtles, alligators, and tropical fish; the shark and piranha feedings, however, are the biggest draw. To see why, go there Monday, Wednesday, or Saturday at 2:00 P.M. to watch the sharks get a late lunch; the piranha dine at 2:00 P.M. on Tuesday, Thursday, and Sunday. Friday at 2:00 P.M. it's the alligators. Keep a close eye on the kids! Fortunately, you won't have to fight for an inexpensive lunch at the Commerce Department cafeteria on the same floor. The aquarium is open from 9:00 A.M. to 5:00 P.M. daily; 482–2825 (information tape) or 482–2826 (live person), fax 482–4946; www.national aquarium.com. Admission is $5.00 for adults, $2.00 for kids two to ten. Metro: Federal Triangle (orange and blue lines).

For the full D.C. experience think about dining at the *Fourth Estate,* where you might find yourself seated next to one of the pundits or talking heads you've seen on TV shows and C-SPAN. Located on the twelfth floor of the National Press Building at 529 14th Street NW, the Fourth Estate was for decades open only to Press Club members, but is now open to all for lunch and dinner. The Fourth Estate gets good marks from local restaurant critics for its seafood entrees and desserts, which are made by Patisserie Poupon and imported from exotic Georgetown. Open Monday through Friday for lunch from 11:30 A.M. to 3:00 P.M. and dinner from 5:30 to 8:30 P.M. 662–7638. Expensive, but prices for members are discounted. For reservations and information about joining, visit www.press.org/abouttheclub/fourthestate.cfm.

There's no way you're going to overlook the **Old Post Office Pavilion** on Pennsylvania Avenue between 11th and 12th Streets, another grand old building that narrowly escaped the wrecker's ball. When it was built in 1899 as headquarters for the Postmaster General and the Post Office Department, this twelve-story fortress of steel and granite was Washington's first "skyscraper," but the Post Office, known to its detractors as "The Old Tooth," fell into disfavor in later years because its massive design overwhelmed that of other buildings in the Federal Triangle area. This Victorian veteran was saved and rebuilt in 1977 and lives on as a combination of government offices and tourist attraction.

Although the building's multistory atrium draws many visitors for its architecture, busy food court, and tourist-oriented shops, the main attraction is the ride up the 315-foot clock tower to the observation deck, where National Park Service rangers will show you around and explain the building's history. If you go, expect a terrific view out over the capital and its suburbs and, on a clear day, even as far as Virginia's Blue Ridge Mountains. While up there you'll also see the Congress Bells, a bicentennial gift from Britain, which replicate the bells in London's Westminster Abbey. The Pavilion (289–4224) is open from 8:00 A.M. to 10:45 P.M. from mid-April to Labor Day; the rest of the year it's 10:00 A.M. to 6:15 P.M. Individual shops may keep different hours. The Web site for the pavilion is www.oldpostofficedc.com and for the tower, www.nps.gov/opot/index .htm. Metro: Federal Triangle (orange and blue lines).

Watch This Space!

In the fall of 2007 you'll be able to visit one of Washington's most dramatic museums when the "Newseum," at Pennsylvania Avenue and Sixth Streets NW will open its doors. The **Newseum,** a six-level tribute to the American news media and the First Amendment, uses interactive displays of journalistic history, many of them fascinating exhibits of broadcast and TV coverage of great events, that may inspire you to clear your D.C. schedule for the rest of the day. It's living history and great for giving schoolkids exciting, highly visual insights into the American past. The Newseum is part of a 600,000-square-foot complex that will also give parents post-museum therapy in the form of restaurants and shops. For a peek at the Newseum project, check out www.newseum.org.

Book Lover's Delight

There's not a dot-com in sight at *Chapters Literary Bookstore,* 445 11th Street NW, (737–5553), one of my favorite Washington bookstores, on or off the beaten path. As its name implies, this is a place for book lovers, with a large selection of fiction and literary biography, along with a good selection of poetry and travel literature. Check with the friendly, well-informed staff about Chapters' extensive program of readings and signings. Open Monday through Friday 10:00 A.M.to 7:00 P.M., Saturday noon to 7:00 P.M., Sunday 2:00 to 7:00 P.M.; www.chaptersliterary.com Metro stop: Metro Center (all lines).

Political junkies visiting our nation's capital will find their special bliss at *Capitol Coin and Stamp,* where they can browse and buy from one of America's greatest collections of political memorabilia. At Capitol, owner Nelson Whitman (no relation to the author) has a huge supply of campaign buttons and stickers, tickets for the Clinton impeachment trials, and presidential Christmas cards from every president since Kennedy. Whitman also has an unparalleled stock of White House gift items reserved for special friends or contributors such as cufflinks and tie clips, plus glassware from Air Force One and a selection of china from Camp David. Lots of posters too, plus videotapes of presidential speeches. Capitol Coin and Stamp, at 1001 Connecticut Avenue NW, Suite 745, is open from 10:00 A.M. to 6:00 P.M. Monday through Friday. 296–0400; www.capitolcoin.com. Metro: Farragut North (red line).

If the words *National Geographic Society* conjure up images of grandma's attic and stacks of dusty magazines with yellow borders, a visit to Society headquarters at 1145 17th Street NW will help bring you up to date fast. In Explorer's Hall, on the first floor, you'll find special exhibits of great explorations or destinations and live music presentations from all over the world. Explorer's Hall is open for self-guided tours from 9:00 A.M. to 5:00 P.M. Monday through Saturday and from 10:00 A.M. to 5:00 P.M. Sunday. No charge.

Nothing demonstrates the "new" National Geographic as much as its bright, colorful store, which sells the Society's excellent travel guides and videos, plus the great photos and maps everyone expects from the National Geographic. If you want to become an intrepid National Geographic Explorer, even if you're just hiking to school, buy yourself an official knapsack or tote. Open Monday through Saturday 9:00 A.M. to 5:00 P.M., Sunday 10:00 A.M. to 5:00 P.M., holidays 9:00 A.M. to 5:00 P.M. Call 857–7588.

The Society also sponsors a little-publicized lecture and film series, often about adventure travel, in the *Grosvenor Auditorium* around the corner at

1600 M Street NW. Tickets, which range from $4.00 to $15.00 per event, can get scarce, so check the schedule and buy in advance by calling 857–7700 (fax 857–7747). The Grosvenor's box office is open 9:00 A.M. to 5:00 P.M. Monday through Friday. Every Tuesday at noon from October to May the Society sponsors a free film program in Grosvenor Auditorium. Call 857–7700 for details. Metro: Farragut North (red line) and Farragut West (orange line). Tickets, along with other information about the National Geographic, are also available at www.nationalgeographic.com.

Across M Street from the National Geographic is the Sumner School, named after Senator Charles Sumner, who was caned on the floor of the Senate after giving a speech against slavery. The school played a historic and crucial role in the education of black students in the District ever since it opened in 1873 as the city's first high school for blacks. In 1979 this classic redbrick schoolhouse became the *Sumner School Museum and Archives,* dedicated to fostering African-American culture, history, and accomplishment. Exhibits of art and history predominate, but you also might find displays of textiles from Nigeria, paintings by black artists, or historic photographs of African-American life in bygone times. Charles Sumner School Museum, 1201 17th Street NW (442–6060, fax 727–6812), is open Monday through Saturday from 10:00 A.M. to 5:00 P.M. Metro: Farragut North (red line) and Farragut West (orange line).

And if during your visit you hear the sounds of strings and chamber music, that's because the school also hosts the *Friday Morning Music Club,* a series of free concerts of classical music featuring top local musicians. The concerts, which are given in the school's museum, begin at noon and are open to the public. Get concert schedules and other information at www.fmmc.org or 333–2075.

Chess buffs should make a series of lightning moves to the *U.S. Chess Center* at 1501 M Street NW, where they'll find one of America's few chess museums. The center's exhibits contain scorebooks of great matches, chess trophies, and art, along with a vast assortment of chess memorabilia. On the walls, photographs and other mementos make up the Chess Hall of Fame, a series of displays honoring American chess champions, and in the center's gift shop,

Homeopathic Heaven

Didn't I tell you that Washington has a statue for everything? Dr. Samuel Hahnemann, who of course you always knew as the father of modern homeopathy, is commemorated with one on the east side of Scott Circle at 16th Street and Massachusetts Avenue NW. A colorful mosaic rounds out the tribute. Metro: Farragut North (red line).

enthusiasts can pick up chess books, boards and sets, and even chess-themed T-shirts. The center emphasizes its instructional programs for children, in which about 2,000 local schoolkids are enrolled. The center also sponsors tournaments and evening games, but I'm told that walk-ins are only rarely able to find a pickup game. The center is open Monday through Thursday nights, starting at 6:00 P.M. and on weekends from noon to 6:00 P.M. Closed Friday. Call 857–4922 or visit www.chessctr.org. Metro: McPherson Square (orange and blue lines).

Places to Stay in Downtown

The Beacon Hotel and Corporate Quarters
1615 Rhode Island Avenue NW
296–2100
http://capitalhotelswdc.com
As the name tells you, the Beacon is aimed at corporate travelers, which explains why 60 of its 199 rooms are spacious suites. Aside from a great location, the Beacon also offers tasteful decor, lots of desk space, along with Wi-Fi connections and all the other electronic goodies that keep road warriors in touch. Even if you're not a guest, drop by the hotel's stylish restaurant, the Beacon Bar and Grill, where the appetizer is likely to be a meeting of the American south with Asia followed by more conventional offerings of steak and seafood. Metros: Farragut North and Dupont Circle (red line).

Hotel Harrington
436 11th Street NW
628–8140 or
(800) 424–8532
www.hotelharrington.com
This family-owned, frill-free hostelry is a Washington institution and a perennial favorite of budget travelers and tour groups. The main reasons are its value and great location, where downtown Washington meets Pennsylvania Avenue and only a short walk from the National Mall. A cafeteria, coin laundry, and pub round out the package. Inexpensive. Metro: Metro Center (red, orange, and blue lines).

Hotel Washington
15th Street and Pennsylvania Avenue NW
638–5900
www.hotelwashington.com
Talk about a great location! This first-rate Italian Renaissance hotel built in 1918 overlooks the Washington Monument and the Treasury; many rooms have great views down Pennsylvania Avenue to the Capitol dome. Expensive. Metro: Metro Center (red, orange, and blue lines).

J. W. Marriott
1331 Pennsylvania Avenue NW
393–2000
Large (773 rooms) and a major meeting/convention place, this is the flagship of the Marriott chain. The J. W. Marriott is located at the crosshairs of downtown Washington, convenient to everything in the city center, including the White House, National Theatre, and Lafayette Square. The hotel sits on top of National Place, a large shopping center with an assortment of stores and restaurants. Expensive. Metro: Metro Center (red, orange, and blue lines).

Mayflower Hotel
1127 Connecticut Avenue NW
347–3000
This National Historic Landmark opened in 1925 with Calvin Coolidge's inaugural ball, and it's been attracting the important and powerful ever since. FDR and Eleanor stayed here while waiting for the Hoovers to move out of 1600 Pennsylvania; Charles De Gaulle and Nikita Khrushchev also signed the register. With its majestic main promenade, top restaurants, and luxurious rooms, it's easy to see why. Molto expensive. Metro: Farragut North (red line).

The Sofitel Lafayette Square
806 15th Street NW
737–8800
This is the downtown Washington outpost of France's top luxury hotel chain, and it is *très magnifique*. Located in a 1920s Art Moderne office building, the elegance starts in the original marble lobby, with its 17-foot ceilings, and continues on upstairs in the Sofitel's 237 sleek and understated guest rooms. Because it's French, the Sofitel has loads of élan, not to mention panache, along with a certain je ne sais quoi. A first-class restaurant, Cafe 15, and impeccable service make this a great, if expensive, experience. Metro: McPherson Square (orange and blue lines).

Places to Eat in Downtown

Beacon Bar and Grill
1615 Rhode Island Avenue NW
(in the Beacon Hotel)
872–1126

This attractive bistro with friendly service is well located for downtown lunches and dinners. American bistro also describes the food, which ranges from sandwiches, large salads, and pizza to grilled fish and steaks. Outside patio is open in good weather. Reserve, especially for lunch, when the National Geographic folks get out their maps and head this way. Moderate. Open daily 6:30 A.M. to 11:00 P.M. Metro: Farragut North (red line) and Farragut West (orange line).

Bobby Van's Steakhouse
809 15th Street NW
589–0060
See page 11 for full description.

Cosi Sandwich Bar
1700 Pennsylvania Avenue NW
638–7101
If you haven't been invited to lunch at 1600 Pennsylvania, don't despair. At Cosi you'll see oodles of White House staff dining decisively on tailor-made sandwiches of tandoori chicken or tuna salad and brie, or you can watch the president's men and women lining up boldly to carry out grilled vegetables

and tasty salads. This branch of a successful New York chain has caught on in a big way in D.C., mainly because of its encyclopedic range of sandwich ingredients and its patented focaccia-style bread. Great for lunch after touring the Lafayette Square/White House neighborhood. No reservations. Inexpensive. Open Monday through Friday 7:00 A.M. to 7:00 P.M., Saturday and Sunday 9:00 A.M. to 5:00 P.M. Metro: Farragut West (blue and orange lines).

Fourth Estate
529 14th Street
662–7638
See pages 14–15 for full description.

Loeb's
832 15th Street
371–1150
If Kosher food had a mecca, this would be it. This storefront deli is for homesick New Yorkers or anyone else who likes thick sandwiches of corned beef, pastrami, or tongue. Cream soda and bagels too—so what's not to like? Just around the corner from Lafayette Square. Open 6:00 A.M. to 4:30 P.M. Monday through Friday. No reservations. Inexpensive. Metro: McPherson Square (orange and blue lines).

M&S Grill
600 13th Street NW
347–1500
www.mccormickand
schimck.com
The atmosphere is late Victorian mansion, with Tiffany glass ceilings, chandeliers, and polished walnut paneled walls. J. P. Morgan would feel right at home. M&S's American bistro menu includes steaks, chops, and well-prepared fish and scampi, which is understandable in a restaurant owned by Seattle's McCormick and Schmick (M&S—get it?). Inventive salads and sides too. The wine list is good and well priced, but could be a tad longer. All this plus friendly, professional service. Open Monday through Friday 11:30 A.M. to 11:00 P.M., Saturday 4:00 to 11:00 P.M., Sunday 4:00 to 10:00 P.M. Moderate. Metro: Metro Center (red, orange, and blue lines).

The Old Ebbitt Grill
675 15th Street NW
347–4801
www.clydes.com
Located across from Treasury this is a big local favorite with a long history, where the decor is early McKinley and the food is refined American bistro. Favorites include steaks, grilled fish of all kinds, great crab cakes, and fresh oysters from all over. The liver and onions will

make you forget mom's forced feeding; the burgers are classics. The Ebbitt's two immense bars are always crowded. First-rate Sunday brunch. Very popular with politicos, real Washingtonians, and visitors, making reservations a must. Moderate. Open Monday through Friday 7:30 A.M. to 1:00 A.M., Saturday and Sunday 8:30 A.M. to 1:00 A.M. Metro: Metro Center (red, orange, and blue lines).

The Palm
1225 19th Street NW
293–9091
See page 11 for full description.

Red Sage
605 14th Street NW
638–4444
This dazzling Southwestern favorite is actually two restaurants in one. The always busy street-level bar and dining area is lively and informal, with a chili bar, lighter fare, and moderate prices; in the grill room downstairs the action is more serious (and expensive) with dishes such as chorizos and black bean terrine or chipotle shrimp on a buttermilk corncake. No reservations upstairs, but essential for downstairs dining. Upstairs hours: Monday through Saturday 11:45 A.M. to 11:45 P.M., Sunday 4:30 to 11:00 P.M. Grill hours: Monday

through Friday 11:30 A.M. to 2:00 P.M., Saturday and Sunday 5:00 to 10:30 P.M. Moderate upstairs; expensive downstairs. If you liked Red Sage and want to take it home with you, go next door to the Red Sage Bakery and Store, practically incandescent with all those spices, hot sauces, and dried peppers. Open Monday through Friday 8:00 A.M. to 3:00 P.M. Metro: Metro Center (red, orange, and blue lines).

Smith and Wollensky
1112 19th Street NW
446–1100
See page 11 for full description.

Tuscana West
1350 I Street NW
289–7300
This downtown Italian is a favorite of the lawyers, lobbyists, and other denizens of nearby K Street's "glitter gulch." Despite its name, Tuscana West offers dishes from all over Italy, including hearty northern risottos and southern pastas with heavy-duty red sauce, along with Tuscany's famed veal chops and seafood. Reservations advised. Moderate. Open Monday through Friday 11:30 A.M. to 10:00 P.M., Saturday 5:30 to 10:00 P.M.; closed Sunday. Metro: McPherson Square (blue and orange lines).

Pennsylvania Quarter and Chinatown

L'Enfant's original plan for Washington envisioned the area around Seventh Street and Pennsylvania Avenue as the hub of the capital's civic life, where the courts, main government buildings, and city hall would be located. And they were. Washington's courthouse and judicial complex, along with great neo-classic public buildings, like the Patent Office and the now abandoned Old Post Office at Seventh and E Streets, were built in this neighborhood and are still there. In later years, the Seventh Street area also became the place to shop for produce at the mammoth Center Market on Pennsylvania Avenue, which operated from 1801 to 1931 on the site of today's National Archives. Seventh Street also became the heart of the city's dry goods district, where Mr. Saks built his first store before moving on to New York's Fifth Avenue. Local department stores like Hecht's, Kann's, and Woodward and Lothrop dominated the area until the 1960s, when the Seventh Street neighborhood fell into disrepair.

The late 1980s saw the Seventh Street corridor, now known as the "New Downtown" or "Pennsylvania Quarter," stage a rebound that's still in progress, thanks in part to the construction of the MCI sports complex and the arrival of trendy art galleries and restaurants. Today the revitalized Seventh Street

N

0   1/4 mi

0   1/4 km

corridor boasts an intense gallery and art scene, some of the city's most innovative restaurants, a world-class Shakespearean theater, and a pair of unforgettable museums. It is also the gateway to Washington's Chinatown.

Two Metro stops serve the Pennsylvania Quarter: at the Chinatown end
through the Gallery Place/Chinatown stop on the yellow, red, and green lines
and at the Pennsylvania Avenue end through the Archives/Navy Memorial stop
on the blue, yellow, orange, and green lines.

Start your visit to the Pennsylvania Quarter at the *Navy Memorial,* which
proves that even well-beaten paths like Pennsylvania Avenue can have hidden
corners. This impressive but simple memorial—with its fountains, ship's masts
with signal flags, and the touching statue of the *Lone Sailor*—commemorates
the Navy's battles, heroism, and achievements. Two curved sculpture walls
record important Navy accomplishments and scenes from Navy history. With
any luck at all, you'll be there for one of the frequent outdoor concerts by the
Navy Band or a visiting musical group.

But less well known, even to many Washingtonians, is the privately funded
Naval Heritage Center. The center's entrance hall adjoins the Memorial on
street level, but the real action is below deck, on an underground floor where
exhibits depict Navy traditions and a "Ship's Store" sells nautical mementos,
prints, and books. The center also has a state-of-the-art theater showing *At Sea,*
an action-packed film about carrier life. And don't miss "Navy Log," where you
can search military records on a 250,000-name computerized database to see if
your Navy or Marine pals haven't been exaggerating their war stories.

The Naval Heritage Center, at 701 Pennsylvania Avenue NW (737–2300), is
open Tuesday through Saturday 9:30 A.M. to 5:00 P.M.; closed Sunday. From
November through February the center is also closed Monday. E-mail

TOP ATTRACTIONS IN THE PENNSYLVANIA QUARTER AND CHINATOWN

National Museum of American Art	Cafe Atlantico
National Portrait Gallery	Verizon Center
Naval Heritage Center	Chinatown
Shakespeare Theatre	National Law Enforcement Officers Memorial
Old Pension Building	
National Building Museum	Morrison-Clark Inn

ahoy@lone sailor.org or visit www.lonesailor.org. Metro: Archives/Navy Memorial (green and yellow lines).

Just off Seventh Street on Indiana Avenue stand a trio of well-preserved 1820 houses that knew Lincoln when the president's carriage took him up Seventh Street to his summer White House at the Soldier's Home. Fine residential dwellings in their day, these antebellum homes have long since been converted to commercial use. The house at 641 Indiana is where you'll find *Artifactory*, a large collection of art and handicrafts unearthed by owner Dominick Cardella on his travels in Africa and Asia. Cardella's shop is packed with an eclectic and tasteful selection of artifacts that includes marionettes from Burma and Indonesia, Balinese masks, and traditional African art and statuary. Artifactory is open Monday through Saturday 10:00 A.M. to 6:00 P.M. Call 393–2727. Metro: Archives/Navy Memorial (yellow and green lines).

The *Touchstone Gallery*, upstairs at 406 Seventh Street NW, is one of the city's original cooperative galleries. In its vast exhibit space you'll see both group and solo shows by its over thirty member-artists, mainly painters and sculptors. And don't be bashful—if you see something you like, why not just write a check on the spot and take it home with you—the artists won't mind at all. Open Wednesday through Friday from 11:00 A.M. to 5:00 P.M.; Saturday and Sunday, noon to 6:00 P.M. (347–2787; www.touchstonegallery.com). Visitors to 406 Seventh Street can browse and buy art.

Even the storefront at 406 offers art, but of a slightly different kind. At *Apartment Zero* you'll find one of D.C.'s hippest home furnishings stores, with cutting-edge office and home furniture, standing lamps of sculptured paper, and, in season, unique Christmas tree ornaments. Nick and Nora Charles would really go for Apartment Zero's collection of '30s era martini shakers, glassware, and other cocktail paraphernalia, minus the olives. Shop here and your house will never be the same. Open Wednesday through Saturday 11:00 A.M. to 6:00 P.M., Sunday noon to 5:00 P.M. Call 628–4067 or visit www .apartmentzero.com. Metro: Archives/Navy Memorial (yellow and green lines).

AUTHOR'S FAVORITES IN THE PENNSYLVANIA QUARTER AND CHINATOWN

International Spy Museum	Jaleo
Hotel Monaco	Teaism
Old Pension Building	Temperance Fountain

Although there's a Starbucks in the next block, ***Footnotes Cafe*** seems to be the coffeehouse of choice for Penn Quarter gallery goers and book browsers. Located in the Seventh Street branch of Olsson's, an outstanding local chain of book and record sellers, Footnotes has a wide range of coffees and teas, a good but short wine list, and a selection of erudite sandwiches for literary noshing. Try ordering the Charles Dickens (traditional roast beef), the Herman Melville ("a whale of a tuna sandwich"), or, if the bambini are along, the Dr. Seuss, which (no surprise here) is peanut butter and jelly. Tables with chairs and sofas round out the picture and, should you feel like falling into a literary swoon, there's a cut velvet chaise longue available in the window. Footnotes, located at 418 Seventh Street, is open Monday 8:00 A.M. to 5:00 P.M., Tuesday through Friday 8:00 A.M. to 7:30 P.M., Saturday 10:00 A.M. to 7:00 P.M., Sunday noon to 7:00 P.M.; afternoon tea from 3:00 to 6:00 P.M. Call 638–4882. Metro: Archives/Navy Memorial (yellow and green lines).

Pua, the shop at 444 Seventh Street NW, takes its name from a natural plant fiber produced in the Himalayas, then spun and woven by hand by Nepalese craftswomen. Pua's designs include quilted cotton coats and jackets, colorful and attractive dresses, and block printed skirts and pants. While you're deciding, have a cup of Darjeeling in Pua's little tearoom. Open Monday noon to 6:00 P.M., Tuesday through Friday noon to 7:30 P.M., Saturday and Sunday 1:00 to 8:00 P.M. Call 347–4543. Metro: Archives/Navy Memorial (yellow and green lines); www.pua-naturally.com.

In Spanish ***Andale*** means "let's go"—not a bad idea if you're in the Pennsylvania Quarter and looking for a delightful place to dine. The cuisine is authentic and professionally prepared Mexican, with familiar dishes like queso fundido and chorizo balanced against fresh and inventive versions of red snapper seviche and zesty pork carnitas. The *Washingtonian*'s food critic gave high marks to the airy Enchiladas Zapotecas and called the Barbacoa de Borrego Andale's "unchallenged gem." And if you go on Monday night, every bottle of wine on the list is half price. Que alegria!! Andale, 401 Seventh Street NW, is open Monday through Friday for lunch from 11:30 A.M. to 3:00 P.M. and for dinner 5:00 to 10:00 P.M., until 11:00 P.M. on Friday and Saturday. Dinner reservations suggested (783–3133; www.andaledc.com).

The ***Zenith Gallery*** is a Pennsylvania Quarter pioneer, having arrived at 413 Seventh Street in 1986. It is also one of the neighborhood's more eclectic galleries, where you'll find sculptures in bronze, steel, wood, and ceramic, abstract and realistic paintings, and other media ranging from light sculptures to wearable art, furniture, and comical figures of papier-mâché and resin. If you have a taste for whimsy, the Zenith is for you. The Zenith Gallery is open Tuesday through Friday 11:00 A.M. to 6:00 P.M., Saturday noon to 7:00 P.M., and

Sunday noon to 5:00 P.M. Call 783–2963, fax 783–0050; www.zenithgallery.com. Metro: Archives/Navy Memorial (yellow and green lines).

Tucked away behind the modest marquee at 450 Seventh Street is the 451-seat *Shakespeare Theatre,* which the *Economist* called "one of the world's three great Shakespearean theatres," and the *Wall Street Journal* dubbed "the nation's foremost Shakespeare company." Since the Shakespeare opened in 1986, its performances have racked up dozens of awards, plus acclaim from the *New York Times* as a "critical and popular success." Outstanding guest actors such as Elizabeth Ashley, Hal Holbrook, and Patrick Stewart often join the resident company in staging Shakespearean and other classical plays during the theater's September to July season. Call 547–1122 for information on what's playing, to book seats, or to ask about the Shakespeare's outdoor summer performances in Rock Creek Park or visit www.shakespearetheatre.org. The box office is open Monday 10:00 A.M. to 6:00 P.M., Tuesday through Saturday 10:00 A.M. to 6:30 P.M., and Sunday noon to 6:30 P.M. Metro: Archives/Navy Memorial (yellow and green lines).

Those walls covered with colorful plates and a giant mural of a flamenco dancer announce that you've arrived at *Jaleo,* a lively storefront Spanish bistro on the corner of Seventh and E Streets. If you're headed for the Shakespeare Theatre next door or the Verizon Center up the street, this bright and bustling restaurant with friendly service is perfect for a pre- or postperformance snack or meal. Choose four or five hot or cold tapas, maybe some garlic shrimp, grilled lamb, or peppers stuffed with goat cheese, and you're off and running. But for a lot of people (like me), that's just the beginning, so they move on to Chef Jose Andres's excellent paellas, grilled fish, or fish stew. Grilled spicy Spanish chorizos (sausages), either as tapas or as a main dish with beans and

The Venerable Bead

Whoever said, "when you've seen one bead museum, you've seen 'em all" clearly had never cast a beady eye at 400 Seventh Street NW. The *Washington Bead Museum*'s spacious loft hosts a continuous round of exhibits of handmade glass beads, period glass, and jewelry from all over, including the United States, the Czech Republic, India, and Africa. Aside from attracting a worldwide audience of bead enthusiasts, the museum also sponsors a series of educational programs to illustrate how beadwork reflects a society's craftsmanship, traditions, and history. Open Wednesday through Saturday 11:00 A.M. to 4:00 P.M., Sunday 1:00 to 4:00 P.M. Closed Monday and Tuesday. Call 624–4500, visit www.beadmuseumdc.org, or e-mail info@beadmuseumdc.org. Suggested donation $3.00.

asparagus, are always a good choice. And, no surprise, the gazpacho and sangria are terrific. As in Madrid, the dinner and bar action goes on until late, when a trendy younger crowd takes over and Jaleo begins to live up to its name—which translates as uproar or revelry—especially on Wednesday nights, when the dancers from Seville perform. Bring castanets. Jaleo, 480 Seventh Street NW (628–7949), is open Sunday and Monday 11:30 A.M. to 10:00 P.M., Tuesday through Thursday 11:30 A.M. to 11:30 P.M., Friday and Saturday 11:30 A.M. to 11:30 P.M.; www.jaleo.com. Although Jaleo accepts a limited number of preshow reservations from 5:00 to 6:30 P.M., seating at other times is walk-in. Moderate. Metro: Archives/Navy Memorial (yellow and green lines).

The neoclassical gem that occupies the block that stretches from Seventh to Eighth Streets between E and F Streets was designed by Robert Mills, who was also the architect of the Treasury Building and the Washington Monument. When it opened in 1842 as Washington's General Post Office, Charles Dickens loved this building, calling it "very compact and very beautiful," making it practically the only thing in Washington that Dickens *did* approve of during his 1842 visit. This is also where the first telegraph message, "what hath God wrought," was transmitted by Samuel F. B. Morse in 1845. During the Civil War the building saw duty as a barracks and hospital. The Post Office ended its official days as the home of the Tariff Commission, after which it stood abandoned for many years until, in 2002, as a prime example of downtown Washington's dramatic renaissance, it was restored, rehabbed, and reopened as the ***Hotel Monaco,*** one of the city's very best hotels. Guests check in at a period reception desk located where clerks sold stamps to 1840s Washingtonians (and maybe even Dickens himself) then stroll down a soaring nineteenth-century corridor to your strictly twenty-first century room with 16-foot ceilings and the sizzle of colorful fabrics. Oh yes, if your bed seems extra-long, you're in one of the "tall rooms" specially configured for the NBA stars who play at the Verizon Center across the street. And the Monaco's Poste-Moderne Brasserie restaurant overlooks the courtyard where the Pony Express riders and Wells-Fargo wagons once brought in mail for sorting by clerks who worked right about where diners now sit.

That massive Greek Revival building on Seventh between F and G Streets is the ***Old Patent Office,*** which dates from the 1830s, when old photos show its elegant columns beginning to rise above the swamplands and meadows of a distinctly rustic Washington. During the Civil War the Patent Office became a Union Army barracks and hospital where two government clerks, poet Walt Whitman and American Red Cross founder Clara Barton, served as volunteer nurses. Lincoln's second inaugural ball was held in the vast, marble-columned

National Portrait Gallery, Old Patent Office

room on the third floor known today as the Lincoln Gallery. The building's Victorian gingerbread Great Hall was once the largest room in America and is still one of the most ornate and beautiful.

Since 1968 this Washington landmark has housed two of the capital's finest museums: the National Portrait Gallery, with stunning portraits of the men and women who shaped American history, from George Washington to Ernest Hemingway, and the National Museum of American Art, dedicated to the entire span of American artistic creativity. After a total six-year makeover, the two museums merged and re-opened as the Reynolds Center for American Art and Portraiture in July 2006, and the result is staggering—a remarkable trove of American art you won't want to miss. Not only has the interior of this venerable building been made even more dramatic, the exhibit space has been greatly enlarged and now includes the Lunder Conservation Center where you can look in on the latest in ongoing art restoration, and a three-story storage facility that allows visitors a behind the scenes look at works not on display in the main galleries. Aside from its permanent collections, the Center hosts many temporary exhibits, including candidates for the prestigious Virginia Outwin Boochever portrait competition. Since you could easily spend the day in this Aladdin's cave of fine art and design, it's fortunate that there are three cafes to revive you before you resume your explorations. The Center is open daily from 11:30 A.M. to 7:00 P.M. (633–1000; www.reynoldscenter.org).

The District's **Recorder of Deeds Building** at 515 D Street NW may not amount to much aesthetically, but it contains a set of wonderful murals representing important leaders and events throughout African-American history. The series begins in the entrance hall by honoring scientist Benjamin Banneker; six others depict Frederick Douglass in his role as adviser to Abraham Lincoln, Col. Robert Shaw and the 54th Massachusetts at the siege of Confederate Fort Wagner, and explorer Matthew Henson at the South Pole with Admiral Peary. These imposing paintings, like many in post offices and other public buildings throughout the United States, were commissioned by the Public Works Administration, which means that they date from the early 1940s. The building is open Monday through Friday from 8:30 A.M. to 4:00 P.M. Metro: Archives/Navy Memorial (yellow and green lines).

Clandestine Collection

It wouldn't make much sense in your average American city but, when you're the "World's Spy Capital" (that's Washington), you've just gotta have a spy museum. D.C. has the first and only museum dedicated to espionage, and it's a good one. Even if you left your cloak and dagger in the drawer back home, you'll still enjoy the *International Spy Museum,* which occupies five landmark buildings, with its main entrance at 800 F Street NW. The museum offers a number of lively exhibits of international intelligence artifacts, including the legendary Enigma cipher machine, an orientation into the world of spy tradecraft, and videos of famous and real-life espionage and counterespionage stories, including historic capers involving the Berlin Wall and some current cases involving turncoats like Aldrich Ames and Robert Hanssen. If you're traveling with children, ask about the Museum's monthly "KidSpy Workshops" where they can play spy, learn the art of disguises, and use some of the clandestine equipment on display. Admission is $25. Reservations for these workshops are essential and adults are not admitted. Sorry.

The Museum also has a nifty spy shop where you can pick up your spy camera, disguise kit, and other spook gear, including how-to-do-it books about making your very own dead drops and scheduling your next *treff.* When you get back home you'll definitely be an International Man (or Woman) of Mystery; just don't get arrested.

The museum has two excellent restaurants, *Zola,* where, under deep cover, you can join James Bond in dining on modern American cooking in a large loft space. Zola (www.zoladc.com) is open Monday through Friday 11:30 A.M. to midnight, Saturday from 5:00 P.M. to midnight, and Sundays from 5:00 to 10:00 P.M. For more casual fare, including salads and sandwiches, try the *Spy City Cafe* (open daily 8:00 A.M. to 8:00 P.M.). Both the museum and its excellent shop specializing in spook lore are open daily from November to March 10:00 A.M. to 6:00 P.M. and until 8:00 P.M. from April through October; 393–7798; www.spymuseum.org. Admission is $13 for adults and $10 for children and students; secret agents under five are admitted free. Red Alert: Since the museum is a major attraction, long lines are frequent so book ahead. Metro stops: Gallery Place/Chinatown (red, yellow, and green lines) and Archives/Navy Memorial (blue, yellow, orange, and green lines).

Honoring the Men in Blue

The *National Law Enforcement Officers Memorial,* across F Street from the National Building Museum, bears the names of the 14,500 American law enforcement officers killed in the line of duty since 1794. Like the Vietnam Memorial, the wall of inscriptions is frequently visited by relatives or colleagues of the fallen officers, who often leave flowers in remembrance. Although the memorial reminds visitors that violence is always just around the corner for law enforcers, it is also a restful, nicely landscaped place to stroll or take a break from gallery- and museum-hopping.

The *National Law Enforcement Visitor Center,* a short walk away at 605 E Street, is the memorial's companion, a collection of exhibits honoring officers killed in the line of duty. There is also a display of legendary policemen, whose ranks include New York Police Commissioner Teddy Roosevelt, "Untouchable" Eliot Ness, and Wild West lawman Wyatt Earp. The visitor center is open Monday through Friday 9:00 A.M. to 5:00 P.M., Saturday 10:00 A.M. to 5:00 P.M., and Sunday noon to 5:00 P.M. Call 737–3213, visit www.nleomf.com, or e-mail info@ nleomf.com.

Tucked away in a tidy little garden at the corner of Third and G Streets NW is the 1876 redbrick synagogue that houses the **Lillian and Albert Small Jewish Museum.** The museum, run by the Jewish Historical Society of Greater Washington, brings together archives and records of Jewish history in Washington over the years. A series of exhibits profile Jewish life in the capital; one of the recent ones, "Kronheim's Washington," was a collection of photographs and other mementos of one of the Jewish community's top movers and shakers. The museum is located at 701 Third Street NW; open by appointment only (789–0900; www.jhsgw.org). Metro: Judiciary Square (red line).

At **Cafe Atlantico** the accent is on Latin America and its exciting *nueva cocina.* Dining is on three dramatically staged levels, each displaying the work of South American and Caribbean artists. Thirsty gringos can belly up to the bar for potent *bebidas latinas* like silky margaritas and tasty but lethal pisco sours. If a few of these Pan-American powerhouses haven't sent you south of the border, order one of the restaurant's imaginative specialties such as Brazilian feijoada with an Asian spin, duck confit, or a plump grilled salmon wrapped in papaya. There's usually a tasting menu, and at Saturday lunch the main attraction is an inventive and popular Latin American dim sum platter. Reservations recommended; to get them, call 393–0812. Cafe Atlantico, at 405 Eighth Street NW, serves lunch 11:30 A.M. to 2:30 P.M. Monday through Friday and dinner from 5:00 to 10:00 P.M. On Friday and Saturday dinner is served from 5:00 to 11:00 P.M. Sunday it's dinner only, from 5:00 to 10:00 P.M.; www.cafeatlantico.com Expensive.

Across the street at 400 Eighth Street, in the bright, airy *Teaism* restaurant, you can dine in utter tranquility on everything from miso soup and soba noodle salad to *ochazuke,* which is Japanese rice and tea soup. Teaism also specializes in "big dishes" of curries and rice, but for a real change of pace, try a "bento" or Japanese meal box based on salmon, beef, or tuna. Teaism's eclectic menu also offers breakfasts of French toast, chicken sausage with naan and raita, and (need we say it?) a vast repertoire of teas and tisanes. Open Monday through Friday 7:30 A.M. to 10:00 P.M., Saturday and Sunday 9:30 A.M. to 9:30 P.M. (638–6010; www.teaism.com).

If you liked Teaism enough to take it home with you, pop into the restaurant's tea shop next door to pick up some Jasmine Pearl or Anxi for your very own, and carry it away in a gorgeous tea box made with colorful washi paper. Here you'll also find all the tea paraphernalia you could ever need, including all of the exotic sweets, jams, and chocolates needed to wow your pals with a great high tea. Open Monday through Friday 7:30 A.M. to 9:00 P.M., Saturday and Sunday 9:30 A.M. to 9:00 P.M. Call 638–7740.

The *Verizon Center,* with its banners and imposing facade, has been the centerpiece of this neighborhood and of the Washington sports and cultural scene since the day it opened its doors in 1998. The center hosts professional teams like the NBA Wizards, the WNBA Mystics, the NHL Capitals, and the Georgetown University Hoyas, along with a variety of concerts.

The Verizon Center, at 601 F Street NW, is open daily 10:00 A.M. to 10:00 P.M. (or one hour after center events conclude), Sunday 10:00 A.M. to 6:00 P.M. For information, call 628–3200; for seats it's 432–7328, or go online at www.verizon center.com. And on the way out, don't miss the photographic exhibit of

Verizon Center

Hooker's Army

When the Civil War brought hundreds of thousands of soldiers to Washington, something occurred that Pierre L'Enfant, the great planner, could never have foreseen. Pennsylvania Avenue, a.k.a. "America's Main Street," turned into America's leading red-light district, where hundreds of Washington hostesses gathered every evening around Seventh Street. Union General Joseph Hooker, concerned about this, ordered the ladies and their activities confined to a nearby neighborhood known today as Federal Triangle, a command that caused them to refer to themselves sarcastically as "Hooker's Army," and so the term "hooker" was born. Archaeological note: Excavations for major buildings in this area have turned up perfume and liquor bottles, combs, and garter hooks.

neighborhood history just inside the F Street entrance. Metro: Gallery Place/Chinatown (red, yellow, and green lines).

You can't miss the **Old Pension Building,** the spectacular redbrick Victorian pile on F Street that occupies the entire block between Fourth and Fifth Streets. The building, inspired by Rome's Palazzo Farnese, is circled by a terracotta frieze of the Union Army and Navy in action, complete with bayonet charges, sea battles, and gallant generals on rearing chargers, your clue that the building was constructed to process Civil War veterans benefits. But this is far from being a maze of cubicles for civil service paper pushers. You'll be astounded by the grandeur of the Pension Building's Great Hall—a 300-foot-long interior courtyard supported by eight colossal marble columns with a fountain in the center. It's the perfect place for a large and elegant party, which is exactly why presidents since Grover Cleveland have been using the Great Hall for their inaugural balls.

The magnificent setting tends to overshadow the **National Building Museum,** which now occupies part of this grand space. The museum, which celebrates the building arts, nevertheless holds its own with a series of lively exhibits ranging from the American country store to the impact of air-conditioning on everyday life. Don't miss the permanent exhibit *Washington: Symbol and City,* an excellent orientation to the history of the Federal City, the evolution of its architecture, and the impact of European cities on Washington's urban plan. The museum shop is one of the city's best—well stocked with imaginative gifts along with books on buildings and architecture. In the museum's cafe, you'll find coffee, salads, and a wide selection of sandwiches. The Building Museum is at 401 F Street NW (272-2448; www.nbm.org). Museum hours are Monday through Saturday 10:00 A.M. to 5:00 P.M., Sunday

11:00 A.M. to 5:00 P.M. Building tours, which last forty-five minutes, are given Monday through Wednesday at 12:30 P.M., Thursday through Saturday at 11:30 A.M., 12:30 and 1:30 P.M., and Sunday at 12:30 and 1:30 P.M. Reservations are not needed and there is no charge. Metro: Judiciary Square (red line).

One of Washington's newest and most thoughtful museums is the *Marion Koshland Science Museum*, located at the corner of Sixth and E Streets NW. The Koshland, which is part of the National Academy of Sciences, features a series of exhibits, many of them interactive and based on studies carried out by the academy. Some will introduce visitors to the wonders of science in general and dramatize the role of science in our everyday world, while others are tar-

Urban Preservation

The *Morrison-Clark Inn* is a prime example of how urban preservation and restoration can enrich the lives of Washington's residents and visitors. This grand Victorian mansion at Massachusetts Avenue and 11th Street actually represents the twentieth-century merger of a pair of handsome homes built in 1864 by wealthy merchants David Morrison and Reuben Clark. A subsequent owner of the Morrison house (obviously a Sinophile) added the grand Chinese Chippendale porch and graceful Shanghai roof visible on the Massachusetts Avenue side of the inn. Through fifty-seven years and two world wars, the house served as an inexpensive residence and club for enlisted men until 1987, when it was extensively renovated and opened as the elegant hotel and restaurant that it is today.

As men of wealth and taste, Messrs. Morrison and Clark would feel right at home in this upscale urban inn. Floor-to-ceiling pier mirrors face each other across a lobby with antebellum furniture and a marble fireplace. The Victorian feel is reflected in the upstairs guest rooms, with their massive armoires, antique furnishings, and imposing mahogany headboards. If you go, ask about room 215, with its private entrance to the porch and a great view up and down Massachusetts Avenue. The inn also offers its guests several French country–style rooms and parlor suites with wicker furniture and pine armoires.

The inn is home to one of Washington's top restaurants, which specializes in imaginative American cuisine. Entrees are seasonal and might include roast quail or Dijon-crusted salmon. All of this culinary delight takes place in an elegant Victorian dining room with tall windows, more full-length gilded mirrors and drapes, and a central banquette of unobtrusive chinoiserie. It is regularly named as one of Washington's most romantic restaurants.

The Morrison-Clark Inn (www.morrisonclark.com) is located at 1015 L Street NW, in the Penn Quarter. Call 898–1200 or (800) 332–7898; fax 289–8576. The dining room is open Tuesday through Saturday 6:00 to 10:00 P.M. The inn and its restaurant are both expensive. Metro: Mt. Vernon Square (yellow and green lines).

geted on subjects like the uses of DNA sequencing and the implications of global warming for the planet. The museum is open 10:00 A.M. to 6:00 P.M. daily except Tuesday (334–1201; www.koshland-science-museum.org). Admission is $5.00 for adults and $3.00 for seniors and students. Metro: Judiciary Square (red line).

In its impressive new space at 641 D Street NW you'll find the **Woolly Mammoth Theater Company,** which the *New York Times* called "Washington's most daring theater company." Woolly mammoths may be slightly antiquated, but that's the last thing you'd say about this cutting-edge theater, which puts on shows with titles like *Preaching to the Perverted* and other edgy American plays. The Woolly is now in its twenty-fifth season and still going strong. If you're interested in seeing some of Washington's most original and talented theater, call 393–3939 for details or go to www.woollymammoth.net.

chinese newyear

If you're in town during early February, call 638–1041 to learn the date and other details about Washington's annual Chinese New Year celebration, which is great fun, with plenty of fireworks and a parade led by a giant dragon.

If you're accustomed to visiting Chinatowns in San Francisco or New York, D.C.'s version is going to seem pretty puny, its main attraction being the ornate and colorful archway at Seventh and H Streets. Chinatown's Metro stop is, logically enough, Gallery Place/Chinatown on the red, yellow, and green lines.

Although it lacks the scale and variety of its counterparts elsewhere, Washington's **Chinatown** does offer a broad array of good and inexpensive Chinese restaurants. My favorite is the modest **Full Kee** at 509 H Street (371–2233), where the fried dumplings and the smoked duck are memorable. If you want to combine dining with history, head for **Wok n' Roll** at 604 H Street (347–4656), a modest but good restaurant located in the house of Mary Surratt, where the Lincoln assassination conspiracy was hatched. Mary was hanged for her role in the plot, but don't let that spoil your General Tso's chicken or shredded beef. Both restaurants are open daily for lunch and dinner.

Then there's the "only in America" block, the 800 block of Seventh Street. Here, in the heart of Chinatown and surrounded by street and other signs in Chinese, you'll find lined up *(a)* an Irish pub and restaurant, *(b)* a Texas barbeque restaurant, and *(c)* the German Cultural Institute, which presents rich programs of German film, music, and theater.

At 707 H Street, literally in the shadow of Chinatown's signature ceremonial arch, **Capital Q** serves up Texas-style chow. Instead of hunkering down around the campfire, you'll grab a tray and load your paper plate with smoky sausages, pulled pork, and chicken with collards and slaw. The decor is Early

Texas Shrine, with license plates and other Lone Star mementos on the walls. Open Monday through Thursday 11:00 A.M. to 7:00 P.M., Friday until 9:00 P.M. and Saturday until 8:00 P.M. (347–TEXN; www.capitalqbbq.com).

The Irish bar is **Fado,** which specializes in boxty (an Irish potato pancake stuffed with salmon or steak), shepherd's pie, and the inevitable corned beef and cabbage. Fado is located at 808 Seventh Street NW, and is open Sunday through Thursday 11:30 A.M. to 2:00 A.M., Friday and Saturday 11:30 A.M. to 3:00 A.M. Call 789–0066, or visit www.fadoirishpub.com. Inexpensive.

The German Cultural Center, the **Goethe Institute,** sponsors a wide selection of art exhibits, lectures, and other cultural programs. And if you've always wanted to learn a little Deutsch, there are courses for that as well. The institute is located at 814 Seventh Street and is open Monday through Thursay 9:00 A.M. to 5:00 P.M., Friday 9:00 A.M. to 3:00 P.M. Call 289–1200 or visit www.goethe.de/ins/us/was for information about exhibits and cultural programs.

That glass building to the right of nearby Mount Vernon Square is the headquarters of **National Public Radio.** If you're an NPR fan you should, all things considered, think about taking the regular weekly tour of this national institution. On the one-hour tour you'll see photos of your favorite NPR personalities and the studios where they broadcast. No reservations are needed—just turn up any Thursday at 11:00 A.M. at NPR's main door, which is 635 Avenue NW. However if you're part of a group of five or more, you should call NPR's Listener Services office at 513–3232 at least a month in advance to ensure they'll have space for you. Metro: Gallery Place/Chinatown (yellow, red, and green lines).

The **Sixth and I Historic Synagogue,** one of Washington's dazzling "new" buildings, was actually built in 1908, when part of what is now Chinatown was the site of a vibrant Jewish community. In 1951, in an ecumenical

Strange Monument to Sobriety

A few steps from the Navy Memorial, on Indiana Plaza at Seventh Street and Pennsylvania, stands the *Temperance Fountain,* one of the weirdest statues in a city where bizarre statuary is as common as fund-raising. Note the intertwined fish under four granite pillars surmounted by a triumphant bronze heron (I am not making this up). This powerful inducement to sobriety was erected in the city's former good-time district by (wait, this gets even more bizarre) a California temperance crusader who made his fortune making false teeth. The fountain once spouted water to give thirsty passersby a big, free drink, but the spigot was turned off long ago and the fountain went dry. The city definitely did not.

leap rarely seen in any city, this 1,000-seat synagogue became the home of the Turner Memorial AME church and its African-American congregation. In 2002, just as it was about to be converted again this time into a nightclub, the synagogue was purchased by a group of Washington's Jewish leaders and, after a $2 million renovation, meticulously restored to its former glory. To see its glorious, stenciled 70-foot dome, the original religious artifacts, some rescued from oblivion, and the gorgeous stained glass windows, take one of the tours given Monday through Thursday at 11:30 A.M., and 12:30 and 1:30 P.M. Reserve by calling 408–3100; www.sixthandi.org. The entrance is at 606 I Street NW. Metro: Mt. Vernon Square/Convention Center (yellow and green lines) and Gallery Place/Chinatown (red, yellow, and green lines).

Places to Stay in the Pennsylvania Quarter and Chinatown

Courtyard by Marriott
Ninth and F Streets NW
638–4600
If, like Gordon Gekko in *Wall Street,* you think that "greed is good," and the idea of spending the night snuggled up with some cash has a certain appeal, then this is just the place for you. The Courtyard is located in an 1891 vintage bank that was clearly designed to impress depositors, with its massive stone facade, coffered ceilings, and marble staircases in the lobby. This classic example of urban conversion features a restaurant, the Courtyard Cafe (located among the safe deposit boxes), and a conference area in the former vault. The rooms are equally imposing. Moderate.

Henley Park Hotel
926 Massachusetts Avenue NW; 638–5200 or (800) 222–8474
www.hotelhenleypark.com
This Tudor-style building began life in 1918 as an apartment house, but it's now the urban equivalent of an English country inn. Its seventy-nine rooms and seventeen suites are mainly done in Chippendale, with four-poster beds, antiques, parquet floors, and overstuffed chairs. Cozy, well-mannered, and chintzy in the nice sense—Edith Wharton will be along any minute. The Henley's restaurant, *Coeur de Lion* is, however, strictly non-British, intimate, and hugely romantic with dim lights, a fireplace, and a tinkling piano. And best of all there's wonderful food from a French-trained chef, including veal and foie gras en croute and a spectacular bouillabaisse. One of the best restaurants in the city. Hotel and restaurant are both expensive.

Hotel Monaco
700 F Street NW
682–7177
See page 27 for full description.

Morrison-Clark Inn
1015 L Street NW
898–1200 or (800) 332–7898
See page 33 for full description.

Places to Eat in the Pennsylvania Quarter and Chinatown

Andale
401 Seventh Street
783–3133
See page 25 for full description.

Austin Grill
750 E Street NW
393–3776
www.austingrill.com
You'll see why this Penn

Quarter outpost of a local chain is so popular when you tuck into the quesadillas and fajitas, not to mention all those silky margaritas. Standard Tex-Mex offerings in a relaxed atmosphere, probably because the decor is early Texas roadhouse. Open Tuesday through Thursday 11:30 A.M. to 10:00 P.M., Friday and Saturday until 11:00 P.M., Sunday and Monday 11:00 A.M. to 9:30 P.M. No reservations. Inexpensive.

Cafe Atlantico
405 Eighth Street NW
393–0812
See page 30 for full description.

Capital Grille
601 Pennsylvania Avenue NW; 737–6200
www.thecapitalgrille.com
The sides of beef hanging in the window say it all. This upscale steak house lures political moguls of both parties from Capitol Hill, probably because of the men's club atmosphere and lively bar scene. All this and terrific steaks and lobsters too. Testosterone levels positively soar in the special cigar areas. Reservations essential. Lunch is served Monday through Saturday from 11:30 A.M. to 3:00 P.M. Dinner from

Sunday to Thursday from 5:00 to 10:00 P.M.; Friday and Saturday 5:00 to 11:00 P.M. Expensive.

Capital Q
707 H Street
347–TEXN
See pages 34–35 for full description.

District Chop House and Brewery
509 Seventh Street
347–3434
www.chophouse.com
Just what its name says, this steak house with billiard tables, oceans of beer, and early twentieth-century kitsch is another good place to know about if you're headed for the Verizon Center or the Shakespeare Theatre. Contrived but fun. Open Tuesday through Saturday 11:00 A.M. to 11:00 P.M., Sunday and Monday 11:00 A.M. to 10:00 P.M. Moderate.

Fado
808 Seventh Street NW
789–0066
See page 35 for full description.

Full Kee
509 H Street
371–2233
See page 34 for full description.

Jaleo
480 Seventh Street NW
628–7949
See pages 26–27 for full description.

Luigino
1100 New York Avenue
371–0595
www.luigino.com
Every meal in this handsome, bustling restaurant brings back memories of my favorite restaurant in Milan. Signor Luigino serves up northern Italian favorites like risotto, sweetbreads, and game specialties, plus pastas made in casa, including my all-time favorite, pappardelle in hare sauce. Open for lunch 11:30 A.M. to 2:30 P.M. weekdays. Dinner is served Monday through Thursday 5:30 to 10:30 P.M., Friday and Saturday 5:30 to 11:00 P.M., Sunday 5:30 to 10:00 P.M. Moderate.

Morrison-Clark Inn
1015 L Street NW
898–1200 or
(800) 332–7898
See page 33 for full description.

Poste-Moderne Brasserie
555 Eighth Street NW
(in Hotel Monaco)
783–6060
See page 27 for full description.

AUTHOR'S FAVORITE PLACES TO EAT IN PENNSYLVANIA QUARTER AND CHINATOWN

Cafe Atlantico	Zola
Coeur de Lion	Luigino
Poste-Moderne Brasserie	Jaleo

Teaism
400 Eighth Street NW
638–6010
See page 31 for full
description.

Tony Cheng's
619 H Street
842–8669
Actually two restaurants in
one. Upstairs the specialty is
dim sum and seafood, such
as stir-fried grouper or
shrimp with asparagus in
black bean sauce. Down-
stairs try your hand at Mon-
golian barbecue or hot pot;
the all-you-can-eat barbecue
involves selecting the ingredients and giving them to the
cooks for grilling, while the
hot pot has you cooking your
own vegetables and noodles
in a pot of boiling stock.
Open Sunday through Thursday 11:00 A.M. to 11:00 P.M.,
Friday and Saturday until
midnight. Inexpensive.

Wok n' Roll
604 H Street
347–4656
See page 34 for full
description.

Zaytinya
701 Ninth Street NW
638–0800
www.zaytinya.com
Dining in this luminous locale,
you'll think you've boarded a
sleek, hip luxury liner that has
mysteriously arrived from the
Aegean with a manifest of
meze—appetizer-size plates
of fish, vegetable, and meat
dishes that the Washington
Post's estimable food critic
called "long and luscious."
You'll also find superb grilled
fish, kebabs, and rich
desserts. Open 11:30 A.M. to
10:00 P.M. Sunday and Monday, 11:30 A.M. to 11:30 P.M.
Tuesday through Thursday,
and until midnight Friday and
Saturday. Moderate to
expensive.

Zola
800 F Street
393–7798
See page 29 for full
description.

Capitol Hill
and Northeast

When Pierre L'Enfant was asked by George Washington to find a site for "the Congress House," he selected Jenkins Hill, an elevation with a commanding view of the future capital, a place he told Washington was "a pedestal waiting for a superstructure." Construction of the Capitol building began in 1793, when President Washington, wearing Masonic regalia, laid the building's cornerstone. The House and Senate wings were completed by 1803 and connected by a wooden bridge erected where the main building and great rotunda now stand. A 1930s guidebook to the District reports that the Hill was so rural in 1809 that, "the British Ambassador put up a covey of partridge" only 300 yards from the Capitol buildings. The unfinished Capitol was torched by the British during the War of 1812. Long story short, the two wings were reconstructed by 1826, but crowned with a low wooden dome; the huge, twin-shelled iron dome that you now see was completed in 1863 by President Lincoln, who saw its completion as symbolic of the survival of the Union.

The area around the Capitol, once you get past the monumental eastern fringe of the Supreme Court and the Library of Congress, is essentially the eighteenth- and nineteenth-century neighborhood that began as a collection of boardinghouses

where representatives and senators lodged during congressional sessions. In fact, in 1793 Thomas Jefferson walked from one of those boardinghouses on New Jersey Avenue along the unpaved streets of the new capital to take his oath of office as president. The Hill, as Washingtonians call it, later became one of the city's prime residential areas, which accounts for the neighborhood's wonderful, large, and completely intact collection of fine homes that trace nineteenth-century residential architecture from antebellum Federal houses to Victorian-era Queen Annes.

Although young and youngish Hill staffers make up a large proportion of neighborhood residents, and crowd the streets during the day and on weekends, the area is surprisingly short of night life. The Hill's restaurant scene, aside from Union Station, is pretty much limited to the restaurant clusters along Pennsylvania Avenue SE and Massachusetts Avenue NE.

Although visitor- and constituent-friendly Capitol Hill has been a major beneficiary of the District's steep decline in crime, you should still exercise the usual street smarts after dark.

Start your Capitol Hill visit at the ***Sewall-Belmont House,*** one of Capitol Hill's oldest and best examples of Federal architecture and one of the top women's history sites in the United States. The small original house on this site, built in 1750, was expanded into the current mansion in 1800 by Robert Sewall and is now its rear wing and kitchen. Because American snipers fired from it on their commanding general, British troops burned the house during the War of 1812, the only private home in Washington to suffer that fate. After rebuilding, the Sewall-Belmont House was home to many distinguished officials, including Albert Gallatin, secretary of the treasury under Jefferson and Monroe, who may have worked out details of the Louisiana Purchase in the house's front rooms, and a slew of U.S. senators. In 1929 the house became the headquarters of the National Women's Party, the militant wing of the feminist movement founded by Alice Paul, the radical strategist who led hunger strikes and

TOP ATTRACTIONS IN CAPITOL HILL AND NORTHEAST

Supreme Court	Eastern Market
Union Station	Library of Congress
National Postal Museum	Kenilworth Aquatic Gardens
Folger Shakespeare Library	

marches and, in 1923, drafted the Equal Rights Amendment on a desk displayed in this house.

The house's feminist library contains a vast and valuable collection of suffragist archives and exhibits celebrating women's history; its rooms are filled with mementos of the early days of the suffrage movement. Your guide will also show you *We Were Arrested, Of Course,* a film chronicling the days before 1920, when the Nineteenth Amendment passed, when a women's right to vote was not only controversial, but insisting on it could land you in the cooler. At the Sewall-Belmont House you'll also look in on some historic rooms, including an elegant front parlor straight out of 1880, with Victorian gilt mirrors, period furniture, and a square 1875 piano. There is also a small gift shop. The Sewall-Belmont House, 144 Constitution Avenue NE, has guided one-hour tours Tuesday through Friday at 11:00 A.M., noon, 1:00, and 2:00 P.M., and Saturday at noon, 1:00, 2:00, and 3:00 P.M. (546–1210, fax 546–3997; www.sewallbelmont.org). Contributions appreciated. Metro: Union Station (red line).

Walk down Maryland Avenue NE to the ***Supreme Court,*** where most visitors troop through the first floor and the tours that go to the building's courtroom, America's ultimate judicial chamber, for a potted lecture. You, however, should head downstairs to the lower level to see lively exhibits that document the fascinating history of the building and its architectural evolution; other displays recount the gypsy nature of the Court, which had no home to call its own for 146 years until this imposing Greek marble temple was opened in 1935. In the theater, also downstairs, every half hour between 9:00 A.M. and 4:00 P.M. you can watch a twenty-four-minute film about the Court's operations and proceedings. Around the corner there's a gift shop selling legal lore, including law books, judicial neckties, and other Court marginalia. Best of all, you'll also find on this level a reasonably priced cafeteria and elaborate snack bar, with good food and (naturally) the most dignified surroundings of any federal government eatery. The Supreme Court building itself is at First Street NE (479–3000; www.supremecourtus.gov). Open 9:00 A.M. to 4:30 P.M. Monday through Friday; closed Saturday and Sunday. The building's cafeteria is open Monday through Friday from 7:30 to 10:30 A.M. and from 11:30 A.M. to 2:00 P.M. The snack bar's hours are 10:30 A.M. to 3:30 P.M. Monday through Friday. Gift shop hours: 9:00 A.M. to 4:25 P.M., Monday through Friday. Metro: Union Station (red line) or Capitol South on blue and orange lines.

When the Supreme Court is in session, which starts on the first Monday in October and ends in April, you can sit in on the one-hour oral arguments the Supremes will hear in each case. Oral arguments are conducted on Mondays, Tuesdays, and Wednesdays for two weeks in each month. To see them, join one of the two lines that form in front of the Court steps before sessions begin

Flying the Flag

Would you like to have that flag flying over the U.S. Capitol for your very own? Ask your congressman or senator to order one from the Capitol's Flag Office, which will fly one from the building, then send it to you. It'll cost about $15, after which you can start building that shiny white dome for your house.

at 10:00 A.M. One is for legal buffs who want to attend an entire argument, while the other is a three-minute line for those satisfied with a brief look at the proceedings. Seating for these events is first-come first-served and begins at 9:30 A.M. so you need to get in line well before that. To see what's scheduled when you're in town, consult the Court schedules in the first section of the *Washington Post*. By the way, one of the Court's attractions that you'll never get to see is its top-floor gymnasium, where the Justices and staffers can work out and play basketball. The gym is, naturally enough, known to Washingtonians as "the highest court in the land."

Inside a classic Art Deco building across from the Supreme Court, is the **Folger Shakespeare Library,** containing possibly the world's greatest collection of works by and about William Shakespeare. The library and its priceless artifacts, the Elizabethan Theater, and the Folger Consort, with its regular programs of early English music, constitute one of the capital's greatest cultural and intellectual treasures. The much-praised facade of this building is worth examining for its carved motifs from Shakespeare's plays.

You'll experience a major time shift beyond that 1930s facade when you enter sixteenth-century England in the Folger's majestic Great Hall, inspired by a grand and historic room of Brasenose College, Oxford. The hall's oak-paneled walls and its high, vaulted ceiling display Shakespeare's coat of arms plus motifs

AUTHOR'S FAVORITES IN CAPITOL HILL AND NORTHEAST

Eastern Market	Johnny's Half Shell
St. Mark's Episcopal Church	Folger Library
Market Lunch	Kenilworth Aquatic Gardens
Capitol Hill Books	Union Station

Rome the Dome

If you want a special and definitely off-the-beaten-path tour of the Capitol, call 223–9800, ext. 27, or visit www.italcultusa.org to find out when the Italian Cultural Institute is running its next tour of the famed *Brumidi frescoes* that adorn the Capitol. Roman artist Constantino Brumidi came to the United States in 1852 after painting murals in the Vatican, and immediately began work on the still-unfinished building. On the tour you'll see many of his masterpieces, including the famed Brumidi Corridors, ornate hallways inspired by designs uncovered in Pompei and by Raffaello's works in the Vatican. Some of Brumidi's frescoes depict events from American history, such as the 1770 Boston Massacre, while others portray North American wildlife and birds. Brumidi also painted the frieze that circles the Rotunda dome. Thanks to a recent restoration, all of Brumidi's work is in top shape—vibrant with brilliant details. Hint: If you go, take field glasses to see details of the higher frescoes. Be advised that since tour groups are small, reservations are essential. While you're in the neighborhood, take a look at Brumidi's home, which still stands at 324–326 A Street SE.

from his plays that the docents call "hints and clues." The Great Hall is also the exhibition space for rare artifacts of Shakespeare's work and his period from the Folger's own collections. During my visit the exhibit subject was *Fortune,* a favorite theme of Shakespeare and his contemporaries and the displays included sixteenth-century playing cards and other ancient gambling devices. Another case contained the only known first folio of *Titus Andronicus.*

The Elizabethan Theater, where the Folger stages educational symposia and an annual cycle of Shakespeare plays, is a timbered replica of an inn-yard theater of Shakespeare's day.

Before leaving check out the Folger's spiffy little museum store, with lots of books and plays by and about the Bard. For information about the Folger's many programs, including the Consort and Theater schedules, call 544–4600. The Folger, at 201 East Capitol Street SE, is open 10:00 A.M. to 4:00 P.M. Monday through Saturday. Tours of the Folger rooms and architecture are given Monday through Friday at 11:00 A.M.; Saturdays at 11:00 A.M. and 1:00 P.M. Tours of the Elizabethan garden occur every third Saturday from April through October at 10:00 and 11:00 A.M.; www.folger.edu. Metro: Capitol South (orange and blue lines) or Union Station (red line).

After leaving the Folger, turn right and get an idea of Capitol Hill as a neighborhood by sauntering along *East Capitol Street.* The Metro stop for this walk is Eastern Market (orange and blue lines).

Heading east toward Lincoln Park you'll pass an eclectic mix of ornate Victorian row houses, Federal beauties from the Hill's earliest days and even a sprinkling of Washington's first apartment houses, most of them dating back to Victorian times. To make this stroll even more pleasant, most houses have deep setbacks, in keeping with L'Enfant's original plan to make East Capitol Street a commercial area; these are now handsome front yards with gardens, trees, and benches for sitting and gazing.

Local shops from another era contribute to East Capitol Street's small-town feel, especially **Grubb's Pharmacy,** at East Capitol and Fourth Streets NE, which, like much of this neighborhood, could have been marooned in a 1900s time warp. Grubb's resembles an old-time general store more than a pharmacy, piled high with medical equipment and supplies of every imaginable kind, plus a huge stock of homeopathic remedies. Grubb's, 543–4400, is open 9:00 A.M. to 7:00 P.M. Monday through Friday and 9:00 A.M. to 3:00 P.M. on Saturday. Closed Sundays.

Nearby at 417 East Capitol Street is the local bookstore, and it's a good one. **Riverby Books** carries an outstanding collection of new, used, and rare books on Washington history. If the Folger has sharpened your appetite for the Bard, you'll also find a trove of Shakespeariana. Open daily 10:00 A.M. to 6:00 P.M.; 543–4342.

greatideas fromthefolger

In the Folger's excellent gift shop you'll find copies of Shakespeare folios and books on Elizabethan times along with busts of the Bard and other period gifts, both serious and frivolous. In the latter category we'd place the Shakespeare bobblehead doll, or would that be much ado about nothing? Other best-selling items are mugs and T-shirts bearing the popular Shakespeare quote "The first thing we do, let's kill all the lawyers." And this just across the street from the Supreme Court?

Mother's Day Tour

A number of those wonderful Federal row houses you'll see on Capitol Hill and their elaborate gardens are open to the public every Mother's Day weekend on the annual "Capitol Hill Restoration Society House and Garden Tour." The tour begins Saturday evening with a Candlelight Tour from 5:00 to 8:00 P.M., then continues on Sunday with open houses from noon to 5:00 P.M. Also on Sunday there's a reception from 3:00 to 6:00 P.M. at the Folger Library, which is a Capitol Hill "must" in itself. Jitneys will take you from house to house. Tickets are $25 in advance and can be purchased at Eastern Market and other Hill locations or by writing to the Restoration Society at P.O. Box 15264, Washington, DC 20003-0264. If you wait until the day of the tour you'll pay $30. Call 543–0425 or check out www.chrs.org for more information.

And at East Capitol and Fifth Streets SE stands *Jimmy T's,* a frill-free zone where you can sit at the Formica counter and join the neighbors for megabreakfasts and basic diner fare. Open Wednesday, Thursday, and Friday 6:30 A.M. to 3:00 P.M., Saturday and Sunday 8:00 A.M. to 3:00 P.M.; closed Monday and Tuesday. Call 546–3646. Farther along, in the 500 and 600 blocks of East Capitol Street you'll pass some of the area's finest examples of Queen Anne houses.

Lincoln Park, a neighborhood hangout for dogs and families, begins at 11th Street. The park contains two great statues—the 1876 Emancipation Monument, a statue of Abraham Lincoln holding the Emancipation Proclamation, and an imposing one of black activist and educator Mary McLeod Bethune. The Lincoln statue was the original Lincoln memorial erected in the District, about fifty years before its far more famous counterpart, the Memorial on the Mall. It was paid for by contributions from freed slaves.

A stroll through the park leads to the charming *Park Cafe,* a bright and attractive restaurant with modern art on the walls and a great view of Lincoln Park. Here the menu includes duck breast, corvina, and choice steaks. The Park also offers terrific paella. The Park Cafe, at 106 13th Street SE, is open Monday through Thursday for lunch from 11:00 A.M. to 2:30 P.M. and for dinner from 5:00 to 10:30 P.M. Weekends the Park is open for dinner from 5:30 P.M. until midnight and for breakfast at 11:00 A.M. Prices are moderate. The nearest Metro is Potomac Avenue on the blue and orange lines (543–0184).

One of the main goals of the D.C. Preservation League is the restoration of the *Old Naval Hospital* at 921 Pennsylvania Avenue SE. This grand old building, which was built to treat wounded Civil War sailors who were carried there from the Navy Yard, is in dire need of restoration. Nevertheless, as you walk by you'll see an urban fly in amber—a virtually intact 1865 building, complete with carriage house and original wrought-iron fence.

capitalquote

"I believe there's something out there watching over us. Unfortunately, it's the government."

—Woody Allen

If you've been missing those terrific European food halls where glistening fish and artistic cuts of meat vie for attention with geometric displays of fruit, exotic cheeses, and vegetables, you'll enjoy visiting the *Eastern Market,* 225 Seventh Street SE (between C Street and North Carolina Avenue). To see Eastern Market's food pageant at its peak, go early on Saturday morning, when trucks packed with crates of fresh produce, game, fish, and meats roll in from Virginia farms and Chesapeake Bay, followed closely by finicky buyers from some of Washington's top restaurants. Eastern Market (www.easternmarket.net) is open from Tuesday through Saturday from 7:00 A.M. to 6:00 P.M., Sunday 8:00 A.M. to 4:00 P.M. Metro stop for the market and its neighbors? Why it's Eastern Market on the orange and blue lines.

Folks from this neighborhood usually head for the market's specialty food shops like The Union Meat Co., for its meats and half smokes on a bun or The Fine Sweete Shoppe. But truckers, locals, and tourists alike usually end up at the **Market Lunch,** a stools-and-paper-plate cafeteria famous for crab cakes, fried oysters, and shrimp, along with immense breakfasts that would horrify your cardiologist. Market Lunch is open Tuesday through Saturday 7:30 A.M. to 3:00 P.M. Expect long lines on Sunday, when the Market Lunch is open from 11:00 A.M. to 4:00P.M.

But the Eastern Market is more than just food; this redbrick food hall and its surrounding stores and stands is also the epicenter of Capitol Hill social and cultural life, especially in the market's north wing, which is given over to exhibits of crafts, wearable art, and jewelry by neighborhood artists and artisans. Outside, surrounding the market building, you'll find a bustling combination of vegetable market and flea market with vendors selling an eclectic mix of everything from prints, clothing, and jewelry to apple pie and flowers. And if you're a tango enthusiast or wannabe, every Thursday evening the Market's gallery building hosts lessons in the world's most sensuous dance, starting at 7:00 P.M. with beginner's classes. Intermediate classes begin at 8:00 P.M., followed by a full-fledged *milonga* at 9:00 P.M. For details about times and prices phone (240) 372–5134 or e-mail tangobuddha@verizon.net.

Across Seventh Street there's a major flea market that fills a large playground every Sunday from 10:00 A.M. to 5:00 P.M.

The Market Lunch

This vibrant neighborhood also boasts a first-class used book store. *Capitol Hill Books,* at 657 C Street SE, is stacked high with books of every vintage and description and literally overflows with language books, which are located in the shop's toilet. Cookbooks naturally are filed in the kitchen sink of this former row house, but owner Jim Toole's excellent collection of District of Columbia history and books on American politics are shelved out front next to the counter. Open Monday through Friday 11:30 A.M. to 6:00 P.M. and weekends 9:00 A.M. to 6:00 P.M.; 544–1621.

Leaving the Eastern Market, a right turn will take you to **Woven History,** worth seeing even if your interest in fine rugs and carpets is only minimal. The shop has a wide selection of dazzling vegetable-dyed, hand-spun wool carpets made in camps in Pakistan by refugees from Afghanistan, Tibet, and Nepal, along with other carpets imported from Turkey and Azerbaijan. Its companion shop, **Silk Road,** under the same management, specializes in exquisite woven goods and tribal and village arts and crafts from all along the route of Asia's fabled Silk Road. These shops—two treasures, one gate—are located at 311–315 Seventh Street SE. Open daily 10:00 A.M. to 6:00 P.M. (543–1705; www.wovenhistory.com).

In this block, at 327 Seventh Street SE, you'll also find one of the Hill's restaurant stars, **Montmartre.** The specialties in this cheerful and intimate French bistro include typical fare such as hanger steak and rabbit served over pasta. This is also the place to come if you like perfectly cooked liver and onions and venison. Open Sunday through Thursday from 11:30 A.M. to 2:30 P.M. and 5:30 to 9:30 P.M., and Friday and Saturday from 5:30 to 10:30 P.M. Closed Monday; www.montmartre.us.

If you're afflicted with "condimentia," the uncontrollable desire to season everything (OK, maybe not ice cream) with a spicy sauce or mustard, then don't miss **Uncle Brutha's Hot Sauce Emporium,** at 323 Seventh Street SE. At Brutha's you'll have your choice of over 300 hot sauces and specialty condiments from all over the world, including a few with names inappropriate to mention in this guide. Brutha's also makes their own line of hot sauces, with repeatable names like Number 10 (smoky and habanero-hot) and Fire Sauce Number 9 (milder and seasoned with a whiff of ginger and scallions). Open Tuesday through Thursday 10:00 A.M. to 7:30 P.M., Friday 10:00 A.M. to 8:00 P.M., Saturday 9:00 A.M. to 7:00 P.M., and Sunday 10:00 A.M. to 5:00 P.M. Closed Monday. (546–3473 (which spells FIRE); www.unclebrutha.com).

When you proceed down Seventh Street to the corner of Pennsylvania Avenue, you'll be standing in front of **Bread and Chocolate,** the local outpost of a highly successful Washington group that specializes in specialty coffees, great pastry, and sandwiches. Bread and Chocolate is also famous for its Sunday brunch and its daily breakfasts, where you'd be well advised to throw dietary caution to the winds and order the divine French toast. Bread and Chocolate, 666 Pennsylvania Avenue SE; 547–2875. Open Monday through Saturday 7:00 A.M. to 7:00 P.M. and Sunday 8:00 A.M. to 6:00 P.M.

In 1871, Frederick Douglass, already distinguished for his writings, his memoirs about his life as a slave, and his wartime role as close adviser to President Lincoln on African-American matters, moved from Rochester, New York, and bought a home on Capitol Hill. His first home in the District is now a small and highly interesting house museum—the *Frederick Douglass Museum and Hall of Fame for Caring Americans.*

The front parlor, Douglass's former study, is a wonderful re-creation of an upper class Washington parlor of the period. The room contains Douglass's

Legislative Lunching

If it's noon and you don't know where your senator or representative is, it's a pretty good bet you'll find them schmoozing with other politicos or, God forbid, even lobbyists, at one of two restaurants where more decisions than you'd like to think are made over top-notch food.

The Monocle
107 D Street NE
546–4488
www.themonocle.com
The atmosphere here is strictly old-time Capitol Hill, with signed photos of national luminaries and walls bearing famous political quotes like, "I give special consideration to everybody," and "Washington is the only city where sound travels faster than light." This is where law-givers from both parties gather for power breakfasts and lunches or dinners of crab cakes, filets, ribeyes and large salads. Jack Kennedy liked the roast beef so much that, after becoming president, he regularly sent a limo over for sandwiches, making the Monocle, according to proprietor John Valanos, "JFK's favorite pickup place." Open Monday through Friday only from 11:30 A.M. to midnight. Metro: Union Station (red line).

Bistro Bis
15 E Street NW
347–4200, (800) 576–8331
www.hotelgeorge.com
The Hotel George's hip and sleek French bistro is a D.C. magnet for fashionistas, celebrities, and Hill powerbrokers. They head there for drinks at the zinc bar, followed by French standbys like cassoulet, duck confit, and scallops Provençal. Or maybe it's the terrific desserts and exceptional cheeses. Open for power breakfasts from 7:00 to 10:00 A.M. Lunch, Monday through Friday from 11:30 A.M. to 2:30 P.M., and dinner 5:30 to 10:30 P.M. daily. Brunch is served Saturday and Sunday from 11:30 A.M. to 2:30 P.M. Reservations are a must. Metro stop: Union Station (red line).

violin, comfortable chairs, and a writing desk with some of his papers, including his "freed man" papers signed by Lincoln, and an invitation to the dedication ceremonies for the Washington Monument. Next door, in the dining room–library, the walls are lined with photographs and mementos of people important to Douglass such as Booker T. Washington, Harriet Tubman, and Sojourner Truth. Next to the original fireplace, which was uncovered during restoration, you'll see the "Paper of Manumission" that gave Douglass his freedom and an 1863 safe conduct pass signed by Lincoln allowing him to pass through Union lines on missions for the president. Douglass moved to Cedar Hill, his Anacostia home, in 1878 (see chapter on Anacostia).

The back half of the ground floor and the upstairs bedrooms are devoted to photographs of and awards to "Caring Americans" who have distinguished themselves through their good works in helping others and in their philanthropic activities.

The Frederick Douglass Museum and Hall of Fame for Caring Americans, 316–320 A Street NE (547–4273; www.nahc.org/fd). Tours by appointment only Monday through Friday from 9:00 A.M. to 6:00 P.M.; Metro: Capitol South (orange and blue lines).

capitalquote

"In your country club, your church, and business, about 15 percent of the people are screwballs, lightweights, and boobs, and you would not want those people unrepresented in Congress."

—Former Senator
Alan Simpson

High on my list of candidates for the city's most glorious church is *St. Mark's Episcopal Church,* built in 1888 and located at Third and A Streets SE, behind the Library of Congress's Adams Building. The tall, high-ceilinged nave of this Romanesque beauty is lined with exposed red brick that makes a simple background for a dazzling collection of stained glass windows that is capped by a splendid Louis Tiffany masterpiece in the baptistery at the north end. A colorful cross made from children's drawings hangs from the nave's beamed ceiling. If St. Mark's should be locked, ask at Baxter House, the church offices at 118 Third Street SE, and someone will show you around (543–0053; www.stmarks.net).

Capitol Hill also includes one of Washington's liveliest specialty stores and a must for anyone interested in the performing arts. *Backstage,* at 545 Eighth Street SE (544–5744; www.backstagebooks.com), is D.C.'s showbiz equipment headquarters, with a large repertoire of ready-made costumes and wigs for sale or rent; theatrical books and scripts; stage makeup and theatrical posters too. Monday through Saturday 11:00 A.M. to 7:00 P.M.

Holiday Concerts

If you're in Washington on Memorial Day, July 4, or Labor Day, be sure to attend the National Symphony's gala holiday concert on the West Lawn of the Capitol. Concerts start at 8:00 P.M., but most people arrive well before that with a blanket and a picnic supper. Prepare for a real patriotic surge and an intensely patriotic experience by tucking a few flags into your hamper.

The *Library of Congress,* the world's largest library, is definitely not an off-the-beaten-path destination, although many of its visitors probably don't take full advantage of its many exhibitions, concerts and lectures. Film buffs shouldn't overlook the free showings of classic films from the library's enormous film archive in the Mary Pickford Theater. To get an idea about what's available, including the superb special and permanent exhibits, watch the twelve-minute orientation film, then take one of the four full tours of the Jefferson Building that begin Monday through Friday at 10:30 and 11:30 A.M., and 1:30, 2:30, and 3:30 P.M.; Saturday every hour on the half hour from 10:30 A.M. to 2:30 P.M. Don't forget to look up every so often to see the murals scattered around the library ceiling, especially those depicting "Government" around the doors of the Main Reading Room.

The facade of the library's main building is inspired by the Paris Opera House, which makes it a bit grandiose for some critics. But the interior, with its grand staircase and the octagonal main reading room, excites the admiration of every visitor, even stodgy Henry James who pronounced it "magnificent." 10 First Street SE (707–5000; www.loc.gov). Metro: Capitol South (blue and orange lines).

Although it's the Jefferson Building that gets all the attention, and with good reason, you might, especially around lunchtime, consider crossing Independence Avenue to visit the library's newish *Madison Building,* at the corner of First Street and Independence Avenue SE. On the sixth floor you'll find one of the best government cafeterias in town, with good food, plenty of space, and a fabulous panoramic view out over southeast Washington and northern Virginia. The cafeteria is open for lunch Monday through Friday from 12:30 to 3:00 P.M. No credit cards. The Madison Building also has an excellent gift shop, where the emphasis is on American history and literature. Open 9:30 A.M. to 5:00 P.M. Monday through Saturday; 707–8300. Metro: Capitol South (blue and orange lines).

After leaving the Library of Congress, walk down Capitol Hill, following Independence Avenue SW past the three House office buildings. That giant glass birdcage you'll spot at the foot of the Hill is in fact the conservatory of the *U.S. Botanic Garden,* one of the city's greatest treasures. The garden was established by Congress in 1820, closed because of general dilapidation in 1997, and reopened in 2001 after a massive and ongoing reconstruction that will be done soon with the completion of a National Garden to the west of the main building.

After entering the garden you'll follow a path through endless summer to visit a number of different plant ecosystems, including Garden Primeval, a mini-Jurassic Park with primitive ferns and plants that have existed for 150 million years; the Desert House, with cacti and other plants from arid areas; and the popular favorite, the Palm House, with a controlled climate similar to that of Washington in August, features a teeming jungle scene of vines, ferns, and palms, along with an example of the tropical pitcher plant, which lures insects with its nectar, then devours them. It's a plant jungle in there. And whatever you do, don't miss the "Jungle Room," a humid and dense rainforest of tropical ferns and palms, and an "Orchid Room" packed with rare blooms and exploding with exotic colors and fragrances. Children have a garden of their own where they can play and learn about plants. The Botanical Garden also has a spot from which you can gaze up at Washington's other hothouse with rare flowerings, the U.S. Capitol. The U.S. Botanical Garden, at First Street and Maryland Avenue SW, is open daily from 10:00 A.M. to 5:00 P.M. (225–8333; www.usbg.gov).

capitalquote

"Reader, suppose you were an idiot. And suppose you were a Member of Congress. But I repeat myself."

—Mark Twain

From the garden, cross Independence Avenue to see the park named for Frederic Auguste Bartholdi, the sculptor of the Statue of Liberty and creator of the elegant and historic fountain located at the center of *Bartholdi Park.* The park is a glorious showcase of contemporary trends in American horticulture and a series of model gardens. If you're a backyard gardener, you might get some ideas from the innovative plant combinations in a variety of styles and design themes. The country villa in Bartholdi Park, the one with the unfortunate paint job, holds the Botanical Garden's administrative offices. Tucked away behind its rear garden you'll find an excellent place to sit on a bench and enjoy the wildflowers and ferns.

Backtracking to the Botanic Garden, stroll down First Street SW along the foot of Capitol Hill past the *Garfield Monument* to the colossal *Ulysses S. Grant Memorial,* with heroic groupings, "Artillery" and "Cavalry," that depict in bronze the heat and anguish of battle. The centerpiece is the statue of Grant, forever astride his horse *Cincinnatus* and coolly contemplating a battle scene. You, however, are more likely to be struck by the general's great and unending view down the Mall past the Washington Monument to the Lincoln Memorial. The Grant Memorial is so grand and complex that it took twenty years to complete and killed its sculptor, Henry Shrady, who died of overwork two weeks before it was dedicated.

Continuing on around the base of Capitol Hill you'll pass the **Peace Monument,** a memorial full of allegorical figures (America weeps on History's shoulder while Mars, the God of War himself, stands by) that honors sailors killed during the Civil War.

At this point you'll see an azalea-lined path winding up Capitol Hill to the rarely visited *"Summer House,"* hidden among the hedges and shrubs of the Capitol grounds. The Summer House was designed in 1880 by Frederick Law Olmsted, the creator of New York's Central Park, as a Victorian-era oasis from Washington's summer heat. You'll find it refreshing too, as you enter this hexagonal redbrick building, then relax on one of the benches and enjoy the sound and sight of the Summer House's ornamental fountain and a stream that bubbles over rocks. For a terrific source of information on the Summer House and other places around the Capitol, visit the Architect of the Capitol Web site, www.aoc.gov.

While you're there you'll hear the bells of the 100-foot-high **Taft Carillon,** just across Constitution Avenue, which forms part of the **Robert A. Taft Memorial,** a tribute to the Ohio statesman and presidential candidate.

Statuary Symbolism

That statue atop the Capitol dome is **Freedom,** cast from a plaster model that sculptor Thomas Crawford made in Rome, but not after considerable political flak. Crawford had originally designed a simple cloth covering for Freedom's head called a Phrygian cap, which was an ancient symbol of freed slaves, who used them to cover their shaved heads. This did not sit well with Secretary of War Jefferson Davis, future President of the Confederacy, who was not exactly a fan of liberated slaves, even symbolically. Crawford was compelled to trade the cap for a crested Roman battle helmet, representing America's victory over tyranny.

After a near-sinking on the way from Italy, the 19-foot statue was set in place in December 1863 as the final touch on the dome, which Lincoln had insisted be completed, despite the Civil War, as a symbol of the continuing Union. If you see the lantern just below Freedom lit, it means that the House or the Senate is in night session.

Johnny's Half Shell is a great restaurant find for anyone seeking sustenance on the Hill. Fish is the specialty, especially Johnny's dense, peppery seafood gumbo, which is almost a meal in itself, but why stop there when you can move on to the fried shrimp po' boys, the terrific crab cakes, or a *fritto misto* of fried shrimp, calamari, and monkfish, or the best fish and chips in town? A short but well-conceived wine list rounds out the pleasure. Johnny's Half Shell, 400 North Capitol Street NW (296–2021; www.johnnyshalfshell.net). Open 11:30 A.M. to 10:30 P.M. Monday through Friday and Saturday from 11:30 A.M. to 11:00 P.M. Closed Sunday. Moderate.

When you see the Irish flag flying from the corner of North Capitol and F Streets NW, it's not the Irish Embassy, but a corner of the old sod that's a lot more fun. Under the Hibernian tricolor is the *Phoenix Park Hotel,* which modestly bills itself as the "center of Irish hospitality in America." Popular with lobbyists and tourists because of its prime location near Union Station, the Capitol, and the Union Station Metro stop, the hotel offers 150 upscale rooms and suites. Irish hospitality obviously extends downstairs; on the hotel's ground level is the *Dubliner Pub,* where the exuberant scene, ably assisted, if not inspired by Messrs. Guinness and Bass, attracts lots of Irish expats along with zillions of Irish wannabes. The fun really heats up every night at nine with the live entertainment, either professionals or customers who, after a few drinks, think that standing in front of an open mike and belting out "McNamara's Band" is perfectly normal. That might be you. The Dubliner will supply the nourishment in the form of Irish comfort food like shepherd's pie and corned beef and cabbage. The Dubliner, 737–3773, at the same address, is open every day for breakfast from 7:00 to 10:00 A.M. and for lunch and dinner from 11:00 A.M. to 3:00 A.M. No reservations. Inexpensive to moderate; www.dublinerdc.com.

And if this isn't enough flaunting of the green, next door to the Dubliner there's yet another Irish outpost, *Kelly's Irish Times,* at 14th and F Streets. A sign over Kelly's door invites "your thirsty, your famished, your befuddled masses" to drop in this no-nonsense pub with a formidable bar and a selection of sandwiches and salads. Call 543–5433. Open Sunday through Thursday 11:00 A.M. to 1:30 A.M. and Friday and Saturday until 2:30 A.M.

You don't have to be a stamp collector to enjoy the *National Postal Museum,* located across from Union Station in what was once the former sorting room of Washington's City Post Office. The monumental Post Office building itself dates from 1914, but the museum only goes back to 1993, when it opened as part of the Smithsonian's network. In it you'll find exhibits that trace the history of America's mail system from its Colonial days down to the present.

A major crowd-pleaser is the series of exhibits called *Moving the Mail,* tracing the growth of postal technology, which leads off with a replica of a 1915

Hill Street Mews

Capitol Hill is also where you can still find some of Washington's famous (or notorious) alleys, which were built into the original city plan to provide tradesmen with backdoor access to substantial homes and mansions. But after the Civil War, the alleys became festering slums where freed slaves squatted and worked under substandard conditions. Some of the few remaining alleys have now been gentrified and turned into smart mews homes for the affluent. Georgetown's Pomander Walk is a good example, but on the Hill, three of the best examples of alleys that have become tiny, tony streets, are Miller's Court, which you can find by following the directional sign in front of the Douglass House at 316 A Street NE; Rumsey Court, off D Street SE, opposite the exit from the Capitol South Metro station; and Terrace Court, just off A Street behind the Supreme Court. Another hidden beauty is Library Court, reachable by the alley next to 315 A Street SE, just behind the Library of Congress's Adams Building.

railway post office car, where clerks sorted letters and parcels to drop off at stations up the line; a film interviews the few remaining post office veterans who worked in these cars. Next door, a 1930 Ford Model A delivery vehicle painted in the old post office green illustrates how urban mail was delivered once it left those trains. And overhead, vintage planes from the U.S. Airmail Service hang from the ceiling to dramatize the beginnings of what is now the standard way of carrying the mail.

The museum is also the home of the Smithsonian's priceless collection of eleven million U.S. and foreign stamps, which can be viewed in a series of sliding vertical files. Your visit will probably end with a stop in the museum shop, which is crammed with books on stamps and stamp collecting, plus the usual branded mugs and T-shirts. The National Postal Museum, at First Street, and Massachusetts Avenue NE, 633–5555, is open daily from 10:00 A.M. to 5:30 P.M. Walking tours anytime. One-hour "highlights" guided tours begin daily at 11:00 A.M. and 1:00 P.M. And for group tour information phone 633–5534; www .postalmusem.si.edu. The museum also contains the world's largest philatelic research library; if you're a serious philatelist and want to visit, phone 633–5544. The museum's Discovery Center has hands-on learning activities for children and adults on the third Saturday of every month.

If you're looking for any of the U.S. government's over 12,000 publications, you'll find them at the **U.S. Government Bookstore,** at 710 North Capitol Street behind the Postal Museum. The bookstore carries publications that will help you get accepted at college, plant your crops, or read all about the findings of the special prosecutors. If you have access to industrial-strength No-Doz, you can also pick up the latest federal budget or the president's latest economic report to Congress. The bookstore is open Monday through Friday 8:00 A.M. to 4:00 P.M.; 512–0132.

Washington's **Union Station** is hardly off the beaten path; with twenty-three million visitors each year, it's the city's most visited site. Most visitors pass through on their Amtrak visits to the District without taking a close look at this monumental Beaux Arts structure patterned after Rome's Baths of Diocletian, with its soaring, vaulted ceilings and, in the magnificent main waiting room, forty-six elaborate statues of Roman legionnaires—one for each state in 1908, when this masterpiece opened. But this glorious restoration has also become one of Washington's most vibrant places, where travelers and locals alike shop, take in a movie, buy a book at one of the five well-stocked bookstores, or dine at one of the station's forty restaurants and cafes. While lots of *mangiare* goes on at the twenty restaurants in the lower-level food court, some of the better choices are located upstairs on the main level and mezzanine and listed on pages 62–64. Also see www.unionstationdc.com

Although the Capitol Hill area includes all four of the city's quadrants, it is also the gateway to the Northeast section, which includes the community known as Brookland. The Northeast is itself diverse, ranging from quiet suburban streets to gritty industrial districts, but it is also, in its Brooklands neighborhood, about the closest thing you'll find to Vatican on the Potomac. About sixty Catholic organizations cluster in Brooklands, which is said to be the highest number in one area outside of Rome; the most significant structure is the **Basilica of the National Shrine of the Immaculate Conception.**

As soon as you spot the Basilica's brightly colored mosaic dome, flanked by a bell tower that seems straight out of Venice's Piazza San Marco, you know

Union Station

that you're in a special place where the operative word is "immense." This is the largest Catholic church in the hemisphere: It can hold 6,000 worshipers in its upper church and 400 in the crypt below, which is modeled after the Roman catacombs. This magnificent church, rich in marble mosaics, is a mix of the Byzantine and the Romanesque, with thirty-two chapels in the upper church that gleam with the vivid colors of their 200 stained glass windows. The effect of the interior can be overwhelming, so don't forget to look in on the Basilica's quiet gardens, especially the restful Mary's Garden, all in white with restful pools and fountains.

The shrine also has an excellent gift shop and bookstore, plus a cafeteria, which can come in handy in this restaurant-free zone. The Basilica of the National Shrine of the Immaculate Conception, 400 Michigan Avenue NE (526–8300; www.nationalshrine.com), is open daily 7:00 A.M. to 7:00 P.M. Mass is celebrated several times a day. Guided tours are given Sundays from 1:30 to 4:00 P.M. and weekdays from 9:00 to 11:00 A.M. and 1:00 to 3:00 P.M. The cafeteria is open from 8:30 A.M. to 2:00 P.M. (until 3:00 on Sunday). If you're interested in a group tour—and there are a lot of them at this national shrine—call 526–8300 and ask for the Pilgrimage Department. Metro: Brookland (red line).

A much lesser known feature of Northeast's "Little Rome" is the **Franciscan Monastery**—modeled on the famed Hagia Sofia church in Istanbul—where Franciscan priests and brothers are trained for work protecting the Holy Land's religious sites and helping its needy. You don't have to spring for a passport or become a martyr to jet lag to visit the Holy Sepulcher or the Grotto of Bethlehem. They, along with reproductions of other Holy Land shrines like the grotto of Gethsemane, are right here in little old Washington, in the monastery's lush rose gardens. There's also a detailed and spooky reproduction of a frescoed Roman catacomb to give you an idea of what early worshipers were up against in the real Rome. The Franciscan Monastery, 1400 Quincy Street NE (526–6800) is open 9:00 A.M. to 5:00 P.M. daily; www.myfranciscan.org. Tours by Franciscan brothers are given Monday through Saturday on the hour (except at noon) from 10:00 A.M. to 4:00 P.M., and hourly on Sunday from 1:00 to 3:00 P.M. The gift shop is open daily 9:00 A.M. to 5:00 P.M.

One of the mid-Atlantic's dance meccas is **Dance Place,** a 200-seat center of contemporary and avant-garde dance. Every weekend, all year long, Dance Place presents programs of original, often experimental dance by top American and international companies. Every June it hosts a "Dance Africa Festival" that attracts large numbers of African and African-American dancers and dance lovers. During the day, Dance Place offers a number of modern and African dance classes for children and adults. Dance Place is located at 3225 Eighth Street NE. Call 269–1600 or visit www.danceplace.org. Metro: Brookland (red line).

Even if your interest in flowers surfaces only every Valentine's Day, you'll have to agree that the **U.S. National Arboretum** is one of Washington's "must visit" sites. The Arboretum, which is run by the U.S. Department of Agriculture as a research and education facility and as a living museum, is located on the city's outskirts, not far from an industrial zone and the high-octane, high-decibel roar of New York Avenue, a.k.a. U.S. Highway 50. But once inside this 444-acre ministate, there's a great sense of beauty and tranquillity.

Most of the Arboretum's main attractions are reachable via the 10 miles of roadways within the park, but start off at the Administration Building for a map, then stroll outside to begin your tour at a large pond dense with lilies, where kids are feeding some of the biggest koi you've ever seen. Move on to the National Herb Garden, with its two-and-a-half acres of 800 herbs, including lavender, sweet bay trees, rosemary, and a formal sixteenth-century knot garden with dwarf evergreens. Visiting the National Bonsai and Penjing Museum, a few steps away, is like entering a corner of Asia, where quiet gardens with stone lanterns showcase ferns, chrysanthemums, and a superb collection of bonsai trees from Japan, China, and North America. The North American contingent is made up of miniature cypress, cedar, and juniper, while the Asian pavilions are lined with 200-year-old yews and wisteria. The area's "Special Exhibits Wing" is located in a Chinese house with an exquisite Chinese scholar's studio in the style of the sixteenth century; nearby you'll find row after row of splashy bonsai azaleas.

You can continue by car or "tram tour" to the outlying displays, such as the dogwood, azalea, and conifer collections; check at the information desk to

U.S. National Arboretum

see which are in flower during your visit. Picnicking is possible at the Arboretum in either the National Grove of State Trees picnic area or in the area behind the gift shop.

No matter where you go, you can't miss the National Capitol Columns, the twenty-two Corinthian columns that from 1826 to 1957 formed the East portico of the Capitol building. These columns, which looked down on the Jackson and Lincoln inaugurations, were dismantled when the building's east front was extended; they were stored at the Arboretum until 1990 when they were reerected in their former configuration.

The U.S. National Arboretum, 3501 New York Avenue NE (245–2726; www.usna.usda.gov), is open as follows: grounds 8:00 A.M. to 5:00 P.M.; Bonsai and Penjing Museum, 10:00 A.M. to 3:30 P.M.; Administration Building, 8:00 A.M. to 4:30 P.M. daily; gift shop, 10:00 A.M. to 3:30 P.M. Monday through Friday and until 5:00 P.M. weekends. Tram Tours, the Arboretum's sightseeing trains, run from mid-April to mid-October, weekends and holidays only; tours leave at 10:30 and 11:30 A.M. and 1:00, 2:00, 3:00, and 4:00 P.M. Tickets are $4.00 for adults, $2.00 for children. No Metro nearby; travel by car or taxi. If you're driving, the Arboretum is reached by taking New York Avenue from the city, then following the directional sign posted just past the intersection of New York Avenue and Bladensburg Road. Because its headquarters is located very near the Arboretum's gate, Yellow Cab (544–1212) is probably the best bet for a return trip by taxi.

When you visit the **Kenilworth Aquatic Gardens,** you're standing in the District's ultimate off-the-beaten-path experience, a unique nature sanctuary that few Washingtonians have visited or even heard of. The gardens consist of twelve acres and forty-five ponds located on the wetlands of the Anacostia River, Washington's last tidal marsh and home to exotic water lilies, ferns, and lotuses; it is the only National Park Service installation devoted entirely to water plants. The gardens are also a sanctuary for a large variety of birds (including the occasional bald eagle), wetland animals from turtles to snakes and fish, which have returned in force, thanks to herculean efforts to restore the once-dead Anacostia.

As you enter you'll be tempted to go no farther, choosing instead to plop down on the porch of the nifty little visitor center and enjoy the vast ponds with lily pads, lavender water hyacinth, and primrose, all surrounded by carpets of daffodils. But press on to follow the Marsh River Trail back into the wetlands and see the riverside sites where fox, muskrat, and deer hang out and wading herons often appear among the cattails. Ranger-led tours are also available, but you must reserve in advance. Field guides and other nature publications are available at the visitor center. Kenilworth Aquatic Gardens, 1900 Anacostia

Avenue NE (426–6905; www.nps.gov/nace/keaq), are open 7:00 A.M. to 4:00 P.M. There are no Metro stops or bus lines that service the gardens. Because of potential security problems, take a cab or your own vehicle to the gardens (there's a good map on the Web site).

You're probably too young to have seen an idyllic, vintage 1870 college campus, but if you ever want to know exactly what one looked like, get in your time machine and warp yourself over to **Gallaudet University,** America's pre-eminent institution for the hearing impaired. There, at 800 Florida Avenue NE, you'll find, preserved like a fly in amber, a glorious collection of Victorian Gothic and Queen Anne houses gathered around a campus with grounds and gardens designed by Frederick Law Olmsted, the same nineteenth-century landscape architect mentioned earlier, who designed the Summer House here in D.C. and created New York's Central Park and dozens of other landscape masterworks.

While you'll want to see the school's College Hall and Chapel Hall, two grand examples of Victorian Gothic style, don't leave campus without visiting the 1889 statue of founder and teacher Thomas Gallaudet and his nine-year-old pupil. The sculptor was Daniel Chester French, whose most famous work is the statue of Abraham Lincoln in the Lincoln Memorial. Like the Lincoln statue, where the president is signing his initials (page 86), Gallaudet and his student are forming the letter *A* in sign language. The statue is just outside Chapel Hall.

Aside from its aesthetics and being the world's only university for the deaf, Gallaudet has a distinction that will never die as long as there are sports trivia nuts. In the nineteenth-century, Gallaudet football players noticed that opposing teams were reading and anticipating all of their plays, which were exchanged among the players in sign language. To thwart this, the team began gathering in a tight circle to sign plays without being observed, thereby inventing the football huddle.

The campus visitor center (651–5000; www.gallaudet.edu) is open Monday through Friday 9:00 A.M. to 4:30 P.M. and offers tours. Metro: New York Avenue–Florida Avenue–Gallaudet U (red line) take a D-2, D-4, or D-6 bus from downtown.

If you're in the Gallaudet neighborhood, find out what an Italian mega-grocery looks like by heading for **Litteri's,** located among the loading docks and warehouses of the Capital City Market, where the city's foods are brought and traded. At Litteri's you'll find Washington's oldest, largest, and best Italian grocery. It's a treat for the eyes and nose, and a still life of all goodies Italian, from shimmering bottles of extra virgin olive oil to thirty brands of balsamic vinegar and every known pasta shape. In the back, a deli counter serves up sandwiches, hunks of Romano and provolone cheese, and glistening slices of prosciutto. Just walking through Litteri's will cost you 300 calories, but it will save you a trip to Rome. Litteri's is at 517 Morse Street NE, near the intersection of New York and Florida Avenues. Open Tuesday and Wednesday 8:00 A.M. to 4:00 P.M., Thursday and Friday until 5:00 P.M., and Saturday until 3:00 P.M. Call 544–0184. Closed Sunday and Monday. Metro: New York Avenue–Florida Avenue–Gallaudet U (red line).

Before you leave the Market, take a stroll through the veritable U.N. of food wholesalers and retail shops that line Morse Street and Neal Place. At **Don Pepe's** (300 Morse Street NE), you'll be tempted by expertly butchered Latin American beef and sausages, while **Obeng International Food**, at the same address, offers West African breads, vegetables, and groceries. **Caribbean Crescent**, at 1280 Fifth Street NE, offers an eclectic but tempting combination of Asian spices and seasonings and halal meats. At 1309 Fifth Street NE you can prowl the **D.C. Farmers Market** for retail meat, poultry, and produce, all at bargain prices. Across the street from the Farmers Market, there's a mammoth weekend flea market selling everything from electronics to clothing and auto parts. The Farmer's Market is open Thursday through Saturday from 7:00 A.M. to 5:30 P.M. and Sunday from 7:00 A.M. to 2:00 P.M.; the flea market is open Friday and Saturday only, from 8:00 A.M. to 5:00 P.M.

Places to Stay in Capitol Hill and Northeast

Capitol Hill Suites
200 C Street SE
543–6000
fax 547–2608
www.capitolhillsuites.com
It's not just a great location—a two-minute walk from the Capitol and the Supreme Court, and across the street from the Library of Congress—that makes this former apartment house so appealing. The 152 suites, studios, and efficiencies, each with a kitchen or cooking facilities, were all remodeled in mid-2000 and the prices are moderate. Judging from the photos and endorsements that line the lobby walls, this is also a big favorite of the congressmen who work just across the street. Moderate. Metro: Capitol South (orange and blue lines).

Hotel George
15 E Street NW
347–4200 or
(800) 576–8331
www.hotelgeorge.com
The sleek, contemporary lobby of glass and stainless steel is your introduction to a boutique-chic, New Yorky world of neomodern rooms and dramatic paintings by Steve Kaufman, a disciple of Andy Warhol. The George's 139 rooms offer intimacy and style along with state-of-the-art in-room communications with the outside world. This all comes at a price, but the George offers some surprisingly low weekend deals. Expensive. Metro: Union Station (red line).

Phoenix Park Hotel
520 North Capitol Street NW
638–6900
www.phoenixparkhotel.com
See page 54 for full description. Metro: Union Station (red line).

Places to Eat in Capitol Hill and Northeast

Aatish
609 Pennsylvania
Avenue SE
544–0931
http://aatishonhill.com
This storefront near Eastern Market is a neighborhood favorite for its fresh, well-prepared Pakistani dishes; its relaxed, friendly atmosphere; and its low prices. Try the clay oven chicken or shrimp tandooris (my personal favorite: the shrimp kebab tandoori). Open Monday through Thursday 11:30 A.M. to 2:30 P.M. and 5:00 to 10:00 P.M., until 10:30 on Friday and Saturday. Inexpensive. Metro: Eastern Market (orange and blue lines).

America
Union Station
682–9555
Everyone wants to be in America, which sports a large menu of regional specialties from all over the United States, including New Mexico's Navaho fry bread, Cincinnati's chili, and Cobb

salad, first produced in Hollywood. There's even something called a fluffernutter sandwich from Las Vegas, which I'm not sure I'll ever order. And is the Reuben sandwich really a "Nebraska specialty"? What happened to New York's Lower East Side? Open Monday through Thursday 11:30 A.M. to midnight. Until 1:00 P.M. on Friday and Saturday. Moderate.

B. Smith's
Union Station
289–6188
www.bsmith.com
Located in the station's former presidential waiting room, this restaurant is a luxurious reminder of the days when presidents traveled only by train. The watchword here is Southern cooking—jambalaya, deep-fried catfish, fried green tomatoes, and a potent seafood gumbo. Feeling adventurous? Order the "Swamp Thing," a wonderful dish of mustardy mixed seafood over collard greens. Try the desserts before you waddle over to your train. Open Monday through Thursday from 11:30 A.M. to 3:00 P.M. and 5:00 to 9:00 P.M., Friday 11:30 A.M. to 3:00 P.M. and 5:00 to 10:00 P.M. Saturday the brunching

hours are noon to 3:00 P.M., while dinner is 5:00 to 10:00 P.M. and the Sunday hours are 11:30 A.M. to 3:00 P.M. for brunch and 3:00 to 9:00 P.M. for dinner.

Bistro Bis
15 E Street NW
347–4200, (800) 576–8331
See page 49 for description.

Bread and Chocolate
666 Pennsylvania
Avenue SE
547–2875
See page 48 for full description.

Cafe Berlin
322 Massachusetts
Avenue NE
543–7656
www.cafeberlindc.com
One of Washington's few German restaurants, and a good one. Springtime is definitely asparagus time at the Berlin, but all year long you can order up schnitzels, goulash, sauerbraten, and all those other Teutonic temptations. The lunch menu also offers up soups, salads, and sandwiches. Open Monday through Thursday 11:30 A.M. to 10:00 P.M., Friday and Saturday 11:30 A.M. to 11:00 P.M., and Sunday 4:00 to 10:00 P.M. Moderate. Metro: Union Station (red line).

AUTHOR'S FAVORITE PLACES TO EAT IN CAPITOL HILL AND NORTHEAST

Bistro Bis

Market Lunch

Pete's Diner

Montmartre

Dubliner Pub
520 North Capitol Street
737–3773
See page 54 for full
description.

East Street Cafe
Union Station
371–6788
http://eaststreetcafe.com
This bright and cheerful cafe,
on the station's mezzanine
level, calls itself "a culinary
journey of the East" because
of its offerings of tempuras,
curries, Pad Thai, and other
classics from eight Asian
nations, including seldom
seen dishes from Malaysia. If
you're in a hurry, try a one-
meal noodle or rice dish.
Open Monday through Friday
11:00 A.M. to 8:00 P.M., Saturday and Sunday 1:00 to
8:00 P.M. Moderate.

Jimmy T's
East Capitol and Fifth Streets
546–3646
See page 46 for full
description.

Johnny's Half Shell
400 North Capitol Street NW
296–2021
www.johnnyshalfshell.net
See page 54 for full
description.

Kelly's Irish Times
14th and F Streets
543–5433
See page 54 for full
description.

Market Lunch
225 Seventh Street SE
Located at the Eastern Market. See page 47 for full
description.

Meyhane
633 Pennsylvania Avenue SE
544–4753
This Turkish delight is a great
place to know about when

you're hungry on the Hill.
Turkish meze (think tapas)
are the specialty, but you'll
also find excellent lamb and
other kebabs, along with
dolma (stuffed grape leaves)
and spicy sausages. Vegans
and vegetarians also have
plenty of choices. Not only is
Meyhane a great value, but a
belly dancer performs Tuesday and Saturday evenings,
right around the time the
baklava arrives as your other
dessert. Moderate. Open
Monday 5:00 to 10:00 P.M.,
Tuesday through Thursday
11:00 A.M. to 3:00 P.M. and
5:00 to 10:00 P.M. Friday
through Sunday 11:30 A.M.
to 10:00 P.M. Metro: Eastern
Market (blue and orange
lines).

The Monocle
107 D Street NE
546–4488
www.themonocle.com
See page 49 for full
description.

Montmartre
327 Seventh Street SE
544–1244
See page 48 for full
description.

Park Cafe
106 13th Street
See page 46 for full
description.

Pete's Diner
212 Second Street SE
544–7335
Pete's is the quintessential
neighborhood hangout that
draws lots of local families
and single Hill staffers who
love its combination of good
food and low prices. It can't
be because of the decor,
which is 50s quirky, sporting
Chinese banners on the wall
next to an award and photo-

graph from the Kiowa tribe
and Hong Kong calendars.
Otherwise Pete's looks like a
typical lunchroom, with
stools and a formica counter,
a row of no-nonsense (i.e.,
beat-up) wooden booths,
and in the middle, a communal table. At first blush the
menu seems pretty much
standard diner—sandwiches,
steaks, pot roast, omelets,
grits, and lasagna—until you
get to the part about the
Asian vegetarian combo
(excellent), the bok choy, and
the smattering of Chinese
dishes and soups. Like a
milk shake to go with that
wild ginger soup? Open
Monday through Friday 5:00
A.M. to 4:00 P.M., Saturday
6:00 A.M. to 3:00 P.M. and
Sunday 7:00 A.M. until 3:00
P.M. Inexpensive. Metro:
Capitol South (orange and
blue lines).

Sonoma
223 Pennsylvania Avenue SE
544–8088
www.sonomadc.com
This sleek, spare, and earth-
toned restaurant-wine bar is
a major favorite among Hill
denizens and staffers. The
Italian-leaning menu com-
bines homemade pastas and
risottos with fresh local vegetables. Wild boar and venison, roast lamb, and pork
loin are available as is a terrific charcuterie board.
Sonoma's wagyu burger has
been dubbed "King of the
Hill" by one critic, but others
also praise the restaurant's
encyclopedic assortment of
cheeses and exceptional
pâtés. You'll also enjoy
Sonoma's thoughtful and
fairly priced wine list.
Upstairs there's a cozy
lounge for sharing drinks and

Hill gossip. Moderate. Metro: Capitol South (orange and blue lines). Open for lunch Monday through Friday 11:30 A.M. to 2:30 P.M., dinner 5:30 to 10:00 P.M. Monday through Thursday, and until 11:00 P.M. on Friday and Saturday. The lounge is open at 5:00 P.M. daily until closing.

Thunder Grill
Union Station
898–0051
Decorated in adobe and turquoise, Thunder Grill offers classic Southwestern U.S. dishes such as burritos, fajitas, and tacos, along with the house specialty, chicken enchiladas with mole sauce. You'll also be offered a wide selection of margaritas served by the yard in a 48-ounce glass, after which you may not even care about getting on that train. Open daily 11:30 A.M. to 11:00 P.M. Moderate.

The Waterfront
and Anacostia

Washington owes its very existence and its role as our capital
to its riverfront location at the head of navigation on the
Potomac, at the point where it meets the Anacostia River. In
selecting this site, George Washington hoped that the new capital, then a Maryland swamp "on the easterly bank of the
Potomac," would be one of the young republic's major deep-
water ports, a transfer point between ocean transport and the
planned canal system that led back into Ohio and other frontier regions. Although the Seventh Street wharf, the current site
of the Washington Marina, was one of the country's busiest
ports in antebellum days and the Washington Navy Yard occupied an important role in the life of the city until well into the
nineteenth century, Washington's long riverfront has slipped
into disuse. That said, the banks of the Anacostia and the
Potomac have some terrific opportunities for anyone exploring
off-the-beaten-path Washington. What they do not offer, however, is a wide selection of places to stay.

Start your waterfront experience by taking the Metro to the
L'Enfant Plaza stop (all lines except red) and walk 4 blocks to
the *Maine Avenue Fish Market,* located well off the beaten
path on the Potomac's Washington Channel in the shadow of

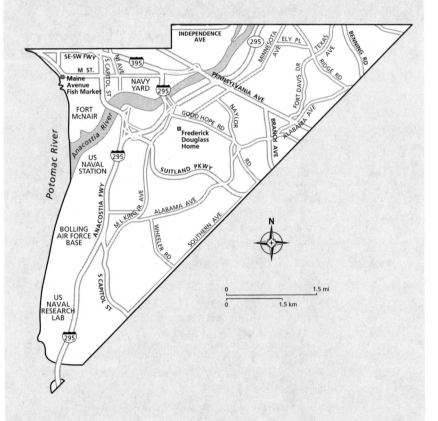

The Awakening

East Potomac Park, located just across the Potomac from the Maine Avenue Fish Market on Hains Point, is a great rest stop and perfect for an urban picnic. But if you go, you'll see one of the city's most unusual pieces of urban statuary, which in a town crowded with statues and monuments like Washington, is really saying something. Even though you're now warned, you'll still do a double take when you first spot the cast aluminum *Awakening,* or as many Washingtonians call it, *The Giant,* which depicts a bearded face, knee, hand, and arm of a man struggling to free himself from the ground. It's very dramatic and more than a little weird, but that doesn't keep kids from using the giant's huge body parts as slides. If you decide you don't like the *Awakening,* you can always gaze out at the Potomac or watch tennis at Hains Point's nineteen courts. But if you do like the sculpture, you'll find more of these "life castings" by J. Seward Johnson also along the Potomac at Washington Harbour in Georgetown.

the 14th Street bridge. Here you'll stroll into an open-air, high-protein scene to find the bounty of the Chesapeake spread out before you on barges, where aproned vendors preside over rows of glistening, freshly caught rockfish, catfish, bluefish, and carp. And since we're talking Chesapeake Bay, there are bushel baskets crammed with oysters and that Eastern Shore delicacy, blue crab. Open daily 7:30 A.M. to 8:00 P.M., the market draws a large number of customers searching for finny friends from other lands and a cadre of chefs from local Asian restaurants.

If all of this triggers a hunger pang or two, no problem. You'll find a number of possibilities for highly informal dining in the market at places like *Captain White's,* where a seafood combo of oysters, shrimp, scallops, and fish tops the bill, and *Jessie Taylor Seafood* for steamed crab legs and shrimp, plus a nifty raw bar. Both are open from 8:00 A.M. to 9:00 P.M. Another option is *Custis and Brown,* open from 8:00 A.M. to 9:00 P.M., which modestly advertises "The Best Hot Cooked Crabs in Town."

TOP ATTRACTIONS IN
THE WATERFRONT AND ANACOSTIA

Maine Avenue Fish Market	Marine Barracks
Arena Stage	Cedar Hill
Washington Navy Yard	

You can explore the waterfront area very nicely and have a picnic in the process by picking up some Fish Market take-out and following the riverside promenade that begins behind Le Rivage and runs along the Washington Marina for several blocks. As you'll learn, the riverside walk is a favorite with fishermen and sightseers who enjoy the views across the Potomac to Hains Point Park and its municipal golf course and, beyond that, the shores of Virginia and Arlington Cemetery. Your stroll will also take you past some of the many luxury powerboats and sailboats that anchor there regularly and a colony of elaborate houseboats, where a number of lucky Washingtonians enjoy life on a permanent cruise on the Potomac.

When you reach Sixth Street, the round (polygonal, actually) building on the left is the *Arena Stage,* a multitheater complex that enjoys a massive local and national reputation for the quality of its productions and of its resident theater company. Of the Arena's three stages, the 827-seat Fichandler (named for one of the Arena's 1950 cofounders), reflects the Arena's origins as theater-in-the-round. Its neighbor, the Kreeger Theatre, which seats 500, is fan-shaped, and the more intimate Old Vat is configured for cabaret. All three serve up a rich schedule that includes contemporary plays, experimental works, and even some musicals. Call 488–3300, visit www.arenastage.org, or consult either the *Washington Post* or *City Paper* to see what's playing when you're in town. The Arena Stage complex is located at 1101 Sixth Street SW. Parking is available. Metro: Waterfront (green line).

capitalquote

"It is very unhealthy. Few people would live in Washington who were not obliged to reside there."

Charles Dickens
—*American Notes,* 1842

Friday night may mean fish for some, especially over at the Maine Avenue market, but at the *Westminster Presbyterian Church,* at 400 I Street SW, it means great live jazz. Every Friday from 6:00 to 9:00 P.M., some of Washington's top musicians jam at Westminster. There's also a buffet served from 6:00 to 8:30 P.M. Admission is $5.00 for adults; if you're under sixteen it's free (484–7700; www.westminsterdc.org).

To the left of the Arena stage, in a charming park vibrant with azaleas, is one of Washington's oldest structures, the *Thomas Law House,* built in 1796 by a wealthy, eccentric land speculator who married into Washington and American nobility when he wed Eliza Custis, Martha Washington's granddaughter. This marriage was not made in heaven, and it ended in 1804 with Washington's first power divorce, but that didn't keep the miserable couple from having President John Adams and King Louis Philippe of France over for dinner in their splendid Federal mansion. Today Eliza would probably cringe at learning that her Washington home is *(a)* named after her disagreeable husband and *(b)* also known as the "Honeymoon Cottage." The Law House is located at 1252 Sixth Street SW and is not generally open to the public. For an appointment to visit the house and its selection of period antiques, call 554–4844 between 9:00 A.M. and 5:00 P.M. Monday through Friday. Metro: Waterfront (green line).

The riverside walk will take you past the piers at Sixth and Water Streets, home port to a pair of the District's leading dinner and sightseeing cruise lines. ***Spirit Cruises*** operates the *Spirit of Washington I* and *II* on lunch and dinner cruises featuring live entertainment, ample buffets, dancing, and a chance to see the District's waterfront and landmarks from an entirely new angle. The company also offers special cruises downriver to visit Mt. Vernon. For schedules and prices, call (866) 211–3811 or 484–2320; or visit www.spirit ofwashington.com.

Odyssey Cruises operates *Odyssey III,* a mammoth version of the glassed-in *bateaux mouches* that take visitors to Paris up and down the Seine. Dancing and live music, plus lunch, dinner, and a Sunday jazz brunch. And for all of you romantics, there's also a moonlight cruise available. Call 488–6000 or visit www.odysseycruises.com.

After passing the docks you'll see the ***Titanic Memorial,*** an impressive statue dedicated to the gentlemen who lost their lives by giving up their lifeboat seats to the ladies in that 1912 disaster. The 18-foot figure forms a forward-leaning crucifix. Don't look now, but isn't that exactly the pose struck by Leonardo DiCaprio, a.k.a. King of the World, and Kate Winslet on the prow of the *Titanic* in the movie of the same name? Every April 14, the anniversary of the sinking, visitors drop by to pay their respects, reportedly including a group of men in black tie who, after their annual banquet, visit the memorial for a mysterious ritual.

A left turn leads to the entrance of ***Fort Leslie J. McNair,*** strategically located on the Potomac to defend the city, which is why it was part of L'Enfant's

AUTHOR'S FAVORITES IN THE WATERFRONT AND ANACOSTIA

Friday Evening Parade	Cedar Hill
Navy Museum	Arena Stage

original plan and one of Washington's first military bases when it opened in 1791 as an arsenal; it is also one of the most beautiful locations in the city. Despite all that fancy strategic planning, the British had no trouble torching the arsenal during their occupation of Washington in 1814, and Fort McNair has gone through many renovations ever since. Today its broad lawns and Beaux Arts buildings are best known as the site of the **National War College,** where military and foreign affairs leaders, in a one-year sabbatical, take courses to improve their professional skills and take a fresh look at their world and its culture.

Fort McNair is a great place to stroll along the river past "Generals Row," the white-columned officers' houses that conjure up memories of those Hollywood frontier forts with their broad parade grounds and tidy military housing. Over by the tennis courts, at the north end of the fort, you'll find a historical marker recording that four of the Lincoln conspirators were hanged on that spot in July 1865. The building next to the courts is all that remains of the 1826 Federal Penitentiary, where the plotters were held until their execution. Fort McNair is located at 103 Third Street SW. Since the events of September 11 visitor access to Fort McNair has been limited, so call 685–3196 to see if it will be possible during your visit.

No matter where you live, the Fourth of July is always a John Philip Sousa show, from the rousing strains of "The Washington Post March" or "El Capitan" and the thrilling conclusion of "Stars and Stripes Forever," followed by enough fireworks to destroy a small country.

When you're in Capitol Hill you're also in Sousaland, where the great composer was born and rose to world fame at the Marine Barracks as leader of the Marine Band. Sousa's birthplace still stands at 636 G Street SE and a few doors away you'll find Sousa's church, the Gothic Revival **Christ Episcopal Church,** which is one of the District's most historic structures. Opened in 1807, Christ Church's earliest worshipers included Presidents Madison and Monroe. When the British seized Washington in 1814, parishioners watched as the invading troops torched the Marine Commandant's residence at Eighth and G, but spared Christ Church. Later, during the Civil War, Union troops were stationed in the church's bell tower to keep an eye on Confederate troop movements just across the Potomac. Inside, a lovely stained glass window over the altar commemorates the mothers of the parish and brightens the spare interior; three other windows around the main entrance add to the glow. F Street Terrace, to the right of the church, leads to Archibald Walk, once one of the city's grim, teeming alleys, but which has now definitely gone upscale. Christ Church, 620 G Street NE, is best reached by taking the Metro to the Eastern Market stop on the orange and blue lines.

Kayaking the Monuments

For a unique look at some of Washington's best-known places, take one of Atlantic Kayak's guided kayak tours of the District's waterside monuments. The tour glides past magnificent views of the Washington Monument, the majestic white colonnades of the Lincoln Memorial, the Kennedy Center, and the Chrysler Airflow swirl of the Watergate. Your guide will also take you for a close-up look at seldom-visited Roosevelt Island, a ninety-acre wilderness park in the middle of the Potomac that was once a farm, then a Union Army camp, and now an urban oasis of wildlife and wildflowers. You'll then cross the Potomac for a water-level tour of the historic waterfront in Georgetown, once one of America's great ports and now a magnet for visitors seeking an eclectic combination of stately Federal mansions and hip street life. And along the way you'll probably cross wakes with rowing teams from local universities, one more sign that recreation is alive and well on the Potomac.

Wherever you've spent the day, you'll find another perspective on the Potomac by paddling over to Georgetown's Washington Harbour complex for a sundowner on the terrace overlooking the river. *Atlantic Kayak,* 1201 North Royal Street, Alexandria, VA, (703) 838–9072, www.atlantickayak.com.

As a child, when asked where he lived, Sousa always replied "near the Navy Yard," which still dominates his old neighborhood. Once America's largest shipyard, the **Washington Navy Yard,** which dates back to America's earliest days, was burned to prevent its falling into British hands during the War of 1812; rebuilt in classic Victorian red brick, The Navy Yard is located at 901 M Street SE; however security considerations have led Navy Yard authorities to close the former main gate and open a visitor gate at 600 M Street. The only visitors admitted to the Yard will be those who have made a prior reservation to see the **Navy Museum,** one of Washington's very best. To reserve, phone the Navy Museum at 433–6897 at least twenty-four hours before your intended visit with as much as a week's prior notice; you'll have to furnish the names of all of the visitors in your party over eighteen and bring a photo ID for checking at the main gate. (*AUTHOR'S NOTE*: Judging from personal experience, you may not need to reserve, especially on weekends, but be sure to bring that ID.)

Once inside, you'll find the Navy Museum along the Anacostia waterfront, in the old Naval Gun Factory. The Museum covers every aspect of U.S. naval history, from the Revolution through both world wars right down to Vietnam. Exhibits range from the gun deck from *Old Ironsides* to a replica of Admiral Byrd's hut from the Antarctic Expedition of 1933. The museum's vast collection of "hands on" World War II exhibits includes film shows, elec-

Visiting the Voice

Although not many Americans ever tune in to their country's official radio station, a lot of other people do. *The Voice of America,* known to all as the VOA, transmits 24/7/365 in fifty-three languages to a worldwide audience of ninety-three million, informing them by radio and television about the United States, its policies, culture, and society. This fascinating tour will begin with a brief video, then show you around the studios and newsrooms of this major international broadcaster. As a bonus, before your tour leaves VOA's C Street lobby, look up at the great Ben Shahn murals representing and dramatizing themes and accomplishments of Franklin Roosevelt's presidency in fighting the Depression. VOA tours are given Monday through Friday at 10:30 A.M. and 1:30 and 2:30 P.M. Reservations are essential. To get them call 203–4990 or e-mail tickets@voanews.com. The VOA Web site is www.voa.gov. The Voice of America is located at 330 Independence Avenue SW. Metro: Federal Center (orange and blue lines) and L'Enfant Plaza (every line except red).

tronic reconstructions of key naval battles, and nostalgic displays of life on the 1942 home front. Even though they may have never seen John Wayne save democracy, visitors can also tour the destroyer *Barry,* another artifact of World War II, which is permanently anchored nearby, and experience life on a submarine with operating periscopes where kids can track enemy carriers to their hearts' content. And if you're a fan of ship's models, this museum is Nirvana. The Navy Museum, in building #76, is open Monday through Friday 9:00 A.M. to 5:00 P.M. Saturday and Sunday 10:00 to 5:00 P.M.; www.history .navy.mil. Metro stop: A twenty-minute walk from the Eastern Market station (orange and blue lines).

Although through the years the neighborhood around the Navy Yard had degenerated into one of the District's seediest areas, that's changing fast, as you'll see during your visit. Construction on the city's new baseball stadium, government offices, and commercial buildings has turned this into some of Washington's primo development regions.

The Navy Yard is a rich oasis of military history located in a restaurant desert, but you won't need to call in the Marines to fight hunger. You'll find William III, an upscale deli with thick sandwiches in building 36 near the Marine Museum, open 6:30 A.M. to 2:30 P.M. If you want a more elaborate lunch, head for the former Officer's Club in building 101 (11:00 A.M. to 1:30 P.M.), and if fast food will do, McDonald's, in building 184, is open 5:00 A.M. to 5:00 P.M.

The **Marine Barracks,** located at Eighth and I Streets, were built in 1801 on a site personally selected by President Thomas Jefferson because of its strategic defensive situation between the Navy Yard and the Capitol. Although

its military significance has long vanished, this massive, walled quadrangle—
"The Oldest Post of the Corps"—remains the epicenter of Marine tradition and
spectacle. This is the home of the Marine Commandant, who lives in an 1805
house on the Parade Ground and the ground zero of Marine history. It is also
the headquarters of the Marine Band, which will always be identified with its
legendary leader, the world's "March King," John Philip Sousa.

Well before Sousa's day, its perfectly manicured Parade Ground was the
scene of the Corps' most hallowed rituals. You'll definitely want to see the most
stirring of those ceremonies, the Friday Evening Parade, an inspiring patriotic
pageant with precision drills, brilliant uniforms, flashing sabers, martial fanfares,
and enough Sousa marches to set the most ardent pacifist ablaze. Speaking of
the March King, Sousa Hall, which looks across the Parade Ground at the Commandant's House, is the sanctum sanctorum for the legions of Sousaphiles
throughout the world. Here, at the headquarters of the Marine Band, you'll see
a wealth of Sousiana, including a library of his original sheet music, personal
mementos, and a large hall where today's band members practice under a large
portrait of Sousa himself.

Guided tours of the Barracks are possible; just show up at the main gate
at Eighth and I Streets at 8:00 A.M. any Wednesday. To schedule a group tour
of the Barracks, you must phone ahead of time: 433–4173. For further information about this and the Friday Evening Parade, call 433–4073 or 433–6060.

The Friday Evening Parade is given only from May through August and
starts at 8:45 P.M. Reservations for the parade should be made in advance, either
online at the Barracks' nifty Web site, www.mbw.usmc.mil, or by writing to:
Protocol Office Attn.: PARADES, Marine Barracks, Eighth and "I" Streets SE,
Washington, D.C. 20390–5000.

Your request should include the names of your party, your return address,
and a point of contact with a telephone number; you should also specify an
alternate parade date in case your preferred date is unavailable. That said,
you'll stand an excellent chance of getting in by joining the general admission
line that forms at the main gate on Friday evenings, but since seating is first
come, first served, plan to arrive at 7:00 P.M. and certainly not after 8:00 P.M.
Another thing: Don't drive. Either take a cab or walk over from the Eastern
Market Metro, which is on the orange and blue lines.

As you exit the Marine Barracks onto Eighth Street SE, you'll be stepping
into one of DC's hottest new neighborhoods—***Barracks Row.*** Thanks to the
dedication of local residents, Eighth Street has been transformed from a dingy
fringe area into a collection of lively restaurants and shops. The revival of Barracks Row has garnered an award from the National Trust for Historic Preservation, but that may not be as interesting to you as some of its top dining

spots, including the high-energy **Belga Café,** where the Dutch Ambassador's former chef serves up a mix of Belgian and "euro-fusion" cuisine that includes Belgian specialties like mussels, coquilles, crab croquettes, and real Belgian fries that make the French variety seem pretty dull. Belga also has a world-class collection of Belgian and other beers and chocolate-based desserts that will remind you of Brussels. Belga Café, 514 Eighth Street. SE; (544–0100; www .belgacafe.com). Open for lunch Tuesday through Sunday from 11:30 A.M. to 3:00 P.M., dinner Tuesday through Thursday 5:30 until 10:00 P.M.; Friday and Saturday 5:30 until 11:00 P.M.; Sundays 5:30 P.M. until 10:00 P.M. Belga also serves Sunday brunch from 11:00 A.M. to 3:30 P.M.

Another Row favorite is **Starfish** at 539 Eight Street SE. This cozy, attractive neighborhood storefront serves up a wide range of seafood, including grilled fish, crab and shrimp salads, and Creole-style gumbo and at reasonable prices. Open Monday through Friday 11:30 A.M. to 3:00 P.M. Dinner: 5:00 to 10:00 P.M. (Monday through Thursday and Sunday) 5:00 P.M. to 11:00 P.M. (Friday and Saturday) Sunday brunch served from 11:00 A.M. to 3:00 P.M. 546–5006; www.starfishcafedc.com.).

Locals also swear by **Ellington's on Eighth,** at number 424A to be exact, a jazz cafe with African, Cajun, and Caribbean specialties. Live jazz and blues concerts are frequent, but check first by calling 546–8308. Open Tuesday through Thursday 6:00 to 11:00 P.M. Friday and Saturday 6:00 P.M. to 1:00 A.M. Sundays there's a jazz brunch 11:00 A.M. to 4:00 P.M. and dinner is from 6:00 to 10:00 P.M.

An eclectic group from every era of American history is buried in the **Congressional Cemetery,** a quiet corner of the capital where American notables have been interred since 1807. The cemetery is the final resting place of military leaders of all wars since the Revolution, as well as Declaration of Independence signer Elbridge Gerry, Pushmataha (the son of Apache chief Cochise), and Civil War leaders from both sides. Many of the cemetery's Congressional guests are buried under peculiar, mushroomlike monuments that prompted one U.S. senator to comment that "the prospect of being interred under these atrocities brings a new terror to death."

The Congressional Cemetery has its share of interesting graves. Between the main gate and the chapel you'll find the obelisk dedicated to noted writer and historian Ruth Ann Overbeck, who was also a teacher. You can tell that when you see "look it up" inscribed where the dates of birth and death usually go. And beyond the chapel a bench on the main road bears the poignant inscription, "Poopsie and Baby Pie. A lifetime together wasn't enough."

After the John Philip Sousa plot, the cemetery's most visited graves include those of Lincoln photographer Mathew Brady, J. Edgar Hoover, and Belva Lockwood, the first woman to run for president. And every November 6,

Furniture Frenzy

If you'd like to do some megashopping, even if it's just the window variety, or if you're looking for some decorating ideas, stop off at one of the East's top design showcases, the **Washington Design Center,** which brings together dozens of major manufacturers of furniture, textiles, and kitchen and bath equipment under one roof.

Although this sumptuous collection is aimed at designers and the trade, the public is welcome in many, but not all, showrooms from 9:00 A.M. to 5:00 P.M. Monday through Friday and from 10:00 A.M. to 3:00 P.M. on Saturday. Purchases, however, can be made only by design professionals.

Having said that, if you've found something you absolutely must have, you can get it by hiring a designer on the spot. The center's front desk will help you find one ASAP. Washington Design Center, 300 D Street SW. Call 646–6118; www.merchandisemart .com/dcdesigncenter. Metro: Federal Center (orange and blue lines).

Sousa's birthday, the Marine Band visits his grave to lay a wreath and play his marches in musical tribute to its former leader. And while you're at the cemetery, don't miss the dramatic arch of healing poles, carved by the Lummi Indian Nation of Washington state to remember September 11. The totem poles, which are covered with sun and moon designs and carvings of eagles and bears, can be found in the cemetery's northwest quadrant. A self-guided tour brochure is available at the office and online at www.congressionalcemetery.org. The Congressional Cemetery, at 1801 E Street SE (543–0539), is open daily from dawn to dusk. Metro: Potomac Avenue (orange and blue lines).

It's not easy finding a lunch spot near the Congressional Cemetery. Your best bet is to head up to Pennsylvania Avenue where *Mangialardo and Sons,* at 1317 Pennsylvania Avenue SE, serves fifteen kinds of whopping submarines (try the "G-man") and pizza Monday through Friday from 7:30 A.M. to 3:00 P.M.; 543–6212; the Metro: Potomac Avenue (orange and blue lines).

Trusty's, at 1420 Pennsylvania Avenue SE, is recommended for those looking for (*A*) one of D.C.'s most unusual sports bars and (*B*) a neighborhood bar with a mega-quirky decor, meaning retro service station. At Trusty's, close to RFK Stadium where the Washington Nationals play, you'll drink under oil-can lamps next to Texaco logos and used hubcaps. Open Sunday through Thursday 4:00 P.M. to 1:30 A.M. and Friday and Saturday until 2:30 A.M. 547–1010. Metro: Potomac Avenue (blue and orange lines).

Across the Anacostia River from the Navy Yard is the section known as Anacostia. Because of its crime rate, out-of-town visitors should exercise caution, especially at night. Its historic significance, however, makes the area worth a visit. An early guidebook called Anacostia "the eastern slice of Washington . . . a place that developed slowly and independently." Because of its physical separation by the river from the rest of the District, Anacostia from its earliest days had a life of its own, starting as a collection of stand-alone villages within the District. Today's Anacostia is an almost entirely African-American residential and commercial community, but in the nineteenth century, Anacostia brought together residents of many backgrounds in settlements like Uniontown, a mainly white community; Stantontown, where free blacks lived; and other villages where German immigrants prevailed.

On a knoll in Anacostia stands *Cedar Hill,* the Victorian frame home of African-American leader Frederick Douglass. Born a slave in 1818, Douglass, after teaching himself to read and write, became a publisher, bank president, diplomat, musician, fiery orator, and the author of hundreds of books, monographs, and speeches; he somehow also found time to learn seven languages and serve as the American Minister to Haiti. This Renaissance man's greatest achievements, however, were in the political arena as an eloquent advocate of abolition, women's rights, and racial justice, and as a trusted adviser to Abraham Lincoln on these issues.

Visitors to Cedar Hill wander through rooms filled with mementos of Douglass's extraordinary life, including his beloved Stradivarius, Abraham Lincoln's cane (a gift from Mary Lincoln), and a leather rocking chair given to Douglass by a grateful Haitian people. The dining room stands ready for one of the formal dinners Douglass gave for fellow members of the Washington power grid of the 1880s, while his library bursts with more than 1,100 books and a massive rolltop desk covered with papers. A visit to Cedar Hill will also give you a spectacular hilltop panorama of the Capitol and other Washington landmarks. Cedar Hill is located at 1411 W Street SE. The House and its adjoining National Park Visitor Center, where you can view a film of Douglass's life, are open from 9:00 A.M. to 5:00 P.M. in the summer, until 4:00 P.M. the rest of the year. Tours are scheduled throughout the day (www.nps.gov/frdo). No Metro.

anacostia farmers' market

If you're in Anacostia and hankering for fresh produce, the Anacostia Farmers' Market convenes every Friday between June and November in the parking lot of the Union Temple Baptist Church, 1225 W Street SE. Hours: 4:00 to 6:30 P.M.

Another showcase of African-American history and culture is the *Anacostia Museum and Center,* located in a former school at 1901 Fort Place SE. The museum reopened in 2002 after a two-year, $8 million overhaul, and the results are well worth the wait. The exterior is now a curvy brick facade with drumlike columns. Inside, the exhibition spaces have been greatly improved, which will enhance your appreciation of the museum's busy schedule of African-American sculpture and art and collections reflecting black cultural history. The museum also displays materials borrowed from private collections of African-American art and artifacts in the D.C. area. The museum is open daily from 10:00 A.M. to 5:00 P.M. No metro. Call 633–4820 for tour information or visit the museum's Web site, www.si.edu/anacostia.

Places to Eat in the Waterfront and Anacostia

Belga Café
514 Eighth Street SE
544–0100. See page 74 for full description.

Captain White's
in Main Avenue Fish Market, Washington Channel at Fourteenth Street bridge. See page 67 for full description.

Custis and Brown
in Maine Avenue Fish Market, Washington Channel at Fourteenth Street bridge. See page 67 for full description.

H2O
800 Water Street SW
484–6300
www.h2odc.com
You'll have lots of company along with great river views at this Washington landmark that has recently undergone a major overhaul. H2O prides itself on its crab cakes, lobster, clambakes, and the mammoth Captain's Platters. Check the Web site for H2O's special events and parties, which include major-league dancing to DJs on Friday and Saturday nights. Open for dinner Tuesday through Sunday 5:00 to 10:00 P.M.; lunch Tuesday through Friday 11:30 A.M. to 3:00 P.M.; Sunday for brunch 11:00 A.M. to 3:00 P.M. Closed Monday. Expensive.

Jenny's Asian Fusion
1000 Water Street, SW
554–2202
www.jennysdc.com
True to its name, Jenny's specializes in fish of all kinds with an Asian accent, including old faithfuls like the ever-present General Tso, who, despite his warrior's title is (or actually was) a chicken. Also a variety of grilled fish salads. And if you want to make a picnic and gaze out at the Potomac, Jenny's has carry-out service. Monday through Thursday open from 11:00 A.M. to 10:00 P.M., Friday and Saturday from 11:00 A.M. to 11:00 P.M. Sunday noon to 10:00 P.M.

Jessie Taylor Seafood
in Main Avenue Fish Market, Washington Channel at Fourteenth Street bridge. See page 67 for full description.

AUTHOR'S FAVORITE PLACES TO EAT IN THE WATERFRONT AND ANACOSTIA

H2O	Starfish
Belga	Pier Seven

Maine Avenue Fish Market
Washington Channel at
Fourteenth Street bridge.
See page 65 for full
description.

Mangialardo and Sons
1317 Pennsylvania Avenue
543–6212. See page 75 for
full description.

Phillips Flagship
900 Water Street SW
488–8515
Takes the self-serve
approach, with huge seafood
buffets at reasonable prices.
Phillips is popular with tour
groups, especially for Sunday
brunch, which is practically
overwhelming. Open Monday
through Thursday 11:00 A.M.
to 9:00 P.M., Friday 11:00
A.M. to 10:00 P.M., Saturday
noon to midnight, and Sunday noon to 9:00 P.M. Moderate.

Pier Seven at Channel Inn
650 Water Street SW
554–2500
This waterside resto near the
Arena Stage draws considerable praise from locals for its
seafood, especially the crab
and lobster dishes, including
crab imperial, and for its
beef. Not to mention the
romantic sunsets. It's also
located in one of the few
hotels in this neighborhood,
which is also reputed to be
quite good. Open Sunday
noon to 9:00 P.M., Monday
through Thursday 11:00 A.M.
to 10:00 P.M., Friday 11:00
A.M. to 11:00 P.M., and Saturday 3:30 to 11:00 P.M. Live
jazz Sunday from 7:00 to
11:00 P.M. Moderate.

Starfish Cafe
538 Eighth Street SE
546–5006. See page 74 for
full description.

Foggy Bottom

Although Foggy Bottom is the home of the State Department, it did not get its name from the torrents of bafflegab and diplospeak that gush forth daily from America's Foreign Policy Headquarters, known locally as "the fudge factory." This neighborhood was originally named Funkstown for Jacob Funk, the German immigrant who founded a small industrial community on the Potomac that clearly would have trouble meeting today's pollution standards. In addition to scads of smoke and pollutants, Herr Funk's riverfront slum also suffered from the gases and other emanations of its surrounding swamps, adding up to a perpetual haze that gave this OSHA paradise its picturesque name. That said, the State Department hasn't helped much.

Today's Foggy Bottom gives new meaning to the term "mixed use." Its tenants include large government agencies, embassies, the Watergate, the Daughters of the American Revolution, and major institutions such as the grandiose Kennedy Center and sprawling George Washington University, along with more human-scale neighborhoods where narrow nineteenth-century row houses line leafy residential streets.

On Pennsylvania Avenue, about 2 blocks from the White House, stands the massive World Bank building and the

M ST
23RD ST
NEW HAMPSHIRE AVE
M ST
L ST
21ST ST
L ST
26TH ST
K ST
WASHINGTON CIRCLE
K ST
25TH ST
PENNSYLVANIA AVE
18TH ST
17TH ST
I ST
22ND ST
I ST
24TH ST
H ST
GEORGE WASHINGTON UNIVERSITY
G ST
19TH ST
20TH ST
F ST
F ST
Watergate
The Octagon
N.Y. AVE
John F. Kennedy Center for the Performing Arts
VIRGINIA AVE
Corcoran Gallery
E ST
Dept. of State
18TH ST
D ST
23RD ST
C ST
21ST ST
DAR Constitution Hall and Museum
C ST
22ND ST
CONSTITUTION AVE
50
HENRY BACON DR
Vietnam Veterans Memorial
17TH ST
Reflecting Pool
Lincoln Memorial
Korean War Veterans Memorial
INDEPENDENCE AVE
West Potomac Park
N
Potomac River
Tidal Basin
OHIO DR
Franklin D. Roosevelt Memorial
Jefferson Memorial

0   1/4 mi
0   1/4 km

Infoshop, the Bank's well-stocked bookstore. The store carries a huge collection of books on international affairs, especially global development issues, along with Bank country reports to prepare you for your next overseas jaunt. This is also the place where foreign affairs mavens can pick up that World Bank polo shirt they've always hankered after. After the Infoshop, at 701 18th Street NW, is open from 9:00 A.M. to 5:00 P.M. Monday through Friday; 458–4500; www .worldbankinfoshop.org. Metro: Farragut West (orange and blue lines) or Farragut North (red line).

The *Breadline,* at 1751 Pennsylvania Avenue NW, has great early morning choices, including a memorable breakfast croissant, along with

funky bottom

Jacob Funk and Funkstown may be ancient history, but their Zeitgeist lives on at Foggy Bottom's United Church, at 1920 G Street NW, which regularly offers services in German.

a lunchtime assortment of imaginative sandwiches and the best lemonade in town. That's probably why you're likely to find lots of White House staff folks and World Bankers perched on those stools, and maybe a few Famous Faces as well. The Breadline also has outside tables that turn Pennsylvania Avenue into Via Veneto (assuming you're into serious self-deception). Open 7:30 A.M. to 3:30 P.M. Monday through Friday; 822–8900. Inexpensive. Metro: Farragut West (orange and blue lines) or Farragut North (red line).

Foggy Bottom is also home to another significant international financial institution, the International Monetary Fund, which serves 183 countries. While you wouldn't want to troop around the Fund's corridors even if you could, its *IMF Center,* at 720 19th Street NW, has permanent exhibits related to the

TOP ATTRACTIONS IN FOGGY BOTTOM

The Octagon	Watergate
Corcoran Gallery	Arts Club
Daughters of the American Revolution Museum and Genealogy Library	Franklin Delano Roosevelt Memorial
	Vietnam Veterans Memorial
Department of the Interior Museum and Indian Craft Shop	Lincoln Memorial
	Korean War Veterans Memorial
State Department Diplomatic Reception Rooms	National Academy of Sciences

global economy, the work of the IMF, and money, almost everyone's favorite subject. A recent show at the center featured exhibits of the objects such as shells, beads, and weapons that once served as currency in Africa and coins from the Silk Road, the Mediterranean, and other historic trade routes. The center also has a global finance-oriented bookstore and a gift shop. Open 10:00 A.M. to 4:30 P.M., Monday through Friday; 623–6869; www.imf.org/external/np/exr/center/index.htm. Metro: Foggy Bottom (orange and blue lines) or Farragut North (red line).

Your next stop is at Foggy Bottom's most elegant home. *The Octagon,* known in its day as "The Palace of Washington," must have seemed wildly out of place among the crude shacks and muddy streets of the young capital. Built by Col. John Tayloe in 1801, this grand Federal town house was designed by William Thornton, the architect of the U.S. Capitol. Jefferson, Monroe, Adams, and Andrew Jackson all passed through the Octagon's circular entrance hall to visit the Tayloes in their splendid home. The Octagon added an entirely new and unwelcome chapter to its history when for six months it served as the Executive Mansion for President Madison after the British burned the White House during the War of 1812. After a long period of decay as a tenement, the Octagon was rescued and restored in 1902 by the American Institute of Architects. The American Architectural Foundation now maintains it as the oldest museum in the United States devoted to architecture.

Your guided tour will start in the drawing room, once covered with 4 feet

of trash, where you'll see the priceless stone mantel that somehow survived those years of neglect. You'll pass through the dining room, with its Chippendale breakfront and Gilbert Stuart portraits of the Tayloes, before climbing the splendid oval staircase. Check out the ivory "amity buttons" on the handrail, which indicated that the house was paid for, an early American custom that few could follow today. Upstairs in the oval study stands the English rent table where Madison signed the Treaty of Ghent, which ended the war with Great Britain. The house's bedrooms, which are regularly occupied by traveling historical and architectural exhibits, are reportedly haunted by the ghosts of two Tayloe daughters who

The Octagon

threw themselves down the staircase when told by their father they could not marry the men of their choice. Odd noises, swaying chandeliers, and mysterious footsteps are not included in the tour.

Down in the basement where President Madison stashed the presidential wine and servants toiled in the large kitchen, this magnificent home shows its human side. The restored (and euphemistically named) "servant's hall" is where the Tayloes' African-American slaves ate and did their household chores, then slept in shifts under impossibly cramped conditions in the small bedroom next door. As you'll see from drawings and cross sections, extensive archaeological research and reconstruction have restored all the original walls and structures of the basement rooms.

The Octagon, 1799 New York Avenue NW (638–3221) is open Tuesday through Sunday 10:00 A.M. to 4:00 P.M.; closed Monday; www.archfoundation .org. Admission is $5.00 for adults, $3.00 for students and seniors. Metro: Farragut West and McPherson Square (orange and blue lines) or Farragut North (red line).

The headquarters building of the **American Institute of Architects,** at 1735 New York Avenue, behind the Octagon, offers regular architectural exhibits in its lobby. The building and its shop, which carries a broad selection of books on architecture, are open Monday through Friday 8:30 A.M. to 5:00 P.M.; www.aia.org.

Although the **Corcoran Gallery of Art** is on a lot of people's "must-see" lists, it's also slightly off the beaten path because it's *(a)* off the Mall, *(b)* generally not as well known as the more publicized National Gallery of Art, and *(c)* one of the few great Washington museums not part of the Smithsonian family. The Corcoran Collection moved to its splendid Beaux Arts building in 1897, when it outgrew what is now the Renwick Gallery. Before entering, take a look at the imposing rotunda and the facade frieze bearing the names of great painters and you'll see why the Corcoran was Frank Lloyd Wright's favorite building in Washington.

Inside you'll find a large, distinguished, and eclectic permanent collection of classic and contemporary American and European art. Here the luminous work of French impressionists mingles with American works such as Albert Bierstadt's epic *The Last of the Buffalo,* the famous Gilbert Stuart portrait of George Washington seen on the $1.00 bill and even a thirteenth-century stained glass window from Soissons Cathedral. Although the Corcoran's famous statue *The Greek Slave* scandalized Victorian-era visitors, who gazed on it in gender-segregated viewings, nobody gives it a thought today, especially anyone who's been to the movies since 1970. The museum also has numerous special exhibits of contemporary American art and photography.

Corcoran Gallery of Art

But for me the star of the Corcoran show is the gilded *Salon Dore,* imported from a Parisian town house. With golden paneling, mirrored walls, and flower garlands, it gives visitors the sense of being transported to a sumptuous, eighteenth-century garden. Our last visit occurred during one of the museum's periodic "family days," which featured performances of Colonial music and dance, children's art lessons, and "appearances" by Abraham Lincoln and a crinkly Benjamin Franklin, who told stories to the kids. The museum shop, well-stocked with art and photography books, is a real treat. So is the Cafe Des Artistes in the museum's double atrium, which offers light fare Wednesday to Saturday 11:00 A.M. to 2:00 P.M., until 8:00 P.M. on Thursday; closed Monday and Tuesday. There's a Cajun-influenced gospel brunch every Sunday 10:30 A.M. to 2:00 P.M., cost $24.95, $10.95 for children. On the first and third Wednesday of every month from 12:30 to 1:30 P.M. a free program of live jazz is presented in the museum's Hammer Auditorium.

The Corcoran, at 500 17th Street NW (639–1700; www.corcoran.org), is open Wednesday through Sunday from 10:00 A.M. to 5:00 P.M. and until 9:00 P.M. on Thursday. The museum is closed on Monday. Docents lead forty-five-minute tours at noon on weekdays, and on weekends at noon and 2:30 P.M. Admission is $8.00 for individuals, and $6.00 for seniors and students. Metro: Farragut West (orange and blue lines).

The block-square ***Daughters of the American Revolution (DAR)*** complex includes a museum, a genealogical reference library, and a series of richly furnished rooms depicting typical upscale American rooms during the period 1770–1840. It also includes one of the city's finest auditoriums, the 4,000-seat Constitution Hall. The DAR may have a fusty image in some areas, but its museum comes up with snazzy displays of American decorative art, most recently an exhibit of colorful and intricately made quilts from colonial times right down to the present. A collection of early American ceramics includes useful medical equipment such as a handsome leech jar to hold the friendly little critters that will happily cleanse that pesky bile from your blood, and you know how important that can be. After all, if it was good enough for (the late) George Washington, it's good enough for you.

Docents also take visitors to the DAR's "period rooms" on tours that depart every forty-five minutes. Among the standouts are the New Jersey Room, with walls paneled in walnut retrieved from a ship that sank in 1777; the California Room, which faithfully reproduces a room of the whaling station in Monterey as it appeared in the early 1800s; and a Maryland Room with wallpaper depicting Baltimore in 1770 that was discovered in a Paris antiques shop by a DAR member.

If you're interested in tracing your colonial-era ancestors, the DAR's vast genealogical library, located in Continental Hall, the building's elaborate theater, is one of the best research sources anywhere. A $6.00 fee will start you off with one of the in-house professional genealogists and a computer to track down your family.

The DAR also offers a "Colonial Adventure" tour: Costumed guides take five- to seven-year-olds on a travel in time back to colonial America, where they play eighteenth-century games, attend a period tea party, and learn what it was like to be a child in pre-Revolutionary days.

The *Daughters of the American Revolution Museum,* 1776 D Street NW; 879–3241; www.dar.org/museum. Open Monday through Friday 9:30 A.M. to 4:00 P.M. and Saturday 9:00 A.M. to 5:00 P.M. Closed Sunday. Tours of the period rooms are offered Monday through Friday 10:00 A.M. to 2:30 P.M. and Saturday from 9:00 A.M. to 4:30 P.M. The genealogical library is open from 8:30 A.M. to 4:00 P.M. Monday through Friday and Saturday 9:00 A.M. to 5:00 P.M. Closed Sunday. For more about the library, call 879–3229. One hour "Colonial Adventure" tours for children from five to seven are given the first and third Saturdays of every month between September and May at 1:30 and 3:00 P.M. Admission is free, but reservations are essential and, because of the tour's popularity, should be made early by calling 879–3240.

The *Organization of American States (OAS),* once known as the Pan-American Union, is an international organization where diplomats from the United States and thirty-four other Western Hemisphere nations come together to promote hemispheric peace, political stability, and social progress. Aside from its many cultural and educational projects and a long list of political initiatives throughout our hemisphere, the OAS's ornate headquarters building, "The House of the Americas," at 17th Street and Constitution Avenue, is a good place to know about if you're walking the neighborhood in any season. In

Memorial Walk

The best way to see the off-the-beaten-path Franklin Delano Roosevelt Memorial and four other important memorials is by taking a half-day stroll that meanders across the National Mall, through the park and polo fields along the Potomac, and winds up at the Jefferson Memorial for a look at the cherry trees around the Tidal Basin.

From the Foggy Bottom Metro exit, turn right on 23rd Street and walk past the State Department to Constitution Avenue, where a left turn takes you to the most poignant spot in Washington, the *Vietnam Veterans Memorial,* with its wall of black granite bearing the names of the 58,000 Americans who died in that war. Offerings, flowers, and mementos of the fallen are often left at the wall and the emotions of their surviving buddies, relatives, and ordinary visitors are always close to the surface.

At the *Lincoln Memorial* at the end of the National Mall, the magnificent Daniel Chester French statue symbolizes Lincoln's greatness. But this memorial is loaded with other symbolic touches. The thirty-six exterior Doric columns represent the number of states in the Union when Lincoln was shot, while the fifty-six steps up to the statue mark Lincoln's age at the time of his death. Then take a close look at Lincoln's hands; one is clenched and the other open, which reputedly represents both his will to preserve the Union and act with openness and compassion. Probably so, but they are also signing his initials, **A** with the left and **L** with the right.

To the right of the Lincoln Memorial you'll pass the *Korean War Veterans Memorial,* which honors the fighting men and women who served in one of America's bloodiest and most frustrating conflicts. The memorial's centerpiece is the group of nineteen stainless steel statues depicting a squad on patrol and the images on black granite of more than 2,400 servicemen and women.

summer, its sumptuous interior courtyard—a shady Spanish colonial patio with a tinkling fountain—is a Latin oasis that's ideal for cooling off and escaping Washington's sizzling temperatures. This sparkling loggia, with tropical flowers, lovely blue tiles, and walls bearing Inca, Maya, and other early Latin American motifs, also makes a great refuge that brightens those winter greys and chills. But there's more. Upstairs you'll see the "Hall of the Americas," the grand meeting room where the OAS Permanent Council gathers under splendid Tiffany chandeliers, and the "Hall of Heroes," with busts of Latin America's greatest figures. The Organization of American States offers self-guided building tours Monday through Friday from 9:00 A.M. to 5:30 P.M. Photo ID is needed. Call 458–3927 for information on group tours; www.oas.org.

Behind the OAS you'll find the *Aztec Garden,* with guava, coffee, date, and other exotic plants collected from all over Latin America. Behind the garden, but facing 18th Street, stands the *Art Museum of the Americas,* in a

Signs will direct you across Independence Avenue to Ohio Drive and a walk along the Potomac through West Potomac Park, past soccer fields, baseball diamonds, and even Washington's only polo fields.

While you're on Ohio Drive you can take a real trip down memory lane back to the days when the United States and Cuba got along. In West Potomac Park next to the 14th Street bridge, you'll spot the ornate marble Cuban Friendship Urn, which the Cuban government gave to President Coolidge in 1929 in gratitude for America's help in freeing Cuba from Spanish rule. The urn was part of a memorial in Havana commemorating American sailors lost during the explosion of the USS *Maine* in 1898, the act that touched off the Spanish-American War. Right now the urn, which once stood in front of the Cuban Embassy (when there was one), was rescued from obscurity in a government warehouse in 1996. Now it's truly off the beaten path, but after Fidel is *no mas, quien sabe?*

At the **Franklin Delano Roosevelt Memorial** you'll walk through four granite-walled spaces, one for each of Roosevelt's four administrations. On the walls are inscribed memorable phrases from FDR's speeches; sculptures dramatize the challenges Roosevelt and other Americans faced in each of his terms. In the first room, haggard and hungry men stand in a Depression breadline for handouts; in another sculpture, a man listens to a radio for inspiration from one of Roosevelt's "fireside chats." In the third room the wartime president sits with his dog Fala, and in the fourth a statue of Eleanor Roosevelt commemorates her role as First Lady and champion of human rights. www.nps.gov/fdrm.

Exiting the FDR Memorial you'll be next to the Tidal Basin and ready to continue your stroll among the cherry trees to the **Jefferson Memorial,** a few yards away. Then head for the Smithsonian Metro stop and your next off-the-beaten-path destination.

charming Spanish colonial building that was once the official residence of the secretary-general of the OAS. The museum showcases contemporary art of Latin America and the Caribbean. You'll always find exhibits of vibrant works from its extensive permanent collection, usually accompanied by at least one temporary exhibit presenting an established or emerging artist from somewhere in the hemisphere. Although the art is always special, be sure to see the fascinating loggia in the back of the museum where two stories of blue and terracotta tiles replicate Aztec figures, legends, and folk themes. Art Museum of the Americas, 201 18th Street NW; 458–6301, fax 458–6021; www.museum.oas.org. Open Tuesday through Sunday 10:00 A.M. to 5:00 P.M. Metro: Farragut West (blue and orange lines).

Although it looks pretty dull from the street, behind its New Deal Modern facade, the Department of the Interior offers visitors a pair of unique places. Exhibits in the **Department of the Interior Museum,** trace the Department's

All About GWU

George Washington University originated in the dream of both Washington and L'Enfant to establish a national university in the District somewhere near the current intersection of 23rd Street and Virginia Avenue. Washington, in fact, held stock in the Potowmack Canal Company, which was founded to create both the university and the C&O Canal. Long story short, Congress never voted to create a national school, but the idea morphed into Columbian College, founded in 1824, which became today's GWU. After the federal government, the university is the largest single private landholder in the city and growing every year.

main areas of activity, which include the protection of wildlife, mine safety, and western lands. The real crowd pleasers, however, are the colorful Bureau of Indian Affairs exhibits of Native American culture, crafts, and heritage. If you're impressed by the exhibits, across the hall there's an authentic off-the-beaten-path find: The *Indian Craft Shop*, one of Washington's top gift shops, has a nifty collection of woven goods, pottery, and jewelry from forty-five tribal groups. The intricate Alaskan carvings from walrus ivory are in themselves worth a visit. The Department of the Interior Museum (208–4743; www.indian craftshop.com) and its craft shop (208–4056) at 1849 C Street NW, are open Monday through Friday 8:30 A.M. to 4:30 P.M. and the third Saturday of every month from 10:00 A.M. to 4:00 P.M. Photo ID required for entry. Metro: Farragut West (orange and blue lines).

If hunger strikes while you're visiting the Interior Department, one floor down from the craft shop and museum there's a cafeteria that serves breakfast, snacks, and lunch at reasonable cost.

Let's be clear—if you take the weekly tour of the *Federal Reserve Bank,* Chairman Bernanke is not going to come out to brief you personally about his innermost thoughts on interest rates or the direction of the stock market. What you will get is a well-organized tour of one of America's and the world's most powerful institutions, which directly influences the health of the economy and interest rates (important only if you're one of the few with a car loan, mortgage, or credit card). You can sample the rarefied air of the Fed's headquarters, with its templelike pillared entrance hall, by visiting the Federal Reserve Board Gallery, a tasteful exhibit of nineteenth- and twentieth-century paintings and sculpture; a recent show featured imaginative sculptures and sketches based on banknotes.

But for a complete look at America's cathedral of cash, take the weekly tour, which visits the gallery, then ascends the graceful stairway to the holiest of holies, the huge Board of Governor's Boardroom. Here, around a 27-foot, two-ton granite table, the world's most influential banker and his colleagues make big decisions that affect you. In fact, you can watch the excellent film describing the Fed's workings from the chairman's chair and think about getting that mortgage paid off. As a souvenir of your visit, your guide will even give you some money, a little bag of shredded cash. (Here's a tip for parents: If the kids are getting fidgety or bored, you can keep them amused for a decade or two by asking them to reassemble the bills). And, oh yes, there's a pay phone outside where you can call your broker. Individual tours of the Federal Reserve building, once given

capitalquote

"If you want to have a friend in Washington, better buy a dog."

—President Harry S. Truman

every Thursday at 2:30 P.M., have been suspended since the September 11 attacks. The bank, however, can accommodate tour groups of ten or more. Call the Fed's visitor center at 452–3126 or 452–3324 for an update and more information. You can still visit the Fed's art exhibits by pre-registering at least twenty-four hours in advance by calling 452–3686 and giving them your Social Security number and date of birth. The visitor's entrance is on 20th Street NW, between C Street and Constitution Avenue. You'll find more information at www.federalreserve.gov.

Someone (I think it was me) once described the huge **Department of State building** at 22nd and C Streets NW as "a '50s insurance office without the charm." You definitely wouldn't want to tour the rabbit warren offices on the first six floors, and even if you could visit the rarefied seventh floor (which you can't), you'd find that even the secretary of state's suite suffers from the klunky boardroom decor so cherished on Planet Eisenhower.

But the eighth floor **Diplomatic Reception Rooms** are a very different story. Here you'll find an unparalleled collection of eighteenth-century American furniture, paintings, and decorative arts that is one of the city's best-kept secrets. The world leaders, foreign diplomats, and other dignitaries that attend receptions and dinners in these opulent rooms wine and dine surrounded by treasures such as Thomas Jefferson's mahogany desk, where he wrote portions of the Declaration of Independence; the secretary on which the Treaty of Paris was signed in 1783, ending the American Revolution; and a large collection of Philadelphia Chippendale chairs. Portraits of John Jay and the Washingtons by Gilbert Stuart look down from the walls, while George Washington's dinner service is displayed in a massive breakfront. The secretary of state's intimate dinners for 250 are held in the vast Franklin dining room, where the carpet is so large that it had to be helicoptered in.

Forty-five-minute guided tours of the reception rooms are conducted Monday through Friday at 9:30 and 10:30 A.M., and 2:45 P.M. and leave from the flag-filled lobby you've seen on every network TV news show. No admission charge, but reservations are required; get them ninety days in advance by calling 647–3241 or faxing 736–4232. Summer tours are fully booked up to three months in advance, so you must plan ahead. Children under twelve discouraged. For an advance peek at some of America's greatest treasures visit www.state.gov. Metro: Foggy Bottom (orange and blue lines).

You don't have to be a rocket scientist to appreciate the *National Academy of Sciences* headquarters building at 2100 C Street NW. The academy's stunning Great Hall, with a four-story ceiling of gold and blue mosaics depicting great moments in the history of science, is similar in form and appearance to a small medieval church. A Foucault pendulum, which illustrates spinning of the earth on its axis, dangles from the center of the dome. The hall and its surrounding corridors usually house small art shows; free chamber music concerts are frequently given under the "Arts in the Academy" program.

capitalquote

"Don't forget, even paranoids have enemies."

—Secretary of State Henry Kissinger

Downstairs, the academy's small, health-conscious cafeteria makes a good lunch stop. Afterward, head for the building's gardens on Constitution Avenue, where you'll find a giant bronze statue of the great scientist Albert Einstein. A celestial map, showing the heavens as they were on April 22, 1979, the day the memorial was dedicated, is spread at Einstein's feet. In his left hand is a paper with mathematical equations that summarize his most important contributions: the theory of relativity, the photoelectric effect, and the equivalence of energy and matter. To round out your visit, offer to explain all three to your spouse and children. The academy (334–2000) is open Monday through Friday 8:00 A.M. to 6:00 P.M. The cafeteria is open 7:00 to 10:30 A.M. and to visitors for lunch from 12:45 to 2:00 P.M. For information on concerts, call 334–2436. Metro: Foggy Bottom (orange and blue lines).

Watergate, where a botched break-in of Democratic party headquarters triggered the investigation and cover-up that led to Nixon's resignation and added a new word to our language, takes its name from the tiers of granite steps still visible along the Potomac just to the north of Memorial Bridge. The steps were originally envisioned as a ceremonial "water gate" where foreign dignitaries would arrive by barge, Cleopatra-like, for a formal welcome to the capital. It never happened. Instead, Washingtonians gathered here on the steps or in canoes for summer evening concerts by the Marine Band and other orchestras playing on a bandshell anchored on the river.

Jazz at the "KenCen"

Although you've surely heard about the Kennedy Center's world-renowned schedule of operas, dance, musical comedy, and classical music, you probably don't know that the center also sponsors a terrific program of live jazz in its very own nightclub. The recently formed KC Jazz Club convenes several times a month from September to June to listen to jazz greats like Cleo Laine, Cassandra Wilson, and the Billy Taylor Trio. The setting is a dimly lit, intimate nightclub in the center's roof-level Terrace Gallery where, aside from great music, you'll also find a buffet table and bar.

KC Jazz Club, John F. Kennedy Center for the Performing Arts, 2700 F Street NW, Washington, D.C. (800) 444–1324 or 467–4600. You'll also find a schedule at www.kennedy-center.org/programs/jazz/jazzclub/home.html. Tickets are $25.

The apartment-office-hotel complex, which resembles a Mussolini–era Italian luxury liner that has mysteriously run aground on the banks of the Potomac, later gave part of its name to the continuing and unfortunate habit of making every minor scandal or passing illegality a "gate" of some kind. But another, real Watergate scandal came along during the '90s when it was the address of Monica Lewinsky; the apartments are also home to her neighbors, presidential candidates Robert and Elizabeth Dole.

The office building where Tricky Dick's "plumbers" broke in is at 2500 Virginia Avenue, while the Howard Johnson across the street that was used by their lookouts is now a George Washington University dorm. Behind the office building, the posh Swisshotel Watergate Hotel contains Aquarelle—an equally pricey restaurant—and a mediocre health club. If hunger strikes in this virtually restaurant-free zone, you could get a loan and head for Aquarelle, but a more reasonable choice would be to take the escalator down to *Chen's,* a small walk-in restaurant in the Watergate's interior shopping mall, where you'll find out why Bob and Liddy go there for the lemon chicken. Chen's is located at 2542 Virginia Avenue NW. Call 965–4104. Inexpensive.

There are at least two good reasons to visit the *Arts Club of Washington,* an organization founded to promote the appreciation of art through a broad range of cultural programs and exhibits. The parlors and public rooms of the club's headquarters

namesake

In 1791 a special panel, acting without the president's concurrence, changed the name of the capital city from "Territory of Columbia" to "the city of Washington." Even though he selected the site and his name is over the door, the ever modest George Washington never called the capital Washington, preferring instead to call it "The Federal City."

The American Meridian

At the corner of 24th and H Streets NW a plaque on the George Washington University campus marks the imaginary north-south line that once was, at least for Americans, zero longitude, which separated the Eastern and Western hemispheres. And, as the center of America's world from 1848 to 1884, the meridian was used to survey the boundaries of the western states.

The American Meridian was an invisible line that ran through the dome of the U.S. Naval Observatory, which you can see (but not visit) on its hilltop a few blocks away on "Navy Hill" at 24th and D Streets NW. Back when 24th Street NW divided the planet, a drive to the Virginia suburbs meant changing hemispheres, which is possibly one reason that, in 1884, America joined the rest of the world in recognizing the Greenwich, England, observatory as the prime meridian. Metro: Foggy Bottom (orange and blue lines).

exhibit paintings by local, national, and international artists and are the scene of a wide range of cultural programs that include literary readings and concerts. The house also contains period furnishings and an old-shoe, book-lined library that will take you back to 1916 when the club was founded. The club offers a free concert series at noon every Friday.

The club's headquarters, located in the Monroe House, one of the capital's oldest and most historic structures, is alone worth a visit. Built in 1806, this handsome Georgian mansion, later expanded to include the house next door, was the home of Secretary of State James Monroe in 1814; in 1817, when Monroe became president, this became the *de facto* White House until restoration of the Executive Mansion could be completed after the fire of 1814. The house was later the British Legation, until the club moved there in 1916.

The Arts Club, 2017 I Street NW (331–7282; www.artsclubofwashington .com) is open Tuesday through Friday 10:00 A.M. to 5:00 P.M., Saturday 10:00 A.M. to 2:00 P.M.; closed Sunday. Metro: Foggy Bottom or Farragut West (orange and blue lines).

Concerts, Compliments of the Kennedy

Although you'll want to join the many who tour the **Kennedy Center,** try to time your visit for 6:00 P.M. That's when, every day, there's a free concert given in the Center's Grand Foyer, and it could be almost anything from ballet to jazz. As Woody Allen once said about life itself, "all you have to do is turn up."

The West End

Just north of Washington Circle, where Georgetown, Foggy Bottom, Downtown, and Dupont Circle all intersect, is the area known as the West End. Once a wasteland of used car lots and warehouses, the West End has become a major center for hotels, most of them pricey, and a variety of restaurants for all pocketbooks. Alas, there's not a lot to see in the West End, but you can't beat the location for lodging or dining. The hotel selection includes upmarket names like the Ritz Carlton (1150 22nd Street NW; 835–0500), the Fairmont (2401 M Street NW at 24th Street; 429–2400), and the Park Hyatt (1201 24th Street NW; 789–1234). However, a less expensive possibility is the moderately priced Best Western New Hampshire Suites at 1129 New Hampshire Avenue NW; 457–0565. The Metro stop is Foggy Bottom on the blue and orange lines.

Good restaurant choices in the West End include:

Agua Ardiente
(translation "firewater")
at 1250 24th Street NW
833–8500
www.agua-ardiente.com
Has the decor of a Latin American country church, but this is a hip chapel with soft light and textures and walls decked out with South American church and Indian art. The Nuevo Latino food includes tapas of pork, chicken, and shrimp and empanadas, those tasty little meat turnovers from the Andes. Try the potent "guarapos" of rum, fruit juice, and sugar. Open for lunch Monday through Friday and daily for dinner. Live music Wednesday through Saturday 833–8500. Moderate.

Courtyard Cafe
BNA Building
1227 25th Street NW
785–1388
For more modest fare when you're wandering the West End, try this self-service cafe where you can choose from a mammoth salad and fruit bar and a zillion sandwich possibilities. Breakfast too. Open Monday through Friday from 7:00 A.M. to 5:00 P.M. Inexpensive.

Grillfish
1200 New Hampshire Avenue NW
331–7310
Casual with very well-prepared seafood. Moderate.

Marcel's
2401 Pennsylvania Avenue NW
296–1196
www.marcelsdc.com
This award-winner combines French subtlety with Belgian robustness, especially in its rich game dishes. After your pre-performance dinner, Marcel's limousine will whisk you to the Kennedy Center, then bring you back for a sumptuous dessert. Expensive.

Meiweh
1200 New Hampshire Avenue NW
833–2288
Excellent Chinese at a moderate price.

Dining at the Kennedy Center

Although most of the restaurants in this chapter, especially Marcel's and the others on Pennsylvania Avenue, are well located for dining before performances at the Kennedy Center, don't overlook the center's two in-house possibilities. Both are located on the center's Roof Terrace level, which will give you a million-dollar view of Washington and the Potomac. Their Web site is www.kennedy-center.org.

The Roof Terrace

416–8555

Dining in New American style. This sleek, newly redecorated restaurant is usually open only Thursday, Friday, and Saturday from 5:30 to 10:30 P.M., but when performances are given on other evenings pre-theater dinners are served from 5:00 to 8:00 P.M. Since the restaurant is often also used for special occasions, it is sometimes closed to the public. The restaurant's renowned Kitchen Brunch is served Sunday from 11:30 A.M. to 2:30 P.M. Reservations recommended. Expensive.

KC Cafe

416–8560

Lighter fare, with salad, coffee, and dessert bars plus gourmet sandwiches and the Chef's Table, which offers daily special dishes. Open daily from 5:00 to 8:00 P.M., making it pretheater only. 416–8560. Moderate.

In good weather you'll see lots of folks picnicking outside on the lower-level terrace overlooking the Potomac. You can join them by either picking up a sandwich from one of the food carts in the Grand Foyer or by brown bagging it from your favorite food shop.

When you're in this area don't miss **Pangea,** a vibrant gift shop, artisan market, and café operated in collaboration with the International Finance Corporation, the World Bank affiliate that promotes economic growth and development in third world countries. At Pangea you'll find home décor items, rungs, textiles, and silks created by grassroots artisans and craftspeople from all over the globe. Pangea's cafe offers specialty coffees and sandwiches to give you much-needed strength while shopping. Pangea, at 2121 Pennsylvania Avenue NW, is open Monday through Friday from 7:00 A.M. to 7:00 P.M. and Saturday from 9:00 A.M. to 5:00 P.M. (458–5360; www.pangeamarket.com).

The ***B'nai B'rith Klutnick National Jewish Museum*** covers the totality of the Jewish experience from antiquity down to the present. The museum's rare and beautiful displays of Judaica include the 1790 corrspondence between George Washington and the sexton of the first American synagogue in Newport, Rhode Island; sixteenth-century European torahs; and collections of historic ritual objects. Other exhibits trace Jewish history, explain dietary laws, and illustrate Jewish holidays and traditions.

There's even "Stars of David," the Jewish American Sports Hall of Fame, a collection of sports memorabilia honoring athletes such as Sandy Koufax, Hank Greenberg, and Mark Spitz. Aside from these exhibitions from its permanent collection, the museum often hosts special shows of Jewish culture, art, and history. The B'nai B'rith National Jewish Museum is located at 2020 K Street NW. Tours are given by appointment only between noon and 3:00 P.M. from Monday through Thursday and can be arranged by calling 857–6583; www.bnai brith.org. Metro: Foggy Bottom or Farragut West (blue and orange lines).

Places to Stay in Foggy Bottom

The George Washington University Inn
824 New Hampshire Avenue NW; 337–6620 or
(800) 426–4455
fax 298–7499
www.gwuinn.com
This well-furnished and well-run hotel is nicely positioned on a residential street close to both the Kennedy Center and the Foggy Bottom Metro stop. Its ninety-five rooms are split between suites and regular guest rooms. Moderate. Metro: Foggy Bottom (orange and blue lines).

Hotel Lombardy
2019 Pennsylvania Avenue NW
828–2600 or
(800) 424–5486
www.hotellombardy.com
Unless you're looking for it, you might miss this European-style urban inn between downtown and Georgetown. Once an apartment house, the Lombardy

has 132 well-appointed suites and guest rooms, many with kitchenettes and dining areas; the best rooms are on the renovated floors. As a bonus, it has the only attendant-operated, door cage elevator you're likely ever to find. Moderate. Metro: Foggy Bottom or Farragut West (orange and blue lines).

Melrose Hotel
2430 Pennsylvania Avenue NW
955–6400
www.melrosehotel.com
This European-style hotel predictably attracts many international visitors as well as performers who like its proximity to the Kennedy Center. Both Georgetown and downtown are a short walk away. Also check out the Melrose's clubby little bar, The Library, and its bistro-style restaurant The Landmark, which is long on big salads and fish. Moderate. Metro: Foggy Bottom (orange and blue lines).

One Washington Circle Hotel
One Washington Circle NW
872–1680 or

(800) 424–9671
fax 887–4989
www.thecirclehotel.com
Overlooks Foggy Bottom Metro. The hotel's moderately priced restaurant, The Circle Bistro (293–5390), routinely draws praise from local food critics for its creative dishes. The cafe is open daily for breakfast, lunch, and dinner.

River Inn
924 25th Street NW
337–7600 or
(800) 424–2741
fax: 337–6520
www.theriverinn.com
Don't be surprised if you find your fellow guests lugging tubas and cellos (this is where it pays to be a flutist); the River Inn is a favorite long-term hideaway for musicians, actors, and other performers at the Kennedy Center just up the street.

State Plaza Hotel
2117 E Street NW
861–8200 or
(800) 424–2859
www.stateplaza.com
Convenient to the State Department, George Washington University, and the Kennedy Center. The hotel's

moderately priced Garden Cafe, a definite find with an outdoor patio and top-notch American cuisine, is popular with American and foreign diplomats. Open Monday through Friday 7:00 A.M. to 3:00 P.M. and 5:00 to 10:00 P.M., Saturday and Sunday 8:00 to 11:00 A.M. and 5:00 to 10:00 P.M., Sunday brunch 10:00 A.M. to 2:00 P.M.

Suite or Apartment Hotels

Conventional hotels attract the most visitor attention, but don't overlook the District's many suite hotels, especially if you're traveling with kids or like the idea of returning to the comfort of your own space after a long day of work or sightseeing. Some of the best are conveniently located in Foggy Bottom. All of the following offer well-appointed suites with kitchens. Prices are moderate, but ask about weekend and other special rates, of which there are many.

Washington Suites
2500 Pennsylvania Avenue NW
333–8060
www.washingtonsuites
georgetown.com
This 124-suite hotel is handy to the Foggy Bottom Metro

(orange and blue lines), the World Bank, and downtown. Georgetown is only a five-minute stroll away. Moderate.

Places to Eat in Foggy Bottom

Agua Ardiente
1250 24th Street NW
833–8500
See page 93 for full description.

Breadline
1751 Pennsylvania Avenue, NW
822–8900
See page 81 for full description.

Chen's
2542 Virginia Avenue NW
965–4104
See page 91 for full description.

Courtyard Cafe
1227 25th Street NW
785–1388
See page 93 for full description.

Dish
924 25th Street NW
338–8707
www.dishdc.com
Located in the River Inn, and not far from the Kennedy Center, Dish serves classic comfort food with a big difference in its ultra-chic quarters. Chef Anthony Chittum's repertoire of regional American dishes with an elegant touch includes great buttermilk fried chicken, grilled venison, and fish from Chittum's native Chesapeake Bay. Lunchtime at Dish might find you facing a plate of the best mac and cheese ever or an oyster po' boy platter. And check out William Wegman's classic photo of a Weimaraner on the back wall. Reservations suggested. Open for lunch Monday through Friday from 11:30 A.M. to 2:30 P.M. and dinner nightly from 5:00 to 11:00 P.M. Moderate. Metro stop: Foggy Bottom (orange and blue lines).

Grillfish
1200 New Hampshire Avenue NW
331–7310
See page 93 for full description.

KC Cafe
The Kennedy Center
416–8560
See page 94 for full
description.

Kinkead's
2000 Pennsylvania
Avenue NW
296–7700
www.kinkead.com
One of America's top food
authorities recently wrote that
when in Washington he
could eat every meal at
Kinkead's. That's no exag-
geration—this American
brasserie consistently makes
the top of most everyone's
list of places to dine in the
capital. Everything is great,
but Chef Robert Kinkead
specializes in seafood dishes
like Scandinavian salmon
stew, baked halibut with crab
and Virginia ham, or maybe
something from the extensive
raw bar. Sinful desserts, Sunday brunch, and a world-
class wine list too.
Reservations essential.
Expensive but worth it. Open
daily 11:30 A.M. to 2:30 P.M.
and 5:30 to 10:30 P.M.
Metro: Foggy Bottom
(orange and blue lines).

Marcel's
2401 Pennsylvania
Avenue NW
296–1196
See page 93 for full
description.

Marshall's
2524 L Street NW
333–1155
www.marshallsbarandgrill
.com

A neighborhood hangout that
visitors find handy for dining
before and after perform-
ances at the Kennedy Cen-
ter. Mainly American food—
burgers and salads—along
with a nice selection of Italian
dishes. Upstairs an English
pub serves drinks, ESPN,
and food. Open Monday
through Thursday 11:00 A.M.
to 2:00 A.M., Friday and Saturday until 3:00 A.M., Sunday
until midnight. Inexpensive.
Metro: Foggy Bottom
(orange and blue lines).

Meiweh
1200 New Hampshire
Avenue NW
833–2288
See page 93 for full
description.

Notti Bianche
824 New Hampshire Avenue
NW
298–9095
www.nottibianche.com
Although it's just a short stroll
from performances at the
Kennedy Center, Notti
Bianche, which received
three stars in a *Washington
Post* restaurant review, is
worth a visit any time, including breakfast. Located in the
George Washington Inn, this
bright and attractive Italian
trattoria offers up great primi
like cheese frittatas, followed
by tasty risottos and pastas.
Also look for imaginatively
prepared grilled fish and veal
dishes, an impressive pastry
menu, and a short, well-
crafted wine list. Notti
Bianche also has special pre-

and post-performance
menus; courtyard dining in
good weather. Since there's
only room for forty-two,
reservations are usually
essential, especially on performance evenings. Open for
breakfast Monday through
Friday 7:00 to 10:00 A.M. and
Saturday and Sunday 8:00 to
10:00 A.M. Lunch: Monday
through Friday 11:30 A.M. to
2:30 P.M. Dinner: Sunday
through Thursday 5:00 to
10:00 P.M.; Friday through
Sunday 5:00 to 11:00 P.M.
Expensive.

The Roof Terrace
The Kennedy Center
416–8555
See page 94 for
full description.

**The Venetian Room and
Cafe Lombardy**
2019 Pennsylvania
Avenue NW
828–2600
The intimate Venetian Room
and the bright and informal
Cafe Lombardy, both located
in the Hotel Lombardy, are
well worth visiting even if
you're not a guest. Open
daily 7:00 to 10:30 A.M.,
11:30 A.M. to 2:30 P.M., and
5:30 to 9:30 P.M. Moderate.
Metro: Foggy Bottom
(orange and blue lines).

Georgetown

A mix of smart shops, historic homes, and hip street life have made Georgetown one of Washington's liveliest and most desirable neighborhoods. But Georgetown was there first: Almost a century before the District of Columbia was created, Georgetown had a life of its own as a wealthy but inelegant Maryland river port that was the commercial gateway to the "west" (i.e., Ohio). In the eighteenth and early nineteenth centuries, an era that saw the founding of Georgetown University, Georgetown was also a slave-trading center and a key player in the tobacco trade at a time when tobacco was the lifeblood of the economy. The decline of the Chesapeake and Ohio Canal siphoned off the once-profitable Western trade and Georgetown fell on hard times, becoming, strange as its now seems, a smelly industrial town and one of Washington's worst slums. Georgetown was rescued in the 1930s when it was rediscovered and rehabilitated by officials of Roosevelt's New Deal. In the 1960s Georgetown was rediscovered all over again when President Kennedy's administration made it their headquarters and an enclave that became nationally known for a glittering lifestyle with chic dinner parties where Important People gathered to make Important Decisions.

N

0 ——— 1/4 mi
0 ——— 1/4 km

Dumbarton Oaks
Park

Montrose
Park

Oak Hill
Cemetery

Dumbarton
House

EAST PL

ROCK CREEK AND POTOMAC PKWY

26TH ST
27TH ST
28TH ST
29TH ST

DENT PL
AVON PL
LA-CAMBRIDGE
ORCHARD LN
W LANE KEYS
31ST ST
32ND ST

R ST
Q ST
P ST
POPLAR ST
OLIVE ST
29TH ST
30TH ST
31ST ST

DUMBARTON ROCK CT

RESERVOIR RD

WISCONSIN AVE

DUMBARTON ST

THOMAS
JEFFERSON
ST

Old
Stone House

M ST

N ST
POTOMAC ST
33RD ST

JONES CT
VOLTA PL
DENT PL
34TH ST

CHERRY
HILL LA

Francis Scott Key
Memorial

WISCONSIN AVE
SOUTH ST
WEST
COPPERWAITHE
AL LA
CECIL PL
GRACE ST
WAREHOUSE PL

K ST
WHITEHURST FWY

S ST
R ST
Q ST

35TH ST
36TH ST
34TH ST
35TH ST
P ST
O ST

RESERVOIR RD

ST MARY'S PL
PROSPECT ST
36TH ST
37TH ST

38TH ST
T ST
S ST
R ST

GEORGETOWN
UNIVERSITY

Glover
Archbold
Park

POTOMAC ST
PAPERMILL CT

Potomac River

Georgetown was a town in its own right until 1871, when it was incorporated into Washington, D.C., and its historic and evocative street names were lettered, numbered, and made part of the city's grid. Georgetown is not integrated into the city's Metro system, however, having opted out to avoid the congestion and crowds that residents thought the Metro would bring. Bad decision—both arrived anyway. Given the problems of parking on Georgetown's narrow streets, when you visit, either walk from the nearest Metro station, which is Foggy Bottom/GWU (it'll take about twenty minutes), take a cab, or hop a Metrobus. Any of the 30-numbered buses (30, 32, 34, 35, 36, 38B) will take you from downtown to Georgetown; you can also transfer to these Metrobus routes from the Metro at 24th Street and Pennsylvania Avenue, near the Foggy Bottom stop. If you're coming from Dupont Circle, catch a D-2 or G-2 bus from 20th and P Streets.

The Georgetown Metro Connection, a privately operated bus service, makes it even easier for visitors to reach Georgetown from Dupont Circle, Foggy Bottom, and northern Virginia. The Connection's Line one runs from the Foggy Bottom/GWU Metro station past the Georgetown waterfront and then follows Wisconsin Avenue uphill as far as the Naval Observatory. Line two connects the Dupont Circle Metro station with the Metro station in Rosslyn, Virginia, just across the Potomac, making several stops in Georgetown's M Street shopping areas along the way. You can transfer between the two lines where they intersect at Wisconsin Avenue and M Street. Fares are $1.00 one-way, 35 cents with a Metrorail transfer. Buses run every ten minutes Monday through Thursday between 7:00 A.M. and midnight, Friday from 7:00 A.M. to 2:00 A.M., Saturday 8:00 A.M. to 2:00 A.M. and Sunday 8:00 A.M. to midnight. Stops are clearly marked with a blue sign. Call 625–7433; www.georgetowndc.com.

Although its main streets—M Street and Wisconsin Avenue—are definitely among Washington's well-worn tracks, this historic district offers a number of opportunities for visitors to leave the usual tourist treadmill behind and explore some often overlooked places that exude American culture and history.

TOP ATTRACTIONS IN GEORGETOWN

Dumbarton Oaks	The Old Stone House
Tudor Place	Chesapeake and Ohio Canal
Dumbarton House	Smith Row
Riggs Riley House	

One of them is **Dumbarton Oaks,** whose ultratraditional Georgian facade conceals a surprising trove of pre-Columbian, Roman, and Byzantine treasures assembled by career diplomat Robert Woods Bliss and his wife, Mildred. In the mansion's pre-Columbian wing, dazzling Inca masks, necklaces, and plates of hammered gold from ancient Peruvian tombs compete for attention with radiant displays of Aztec artifacts of solid gold and jade. Incidentally, the museum building, designed by Philip Johnson, is itself a gem—an octagonal structure of glass, marble, teak, and bronze surrounding a lovely little garden and fountain.

Other rooms contain a priceless collection covering more than eleven centuries of Byzantine art: luminous bronzes, mosaics, and ivories that turn their display cases into jewel boxes. Its centerpiece is the magnificent Sion Treasure, a collection of liturgical silver from sixth-century Constantinople that lay hidden for fourteen centuries.

Most of Dumbarton Oaks is given over to staff offices and research libraries for Byzantine and pre-Columbian studies that are administered by Harvard, which was deeded the house, gardens, and collections in 1940. Visitors may, however, wander through the house's sumptuous music room, with El Greco's *Visitation,* tapestries, and memories of the 1944 Dumbarton Oaks Conferences, where the Allies planned and shaped the United Nations.

Lovers of fine gardens will also want to stroll through Dumbarton Oaks' ten acres of formal gardens, among America's best, and one of Washington's truly special places. The gardens unfold downhill on a series of broad terraces with colorful blooms that change with the seasons. Better yet, lots of tree-shaded walks and benches make the gardens an inviting R&R stop, but picnics are out. Be sure not to miss **The Orangery,** a joyous collection of orange and lemon trees attached to the main building. The Orangery, a winter greenhouse that dates back to 1810, also houses jasmine trees and creeping fig. The Museum at Dumbarton Oaks, 1703 32nd Street NW; 339–6401; www.doaks.org, is open Tuesday through Sunday 2:00 to 5:00 P.M.; donations accepted. The garden entrance is at 31st and R Streets; open April through October 2:00 to 6:00 P.M.; November through March 2:00 to 5:00 P.M. Garden admission $7.00 for adults, $5.00 for children and seniors. For docent tours, call 339–6409.

Back in 1816, when **Tudor Place** was completed, Georgetown was a thriving but noisy and disheveled tobacco port that Abigail Adams dismissed as "a dirty little hole." She could get pretty nasty, that Abigail, and she sure wouldn't say that today. While traffic and tumult may have lurked outside the massive gates of Tudor Place for nearly two centuries, this yellow stucco neoclassic mansion and its formal gardens have always been an oasis of urbanity and tranquillity.

AUTHOR'S FAVORITES IN GEORGETOWN

Dumbarton Oaks	Clyde's
Chesapeake and Ohio Canal	Wisconsin Avenue Shops
Martin's Tavern	

Tudor Place was designed by William Thornton, the architect of the Octagon and the Capitol, for his friend Thomas Peter, a wealthy tobacco merchant and relative of Martha Washington. The Peter family then proceeded to make this estate their home for almost 200 years, which must be some kind of record for nomadic Americans. Through all of those years, Tudor Place was a distinguished home with distinguished visitors, including Robert E. Lee (also a Peter relative), Lafayette, and Henry Clay. Although it is one of Washington's finest Federal homes, Tudor Place is far from being a period house. The Peter family's long ownership and discerning tastes have created there a continuum of rarities acquired throughout the span of their occupancy, ranging from George Washington's furniture, silver, china, and other memorabilia to rare Oriental rugs and glass paintings collected in this century by Armistead Peter, the last of the family to reside there.

Before entering to start your guided tour, take a few minutes to see the mansion's historic North Garden, where, in azalea season, secluded walks lead to outbursts of showy whites and fiery pinks. But this southern formal garden, with its English boxwood hedges, also holds many year-round pleasures, including colorful magnolias, sprawling oaks that saw the mansion's first days, and an elliptical bowling green that dates back to the early 1800s.

Once inside, you'll surely be taken by the elegant simplicity of the "Saloon," a sitting room with a two-story wall of concave windows and a staggering view out over the Potomac and Virginia. Outside, overlooking the south lawn, a columned rotunda creates a templelike porch that is Tudor Place's signature architectural feature.

Although the drawing rooms and parlors, with their priceless portraits and Colonial-era furniture, are splendid indeed, your real favorite is likely to be the mansion's handsome dining room, where chairs that once belonged to George Washington grace a grand mahogany table set with gleaming silver and period china. Upstairs all visitors, especially those from the other side of the Potomac, are thrilled to see the guest room and four-poster that Robert E. Lee used on

Pleased as Punch

A plaque on the wall at 1054 31st Street commemorates Herman Hollerith, hardly a household name, but this gifted inventor launched the computer age from his workshop on this site. In 1880 Hollerith invented the punch card tabulating machine, after getting the idea of storing data on punched cards by watching a train conductor punch tickets. His machines took off in a big way, especially when the government used them to replace hundreds of clerks and save months of labor in tabulating the 1890 census. Still wondering why you should be interested in all this? To help you sort it out, I'll just mention that, in the early 1920s, Hollerith's Computer Tabulating Machine Company changed its name to International Business Machines.

his frequent visits. Tudor Place is located at 1644 31st Street NW; 965–0400. The Tudor Place Web site, www.tudorplace.org, carries a schedule of special events, including lectures and art exhibits. House tours, which last forty-five to sixty minutes, are Tuesday through Friday at 10:00 and 11:30 A.M. and at 1:00 and 2:30 P.M. Saturday and Sunday tours are given on the hour from 10:00 A.M. to 3:00 P.M. No tours on Mondays or major holidays. The garden is open Monday through Saturday 10:00 A.M. to 4:00 P.M. and Sunday noon to 4:00 P.M. Admission: $6.00 for the house, $2.00 for the garden.

Back on R Street you'll find two other oases of tranquillity. *Montrose Park* is a preferred outdoor destination for Georgetowners looking for a little urban R&R—a primo place for dog walking, Frisbee flipping, sunbathing, or just getting the kids out of the house. Tennis courts are also available, but you can't reserve. And then there's *Lover's Lane,* a quiet walking path along the wall that separates the park from Dumbarton Oaks. Although it definitely has romantic connotations, Lover's Lane also has its practical side. If you follow it to the end, then walk through Dumbarton Oaks Park and follow the path upward, you'll surface near the Italian Embassy on Massachusetts Avenue and will have discovered a nifty (and scenic) shortcut between Georgetown and Embassy Row.

Farther along R Street, *Oak Hill Cemetery* may be a little too restful for some, but it has an elaborate redbrick gatehouse that looks like an Italian villa and a gorgeous little Gothic chapel that dates from 1850, but looks like it was built in the thirteenth century; both are easily reachable from the main gate at 30th and R Streets. For a map of the cemetery and the graves of the many notables that are buried there, including Abraham Lincoln's son, Willie, and Edwin M. Stanton, his Secretary of War, visit the superintendent's office in the gatehouse. Visiting hours; Monday through Friday 10:00 A.M. to 4:00 P.M. Closed evenings and weekends.

On your way down 28th Street, crane your neck to get a glimpse through the boxwoods and azaleas of *"Evermay,"* at number 1623. This Georgian mansion was considered the most elegant house in the city when it was built between 1792 and 1794, and it still is. Although no visitors are permitted except once a year as part of the Georgetown Garden Tour, a bronze plaque outside the entrance will fill you in on the history of this grand estate and the distinguished families that have lived there.

Architectural historians view **Dumbarton House** (not to be confused with Dumbarton Oaks) as a perfect example of the great Georgian manor houses built by wealthy Washington and tidewater Virginia merchants during the late 1700s. Dolley Madison fled to Dumbarton House when the British torched Washington in 1814. However, you'll probably remember it more for its wonderful collection of American cabinetry and furniture-making. In the library there's a gleaming secretary bookcase from 1775 New York, flanked by a pair of English globes showing the world of 1800. And if you want to see what Georgetown's busy port looked like in 1789, take a look at the background of the Peale portrait of the Stoddert children in the dining room.

In the music room, where women guests were exiled after dinner while husbands talked serious stuff, a 1795 Pembroke table is set for tea, consolation, perhaps, for missing all that early American guy talk; across the room a harp, piano, and violin of the same era stand ready for an eighteenth-century musicale.

In the upstairs bedroom you'll see that Washington political kitsch didn't begin with those Jack and Jackie drugstore plates when you spot the allegorical print of *America Paying Homage to France,* showing a native American princess in full headdress saluting an elegantly reclining France. This print was,

Out of Spite

If you're like me you've never heard of a "spite house," a home built by someone solely to enrage their neighbors, usually to block their view, their sunlight, or access to a street. But now, thanks to the *Washington Post*'s "Answer Man" column, which covers the District and its history like a hot sauce, we find that you can see two of these houses on your stroll through Georgetown. The narrow three-story house squeezed into 11 feet of space at 1239 30th Street was reportedly built to cut off a neighbor's light while the equally skinny home at nearby 3047 N Street was allegedly, says the Answer Man, designed to deny access to a shared garden.

naturellement, made in Paris. In addition to its elegant furnishings, Dumbarton House is the headquarters of the National Society of Colonial Dames. Dumbarton House, 2715 Q Street NW (337–2288; www.dumbartonhouse.org), conducts forty-five-minute tours Tuesday through Saturday at 10:15 and 11:15 A.M., 12:15 P.M., and 1:15 P.M. Admission is $5.00.

Next to Dumbarton House, tucked away on the grassy space behind the apartment house at 27th and Q Streets, is **Mt. Zion Cemetery,** the oldest predominantly black burial ground in Washington. The property originated in 1809 as a cemetery for slaves and freedmen, as opposed to the ritzy whites-only Oak Hill Cemetery visible next door. Mt. Zion was neglected for years, and its wooden markers disappeared; trustees, however, have removed most of the remaining grave markers, which have been recorded and stored pending eventual restoration of this historic site as a memorial to the historic and large black presence in Georgetown. If you look carefully at the back of the cemetery, you'll find the redbrick underground vault used as a hideout for slaves escaping north to freedom on the Underground Railroad.

The **Mt. Zion United Methodist Church,** at 1334 29th Street NW (www.fm2forministry.com), is the oldest African-American congregation in the District, having been organized in 1816 by slaves and freedmen of Georgetown's thriving black community that were subjected to segregation by their original, mainly white church. The first Mt. Zion Church, which was a major stop on the Underground Railroad, burned down in 1880. Over the years many of the black parishioners either had moved away or were, before that, "sold to Georgia traders," but Mt. Zion retains its unique character. Its historic role in Georgetown's African-American community is commemorated in its **Heritage Center,** a cozy English cottage built in 1810 and located just around the corner at 2906 O Street. Admission to the Heritage Center and its archives is by appointment only; to set up a visit call 234–0148.

The "Social Safeway"

The seemingly standard mega-grocery at 1855 Wisconsin gets its nickname from the Washington notables who flock there. Where else are you going to routinely find cabinet officers squeezing the lemons, pundits prowling the produce, or a certain very well-known TV news anchor sniffing the cantaloupe? The Safeway is also a meeting place for zillions of single Georgetowners who over the years have met, not really by chance, among the cleansers or condiments, then made plans for dinner, a movie, and who knows what else. I once spotted Elizabeth Taylor shopping at the Social Safeway and still haven't gotten over it. Visiting hours: 5:00 A.M. to 11:00 P.M. daily. Black tie optional.

Camelot on the Potomac

Jack Kennedy loved Georgetown and lived there in five different houses. As a freshman congressman, the future president established bachelor quarters at 1528 31st Street, then, after his 1950 election to the Senate, moved to 1400 34th Street. As newlyweds, Jack and Jackie set up their first Georgetown home at 3321 Dent Place. Later in his senatorial term the Kennedys rented the house at 2808 P Street. Jack and Jackie's longest residence in Georgetown was at 3307 N Street, where they lived from 1957 until they moved to 1600 Pennsylvania Avenue. The doorstop of the N Street house became famous as the place where the president-elect announced his cabinet choices. Across the street, on the wall at 3302 N Street, you'll see the plaque presented to the owner by a White House press corps grateful for the shelter, coffee, and doughnuts she supplied them during their long waits for Kennedy's appearances during the icy winter of 1960–61.

Behind a modest facade at 2613 P Street lurks one of D.C.'s most intriguing and colorful boutiques. At **Bobbie Medlin** the walls are lined with colorful and imaginative necklaces designed and crafted by Ms. Medlin from lapis lazuli, jade, and many vibrant semiprecious stones. The star of the Medlin show may be the Moroccan necklace of handcarved jasper beads adorned with silver talismans. This may also be your only chance to bring home a necklace of wedding beads from Mali or a dynamite bracelet fashioned from Tibetan silver. Open from 11:00 A.M. to 5:00 P.M. Wednesday to Saturday (333–2630).

As you wander around on the east side of Wisconsin Avenue, you'll find plenty of mansions and row houses you'd like to wrap up and take home, but keep an eye out for some really special places such as the **Colonial House,** at 1305 30th Street, home of Miss Lydia English's tony finishing school for wealthy young women until the Civil War, when the army threw out the girls and brought the wounded of Bull Run there to recuperate. The building was later turned into an apartment house, which it is today.

Cooke's Row, which extends from 3007–3027 Q Street, is a cluster of four duplexes built in 1868 in, atypically for Federal Georgetown, the Italian style. These grand and luxurious Victorians, with their ornate dormers, mansard roofs, and bay windows, were patterned after an Italian villa and are among Georgetown's grandest homes.

In the backyard of **2726 N Street,** you'll find a large and beautiful Chagall mosaic on the back wall of the garden. The story is that Marc Chagall was a close friend of the owner and, after a visit, bestowed this wonderful gift on his host. You and I should be so lucky. The mosaic is best viewed from the 28th Street sidewalk. The house also has a handsome bronze sculpture in its front garden.

The houses at *2806–2812 N Street* represent three of the finest examples of Federal architecture in Georgetown. All three were built between 1813 and 1817; number 2812 is where Susan Decatur, the widow of naval hero Stephen Decatur, lived after her husband was killed in a duel.

The *Riggs Riley House* at 3038 N Street is a splendid Federal home built in 1816 by a prominent banker, but better known more recently as the home of Averell Harriman and his wife, Pamela. The Harrimans turned the house over to their friend Jackie Kennedy after President Kennedy's assassination. After living there a month, she bought the house across the street at 3017 N Street.

At the corner of N and 30th Street, you'll visit a medical compound from Washington's Civil War days, when Georgetown was an important center for treating thousands of the wounded. Those bright, narrow little row houses from 2916 to 2924 N were nurses' housing for the hospital across the street at 2929 N, now a private residence. Down the block, the nicer houses, starting at 2903 N, were reserved for the hospital's doctors.

At 1220 31st Street, you can browse through one of the city's most distinguished collections of antique prints and maps from all over the world at the *Old Print Gallery.* The gallery specializes in city views and maps from the nineteenth century and earlier, including Brooklyn in 1816 and a bird's-eye view of Abraham Lincoln's Washington of 1861 and a spectacular 1720 city map of Rome (965–1818; www.oldprintgallery.com). Open Monday through Saturday 10:00 A.M. to 5:30 P.M.

The *Old Stone House,* at 3051 M Street, is Washington's oldest dwelling. The house started out in 1765 as a cabinetmaker's workshop, after which it was used variously as either a private home or place of business. It's now run by the National Park Service, which uses it as a small house museum of pre-Revolutionary life, with the spinning wheels and furniture of the period; check to see about taking in one of the frequent craft demonstrations. In the front room you'll find a gift shop with travel guides. The house's garden/orchard

Black History Tour

One weekend a month a guided walking tour takes visitors on a stroll to places that dramatize Georgetown's long and rich African-American heritage. One of these is "Herring Hill," the large black enclave between Rock Creek Park and 29th Street, that was named after the fish that residents used to catch in the creek. Mt. Zion and other local churches are also on the itinerary. Tours leave from the Old Stone House; call 426–6851 for dates and times. You can get a preview and a map for a self-guided tour by logging on to www.nps.gov/rocr/olst/black.htm.

Art and Antiques on M Street

You'll find some of Washington's top galleries and antiques stores along M Street, in the blocks between 28th and 30th Streets. Among the best:

American Studio+
2906 M Street
965–3273
For the latest from Alessi and other cutting-edge U.S. and European designers of tableware and ceramics. Also the latest in zoomy watches and pens. Monday through Saturday 11:00 A.M. to 6:00 P.M., Sunday 1:00 to 5:00 P.M.

Grafix
2904 M Street
342–0610
For vintage posters and an encyclopedic collection of *New Yorker* and *Fortune* covers dating back to the '20s. Ask to see the posters for the long-vanished transatlantic luxury liners of the '30s and '40s. Thursday through Saturday noon to 7:00 P.M., Sunday noon to 6:00 P.M.

Spectrum Gallery
1132 29th Street
333–0954
www.spectrumgallery.com
For colorful posters and prints, along with a selection of nice oils and photographs. Tuesday through Saturday, noon to 6:00 P.M.; Sunday noon to 5:00 P.M.

Justine Mehlman
2824 Pennsylvania Avenue
337–0613
www.justinemehlmanantiques.com
The place to find antique jewelry of all kinds, along with art deco ceramics from Paris and art nouveau picture frames and candlesticks. Open Tuesday through Saturday 11:00 A.M. to 5:30 P.M.

Bridge Street Books
2814 Pennsylvania Avenue
965–5200
One of those bookstores every neighborhood should be so lucky to have. This one's for lovers of serious nonfiction; heavy on politics, literature, history, and film; remainders table out front. Open Monday through Thursday 11:00 A.M. to 10:00 P.M., Friday and Saturday until 11:00 P.M.; Sunday noon to 6:00 P.M.

makes a great place to take it easy or even picnic with the locals. Open Wednesday through Sunday noon to 5:00 P.M. (426–6851; www.nps.gov/rocr/oldstonehouse).

Washington's legendary ***Blues Alley,*** true to its name, is tucked away off the alley at 1073 Wisconsin Avenue. World-class jazz artists like Wynton Marsalis, Benny Green, and Nancy Wilson have performed there, which is one reason that the *New York Times* called it "the nation's finest supper club." The food is almost as good as the music, which is saying a lot. With all this good stuff going on, you must reserve by calling 337–4141 or visiting www.blues alley.com. Open seven days a week, with nightly shows from 8:00 to 10:00 P.M. and a third show at midnight on Friday and Saturday. Dinner from 6:00 P.M.

With a little historical imagination, you can get a sense of the long-vanished port of Georgetown at the corner of Wisconsin Avenue and K Street, which 200 years ago was the heart of the town's busy waterfront. This cluster of redbrick commercial buildings is the Old Dodge Warehouse, which was built in 1800 next to the Potomac docks as warehouses for Havana "seegars," Cuban molasses, Santo Domingo coffee, and the other cargoes of a busy port.

Washington Harbour, on the Georgetown waterfront at 3000 K Street, between 29th and 31st, is a major residential and office complex, which will interest you chiefly for its lively restaurant scene and riverside promenade. In good weather it's great fun to dine outside next to the Potomac and gaze out at the Lincoln Memorial, the Kennedy Center and, across the way, Theodore Roosevelt Island, now a wooded park but once an important Civil War encampment used for the defense of Washington. But it's the river that's the big attraction for diners, who enjoy the nonstop aquatic pageant of racing sculls from Georgetown and other schools, frequent sightseeing ships, and a luxury yacht or cabin cruiser tied up across the way. The Washington Harbour restaurants are **Sequoia,** with a large glassed-in dining room with great river views and lots of action at the outside bar and tables, **Tony and Joe's** with seafood specialties (none from the Potomac), and **Bangkok Joe's** (no relation) for Thai street food with an elegant twist. All serve great Sunday brunches Sequoia, 944–4200, is open Monday through Saturday from 11:30 A.M. to 3:30 P.M. and Sunday from 5:30 to 11:30 P.M.; weekend brunch 10:00 A.M. to 3:30 P.M. Tony and Joe's (944–4545; www.dcseafood.com/taj), is open Monday through Friday from 11:00 A.M. to 10:00 P.M. and until midnight on Friday and Saturday. Bangkok Joe's (333–4422; www.bangkokjoes.com), is open Sunday through Thursday 11:30 A.M. to 10:30 P.M. until 11:30 P.M. Friday and Saturday.

Washington Harbour is also home port or a stop for the fleet of sightseeing boats that cruise the Potomac, giving passengers a unique look at some of Washington's best-known places. Boat tours of the District's waterside monuments glide past magnificent views of the Washington Monument, the majestic white colonnades of the Lincoln Memorial, the Kennedy Center, and the Chrysler Airflow swirl of the Watergate. Some will also take you for a close-up look at seldom-visited Roosevelt Island, a ninety-acre wilderness park in the middle of the Potomac that was once a farm, then a Union Army camp, and is now an urban oasis of wildlife and wildflowers. Some will take you downriver to historic Alexandria, Virginia, and its Old Town of stately Federal mansions and lively street life. Cruises run from April 1 through October. For information about *Capitol River Cruises,* which offers narrated fifty-minute trips within the District only, phone (800) 405–5511 or visit www.capitolrivercruises.com. Adults $12.00, children $6.00.

Boats of the Alexandria-based *Potomac Riverboat Company* (703–684–0580; www.potomacriverboatco.com), call at Washington Harbour, then cruise past the District's monuments on their way back to Alexandria. Some boats continue from Alexandria to Washington's home at Mt. Vernon. Prices range from $8.00 to $32.00 for adults, $5.00 to $16.00 for children, depending on the route you choose. Potomac Riverboat operates cruises on weekends only in April and October and up to six daily from May through September. Both lines sell refreshments aboard, but think about bringing your own lunch or snacks from one of Georgetown's patisseries. You'll find more information about both lines at the ticket booth on the water at the foot of 31st Street NW.

If you're on a spring visit, you should know that Washington Harbour is the best place to watch the annual *Dragon Boat Festival,* one of Washington's most exciting and colorful spectacles. The boats themselves are worth the trip—these are ornate boats in red, blue, green, yellow, and other shades, with dragon's heads on the prow, dragon's scales on the side, and a forked tail at the end. And they're 45-feet long, with a crew of twenty who paddle in unison, plus two members who mark the strokes with a drum. About forty-five teams compete in a series of heats over a 1,500-meter course between the Key Bridge and Thompson's Boathouse. The race continues an ancient tradition that began in the third century B.C. and begins when the dragonheads are brought to life symbolically by dotting the eyes with paint. The ceremony is held on the fifth day of the fifth month of the lunar calendar. If your terrestrial calendar doesn't stretch that far, find the exact dates and more details by going to www.dragon boatfestivaldc.com, or phoning the Georgetown Visitor Center for information at 298–9222. Hint: In 2004 this was the third week in May. The races are held over a weekend on Saturday from 10:00 A.M. to 5:00 P.M. with the finale the following day from 10:00 A.M. to 4:00 P.M.

In season, which is April to November, you won't want to miss the *Georgetown,* a replica of an early canal boat, for a ride on the *Chesapeake and Ohio Canal,* which is now a National Historic Park. During these one-hour, mule-drawn excursions, you'll pass through locks and hear from period-costumed guides about life on the canal in the 1800s in talks that are both fun and knowledgeable. You'll also see some of the Canal's original warehouses, built in 128 and now reincarnated as sales and office space, and envy the Washingtonians who jog, bicycle, or amble along the towpath. The *Georgetown,* thanks to the efforts of mules Lil and Ada, hurtles along at speeds reaching 4 miles per hour, so fasten those seat belts! While you'll enjoy the leisurely pace, the slow speed

Paddle Your Own Canoe

If gazing at the Potomac and the C&O Canal has started you thinking about your own nautical expedition, you're in luck. Next to Washington Harbour, on the river at 2900 Virginia Avenue, NW, you can rent canoes, bikes, and kayaks at *Thompson's Boat Center,* a National Park Service boathouse. At the Center (333–9543, www.thompsonboatcenter.com) canoes and kayaks rent for $8.00 an hour, $22.00 for a full day, while bikes run $4.00 to $8.00 an hour or $15.00 to $25.00 all day, depending on whether the bike is a one-or two-speed model. The Center is open from 8:00 A.M. to 5:00 P.M. daily; during the year it is open for boat rentals from about March 1 to November 15, or when the water temperature reaches 55 degrees, and from March to mid-October for bike rentals.

Nearby, at *Jack's Boathouse,* right on the water at 3500 Water Street, not far from the foot of Wisconsin Avenue, you can rent a canoe or kayak and paddle the Potomac for $15.00 an hour or $35.00 per day. Just be sure and get some river safety instructions first—the Potomac can be hazardous. Jack's is open between April 1 and November 1 from 8:00 A.M. to sunset (337–9642). If you're hoping to view the July 4 fireworks aboard one of Jack's boats on the Potomac, you'll have a lot of company.

Just beyond Jack's, at 3530 Water Street NW, you'll see the *Potomac Boat Club,* a private rowing club founded in 1869; for information about viewing their annual September regatta, check their Web site at www.rowpbc.net. The Club stores its sculls in the massive arches of the historic *Aqueduct Bridge,* one of the main bridges across the Potomac from 1844 until it was dismantled in the 1920s. As its name suggests, the bridge originally carried barge traffic from Washington to Alexandria, Virginia, then was

is the reason that the Canal, which was conceived as a 185-mile freight artery connecting the port of Georgetown with the West, never panned out commercially, losing out to the railroads despite the political and financial support of heavy hitters like George Washington and Thomas Jefferson. No reservations, but to hear more, call the Park Service at 653–5190 for sailing times, which vary during the season. You can also visit www.nps.gov/choh/boatrides/public boatrides.html. Get your tickets at the visitor center at the rear of 1057 Thomas Jefferson Street NW: $8.00 adults, $6.00 seniors, $5.00 children. The visitor center is open in season from 9:00 A.M. to 4:30 P.M., and from November to March on weekends only from 10:00 A.M. to 4:00 P.M. While you're there, check to see if you're in time for one of the Georgetown walking tours, which in the summer start there every Saturday and Sunday at 12:15 P.M.

Across Thomas Jefferson Street from the visitor center, you'll find *Snap,* the perfect place to pick up stuff for a canal-side snack or lunch. This vest-pocket creperie offers a long menu of crepes, from fruit jam and Nutella-filled drained for wheeled traffic; during the Civil War it was a vital military link connecting the Capital with Union forces fighting in the states of the Confederacy.

Those green buildings after the bridge belong to the **Washington Canoe Club,** a members-only organization that dates from 1904.

The Boathouse at Fletcher's Cove is 2 miles upriver from Georgetown, so you can either drive or, better yet, stroll there along the C&O Canal towpath; it'll take about forty minutes. When you arrive you'll find one-stop shopping for recreation involving the river or the canal. The Boathouse will rent you a canoe ($11.00 an hour, $21.00 per day) or rowboat ($11.00 and $20.00). You can also rent a bike to ride the towpath for $6.00 an hour (two hour minimum) or $25.00 per day.

If fishing is your passion, Fletcher's Cove is just the place for you. It was near this secluded cove that, in 1608, Captain John Smith (who had earlier hooked Pocahontas) saw fish "lying so thick with their heads above water . . . we attempted to catch them with our frying pans." Well, the Potomac hasn't come back *that* strongly, so you can leave your skillet at home. Instead, head for Fletcher's Cove to rent a rowboat, and buy bait, tackle, and a D.C. fishing license, then join Boathouse regulars and a surprising number of foreign and American visitors in fishing for white perch and fat striped bass. You can e-mail fletchers@guestservices.com or phone 244–0461 to find out how the fish are running during your breakaway, especially if you're in town during the spring spawning run, when these waters teem with shad and you can watch the cormorants swoop down to dive underwater for herring. There's also a large picnicking area. Ask about fly-fishing lessons. The Boathouse at Fletcher's Cove, at 4940 Canal Road. (corner of Reservoir Road NW; www.fletcherscove.com). Open daily 7:00 A.M. to 7:00 P.M. from early March to around Thanksgiving.

to meats and vegetables. Snap also has a wide selection of coffees, designer waters, and soft drinks. Snap, at 1062 Thomas Jefferson Street, is open daily for breakfast, lunch, and dinner. (965–7627). Inexpensive.

From here it's only a short stroll to Wisconsin Avenue, where you'll find a profusion of stores with the usual names offering the usual running shoes, designer jeans, and legible clothing. But if you look selectively, you'll be rewarded with visits to the fine specialty shops and restaurants for which Georgetown has long been renowned.

Start just below the intersection of Wisconsin and M at *Ching Ching Cha,* a corner of perfect repose and serenity on busy Wisconsin Avenue, Ching Ching Cha, a Chinese tea house, has everything for the lover of fine teas and the ancient rituals that go with them. The shop serves and sells every kind of tea imaginable, along with tea meals of miso salmon and curried chicken, and a wide assortment of kettles, cups, and other tea paraphernalia you'll need to hold a special tea ceremony in your own home. If that's your plan, you'd better snaffle up a few of Ching Ching Cha's low rosewood tables and pillows, then figure out how to slip them into your car or onto the plane. Tea with sweets and dumplings is served on those tables Monday through Friday from 2:30 to 5:30 P.M. Ching Ching Cha, at 1063 Wisconsin Avenue NW; 333–8288. Open 11:30 A.M. to 10:00 P.M. daily.

Martin's Tavern has been a Georgetown tradition since it opened on the day after Prohibition was repealed in 1933, which in Washington restaurant years is equal to being in town since the Van Buren administration. In the '50s, when they lived just up O Street, Martin's was Jack and Jackie's neighborhood hangout. Want to sit in JFK's usual booth when he was a bachelor? Of course it's number one, the "rumble seat," immediately to the right of the entrance. But when they began dating, Jack and Jackie usually dined in booth number three (number two is Nixon's former favorite), known as "the proposal booth," because it was there that Jack allegedly asked Jackie to marry him. The Kennedys, like today's regulars, probably liked Martin's cozy atmosphere where Tiffany glass drop lamps hang over cozy wooden booths and a real bar where patrons are just as likely to order martinis or scotch as chardonnay. So slide into a battered wooden booth, and enjoy the clubby atmosphere of a Georgetown institution. Martin's menu is also special—where else these days can you find comfort food like the elusive welsh rarebit or shepherd's pie and local specialties like shad roe and first-rate crab cakes? And the hamburgers just might be the best in the city. Also great for breakfast and weekend brunch. Martin's Tavern, at 1264 Wisconsin Avenue NW, is open from 10:00 A.M. to 11:00 P.M. Monday through Thursday, from 8:00 A.M. to 12:30 A.M. on Friday and Saturday, and from 8:00 A.M. to 11:00 P.M. Sunday (333–7370; www.martins-tavern.com).

The Tomb of the Well-Known Mascot

This is very weird, but you shouldn't leave Washington without knowing about that stone tablet on the wall of 1066 Wisconsin that memorializes a dog. This was not just your everyday pooch, but "Bush, the Old Fire Dog," beloved mascot of the Vigilant Volunteer Fire Company, which occupied this site in the 1860s. Bush died in July 1869 under mysterious circumstances, probably poisoned by a rival fire company in a day of cutthroat competition between the city's firefighters. Although RIP is inscribed on the tablet, the site of Bush's grave is not definitely known; a recent *Washington Flyer* story speculates that the murdered mutt was buried by his bereaved owners under the firehouse, minus his tail, which for years was reverently kept in the firehouse in a glass case. The building is the oldest firehouse in the city; over the door you can still see the "V" for Vigilant. Today it is home to Papa Razzi, a popular Italian restaurant. If you ask about Bush's tail, they will smirk, then deny knowing anything about it. Obviously, this is another Washington cover-up.

"Georgetown Bazaar"

Although the neighborhood is much more suitable for *Harper's Bazaar*, rather than the Algiers version, you'll find strongholds of collective bargaining scattered among Georgetown's tony shops. All along Wisconsin Avenue, especially at the corners of N and Potomac Streets, street merchants with folding tables will offer you their wares, mainly knockoff Kate Spade handbags, Gucci purses that never saw Rome, and Swiss Army watches crafted with care in New Jersey.

Random Harvest is the place to find antique furniture, especially restorations of period pieces ranging from antebellum to New Deal. The selection includes American-made hutches and tables of pine, along with a wide selection of vintage prints, especially botanicals. You'll also find European armoires, commodes with wood inlaid tops, and maybe even a mega-bed with posts that look like the pillars in St. Peter's in the Vatican. Random Harvest also offers distinctive outdoor chairs, tables, cachepots, and a lot of other excuses to start furnishing your garden. Random Harvest, at 1313 Wisconsin Avenue, is open Monday through Saturday 11:00 A.M. to 6:00 P.M. and Sunday, from noon to 6:00 P.M. (333–5569; www.randomharvesthome.com).

Big Planet Comics, at 3145 Dumbarton Avenue NW, just off Wisconsin Avenue, is one of the city's top comic book outlets, where the motto is "we're serious about comics." This is where you'll find every comic and cartoon book you've ever heard of or remember, including my favorites, those eternal sweethearts, Archie and Veronica. Great for reliving your youth or finding out what's new in comics (342–1961; www.bigplanetcomics.com). Open 11:00 A.M. to 7:00 P.M. Monday through Friday, but until 8:00 P.M. on Wednesday, 11:00 A.M. to 6:00 P.M. Saturday, and noon to 5:00 P.M. Sunday.

If you shop at *Baldaquin* you'll not only sleep better, but you might (no offense meant) even smell better. Downstairs you'll find imported linens, duvet covers, and sheets from upscale European producers such as Frette and Porthault. Upstairs, Baldaquin offers choices for your table, such as Herend china and Baccarat crystal. Owner Lisa Mullins Thompson will also sell you the bed of your dreams (so to speak), perhaps one handmade and carved by Simon Horn, said to be England's top bedmaster (if that's a real word). To round out all of this pampering, Baldaquin also sells a definitely upscale line of French bath oils and gels. And if all this nighttime luxury is making you think harder about marriage, Ms. Thompson will happily help you assemble your wedding list because "Baldaquin is changing the way Washingtonians are getting married," a goal not to be snoozed at. Baldaquin, 1413 Wisconsin Avenue NW; 625–1600, fax

625–1631, is open Tuesday through Saturday 10:00 A.M. to 6:00 P.M.; and until 5:00 P.M. Saturday. Closed Sunday and Monday; www.baldaquin.com.

Although Baldaquin specializes in European craftsmen, next door, at **Appalachian Spring,** the emphasis is strictly all-American, with works by homegrown designers and craftspeople. This is the place to find a huge assortment of cutting boards and other housewares of hand-carved woods, along with handmade designer pottery and ceramics. Appalachian Spring's artisan collection also features textiles, including colorful place mats, quilts, and rag dolls for the kids. Appalachian Spring, 1415 Wisconsin Avenue NW; 337–5780. Open Monday through Friday 10:00 A.M. to 8:00 P.M. Saturday 10:00 A.M. to 6:00 P.M., Sunday noon to 6:00 P.M.

georgelivesonin georgetown

At the corner of 33rd and Prospect Streets you'll find a former police call box that has been rescued, repainted, and remade into a brightly colored mini-shrine to Beatle George Harrison.

For a smallish shop, **Phoenix,** at 1514 Wisconsin Avenue NW, carries an astonishing and vibrant array of quality Mexican jewelry, Latin American ceramics, and contemporary clothing in natural fibers by noted designer Eileen Fisher. Local diplomats and lots of savvy Georgetowners flock to this local landmark every time owner Sharon Hays returns from Mexico with her usual haul of silver, antiques, and fine art. Find out why from 10:00 A.M. to 6:00 P.M. Monday through Saturday. Sunday hours in winter are noon to 5:00 P.M. and in summer from 1:00 to 6:00 P.M. (338–4404).

Amid all of these tough choices, you might want to wander across the street into **Marvelous Market,** at the corner of Wisconsin and P for a little R&R and give your credit card a chance to cool off. Essentially an upscale grocery and bakery, the market has a battery of coffee machines ready to re-caffeinate you with the most exotic concoctions along with the croissants, Danish, and other goodies you'll need to go with them. The market also offers a variety of pizzas and some great in- and outdoor people-watching tables. 3217 P Street NW; 333–2591. Open from 8:00 A.M. to 9:00 P.M. Monday through Saturday, 8:00 A.M. to 8:00 P.M. Sunday.

Proper Topper, at 3213 P Street NW, gives new meaning to the word eclectic. True to its name here you'll find hats of every era—cloches, fedoras, and lids from your favorite '30s movies. But there's also an exciting assortment of hip and imaginative gifts, women's dresses from the Roaring Twenties, great jewelry, retro sunglasses, and books. Call 333–6200; www.propertopper.com. Open Monday through Friday from 10:00 A.M. to 7:00 P.M., Saturday 10:00 A.M. to 7:00 P.M., Sunday noon to 6:00 P.M.

Hollywood on the Potomac

If you get a sense of déjà vu on your wanderings through Georgetown, it's probably because this charming and photogenic neighborhood has appeared in many Hollywood films.

The best-known film location of all are the *The Exorcist* steps, from that memorable scene where Father Damien takes a fatal header down a steep flight of ninety-seven stairs. You'll find these steps, now used by students and seekers of cardiovascular perfection, at Prospect and 36th Streets NW, next to the Victorian D.C. Transit car barn. *The Exorcist* also included other scenes shot on the nearby Georgetown campus and at Holy Trinity Church at 3513 N Street NW.

Some of the many other films with Georgetown footage:

Suspect, in which Cher and Dennis Quaid investigate a murder in Georgetown's waterfront parking lot along K Street.

No Way Out, in which Kevin Costner jogs along the Chesapeake & Ohio Canal and later bails out of a moving car on the Whitehurst Freeway (involving Kevin in a fall of at least 100 feet), then heads for the equally fictitious "Georgetown metro station" (actually Georgetown Park Mall).

Georgetown Park Mall was also used in several scenes from Governor Arnold Schwarzenegger's *True Lies* and in Jean Claude Van Damme's *Time Cop.*

And let's not forget TV's *West Wing,* which often filmed in Georgetown, including Josiah Bartlet's mawkish commencement speech on the Georgetown campus.

A few steps from Wisconsin Avenue, at 3241 P, you'll find the **Bryn Mawr Lantern Bookshop,** which lives up to its name by operating for the benefit of the famous college. This bright and attractive shop is well-stocked with lightly used books and well-run by volunteer staff, all of whom would be happy to see you walk in with a few hundred books to donate to their favorite cause. Call 333–3222; www.his.com/~lantern. Open Monday through Friday 11:00 A.M. to 4:00 P.M., Saturday 11:00 A.M. to 5:00 P.M., Sunday noon to 4:00 P.M.

Just Paper and Tea, across the street at 3232 P, sells just that—luxurious stationery, invitations for classy weddings, exotic teas, and a wide selection of Florentine paper seldom seen this far from the Arno. Call 333–9141. Open Monday 10:00 A.M. to 5:00 P.M.; closed Sunday.

Back on Wisconsin Avenue, you'll find a slew of great antique and decorative arts shops in the blocks between Q Street and Reservoir Road. **August Georges,** at 1523 Wisconsin Avenue, will sell or show you everything you'd want for your home, from sixteenth-century prints to upscale bed linens from

Flea Market, Georgetown Style

Addicted to flea markets? Georgetown's may not be the cheapest you've ever seen, but it's probably one of the toniest and most socially acceptable. This is just the place to pick up Muffy and Jason's castoffs, along with a lot of other stuff. You'll find it across from the "Social Safeway," natch, in the schoolyard at the corner of Wisconsin and 34th. Open Sunday 8:30 A.M. to 5:00 P.M. (Note: Because of construction and paving, the flea market will be closed until the fall of 2007.)

Pratesi and even some snazzy, belt-driven "architectural fans." Wonderful furniture, too; just check out the George Smith chairs and the other top-quality, top-designer pieces. Call 337–5110; www.augustgeorges.com. Open Monday through Friday 9:00 A.M. to 5:00 P.M.

My vote for most beautiful shop in D.C. goes to **Marston Luce,** a storefront luminous with eighteenth- and nineteenth-century French antiques, especially pine armoires and tables. This citadel of exquisite taste will also gladly sell you a nice Provençal buffet, a lovely flowered screen from Louis Napoleon's Paris, or a peaceful French landscape painting. As a nice touch for your garden, snap up that bucket of vintage petanque balls so you'll be the first in your neighborhood to lawn bowl, French-style. Expensive, but lots cheaper than a trip to France. Marston Luce, 1651 Wisconsin Avenue NW; 333–6800. Monday through Saturday 11:00 A.M. to 5:00 P.M.

Patisserie Poupon, at 1645 Wisconsin Avenue, 342–3248, is a great place to know about for a break or a light lunch. Favorites include wonderful croissants, light salads, a plate of charcuterie, or baguette sandwiches. Open Tuesday through Friday 8:00 A.M. to 6:30 P.M., Saturday 8:00 A.M. to 5:00 P.M., and Sunday 8:00 A.M. to 4:00 P.M. Before leaving try a slice of a chocolate cake, which will provide a sugar surge powerful enough to last until at least the next stop, which is:

Addison/Ripley Fine Art, at 1670 Wisconsin Avenue, is one of the city's most renowned galleries, with regular exhibits of contemporary art, sculpture, and photography. To find out what's on when you're in D.C., go to their Web site; www.addisonripleyfineart.com or give them a call at 338–5180. Open Tuesday through Saturday 11:00 A.M. to 6:00 P.M.

Carling Nichols is an Aladdin's cave of rare and exotic Chinese antiques. Treasures in the classical and graceful Ming style, mostly from the eighteenth and nineteenth century, including lacquer boxes, stone statues, tables, and screens. 1675 Wisconsin Avenue; 338–5600. Open Tuesday through Sunday noon to 5:00 P.M.

And at the end of this sumptuous strip, you'll find *A Mano,* at 1677 Wisconsin Avenue, where, for a few (well, maybe more than a few) bucks, you can buy yourself the snazziest ceramics in town. True to its name, A Mano specializes in handmade tableware, especially Italian majolica and French faience; it also carries a broad selection of linens and decorative objects, including wonderful cachepots and rooster-head wine carafes from Umbrian workshops. Open Monday through Saturday 10:00 A.M. to 6:00 P.M., Sunday noon to 5:00 P.M. (298–7200; www.amano.bz).

At 1524 33rd Street you'll find a survivor of Georgetown's earliest days, the eighteenth-century *Yellow Tavern* or *White Horse Inn,* its name depending on what year you did your drinking. Back in the 1700s, Georgetowners gathered in taverns like these, then known as "ordinaries," which were in fact the municipal centers of their times. Here colonials held town meetings, plotted to give King George III the heave-ho, and guzzled the drinks of the day, including rum punches and "flips" (ale sweetened with sugar, molasses, and rum). As a plaque points out, this tavern, back in the colonial days when 33rd Street was called Market Street, was a favored hangout for travelers, merchants, and even Thomas Jefferson. Next door you'll see the innkeeper's house, also clearly marked. Beyond that look sharp at 1528 33rd Street, where you'll discover, tucked away in a tiny courtyard, one of Georgetown's hidden houses.

For a perfect example of Georgetown's ability to come up with hidden nooks and crannies, stick your head into *Pomander Walk,* a tiny dead-end mews just off Volta Place between 33rd and 34th Streets. Pomander Walk, which consists of ten cozy row houses, each painted a different pastel color, started out as Bell's Court, a group of homes rented by African-American laborers and named for inventor Alexander Graham Bell, who lived in the neighborhood and owned a sizable chunk of nineteenth-century Georgetown. It's hard to believe

Stars and Fire Marks

On the walls of many old Georgetown buildings you'll spot large metal stars, which were not meant just to be decorative. Instead these "rod stars" secured the ends of iron poles that ran through each end of a building and held them together.

As you stroll through Georgetown you'll also see little oval plaques on the walls of many houses, some with a hose, tree, or eagle, each symbol representing a different insurance company. Those "fire marks" indicated to volunteer firemen that the house was insured, thus assuring them that they'd be rewarded for saving that home. History records a number of occasions when firemen allowed uninsured houses to burn or even, some say, would themselves do a little selective torching.

now, but these charming dwellings were condemned in the 1950s; thanks to Georgetown's post–World War II housing boom, they were rescued and restored.

Continue down Volta Place to the **Volta Bureau,** that Greek Revival temple at the corner of 35th Street, across from the idyllic campus of Georgetown Visitation School, which was founded in 1799. The Bureau was built by Alexander Graham Bell, who invented the telephone, and named after Alessandro Volta, the Italian physicist who invented the storage battery. After its construction in 1893 Bell, who was also a prominent educator of the deaf, moved his workshop and library from his father's carriage house (it's the pink house still standing at 3414 Volta) into the current building, and there set up the Volta Bureau for "diffusion of knowledge relating to the deaf." As the home of his extensive library and the Alexander Graham Bell Association for the Deaf, which he founded in 1905, the Bureau is a must for anyone interested in the education of the hearing-impaired. Inside you'll find a collection of exhibits about Bell's life and work, wax discs, examples of his "visible speech" method, and earphones and other examples of early hearing technology; other displays dramatize the work of the Bureau among the hearing-impaired. The Volta Bureau, at 1537 35th Street NW, is open from 8:30 A.M. to 4:30 P.M. Monday through Friday (337–5220; www.agbell.org)

Following 35th Street to the left you'll pass **Greenworks Florist,** at 3428 O, a haven for anyone seeking plants, blooms, and thoughtful, imaginative gift items. Greenworks also offers an assortment of exotic teas, wicker furniture, and lively ceramics. Open Monday through Friday from 9:00 A.M. to 5:00 P.M. and on the weekends from 10:00 A.M. to 3:00 P.M. (333–3366; www.green worksflorist.com).

Leaving the Bureau, follow 35th Street to the left down to Prospect Street, where you'll find yourself at the top of the *"Exorcist Steps"* famous because of that memorable scene in the 1973 movie, *The Exorcist* (see Hollywood on the Potomac on page 117.) The house at 3600 Prospect, which was a filming location, is owned by Georgetown University.

If you descend the steps to M Street (voluntarily, we hope) you'll find yourself standing next to one of D.C.'s great Victorian relics, which was built in 1897 as a luxurious, multilevel trolley car terminal and turnaround; you can still see the tracks entering the barn, along with the embedded tracks on Georgetown's O Street, all that remains of the city's once extensive rail network.

If you'd been standing on Prospect Street a couple of centuries ago, you'd instantly know how the street got its name. The mansions (some of them still standing) that were built here by our nation's early leaders had a command-

Tours for Voyeurs

If you're frustrated at not being able to peek inside all those splendid Georgetown homes, try to arrange your visit for the Saturday after Easter and take the annual *Georgetown House Tour,* the only time that some of the neighborhood's finest homes open their doors to visitors. The tour, which runs from 11:00 A.M. to 5:00 P.M., takes visitors to eight homes. Tickets are $40 per person if purchased in advance, but $45 on the day of the tour; buy them at St. John's Episcopal Church, 3240 O Street NW (page 122). A sumptuous afternoon tea at St. John's Church is included in the ticket price. Children under ten are not permitted. To order tickets, call 333–2287, ext. 50 or fax 338–3921. Tickets may also be ordered at www.georgetownhousetour.com.

And if you're interested in flowers, the first Saturday in May is *Georgetown Garden Day,* when self-guided tours will take you to twelve of Georgetown's finest private gardens between 10:00 A.M. and 5:00 P.M. Tickets cost $25 if purchased in advance or $30 on tour day. Get them by turning up at Christ Church, 31st and O Streets; on the day of the tour or reserve by either calling 965–1950 or visiting www.georgetowngardentour.com.

ing view out over the thriving port of Georgetown and the Potomac River. One of them, **Prospect House,** at 3508 Prospect, was built in 1788 by William Thornton, the designer of the Capitol, and back then its guests included the Marquis de Lafayette and President John Adams. Check out the octagonal watchtower just behind the house—it was used by one early owner to watch his ships sail into Georgetown harbor. And, although Prospect House is not open to visitors, you can get an idea of its lovely garden by peering through the gate on the side.

There's some eclectic art displayed in front of the elegant home at 3421 Prospect, where you'll find the unlikely combination of a Roman centurion standing his watch accompanied by his attack panda.

Another grand mansion, **Halcyon House,** built in 1790 by Benjamin Stoddert, the first Secretary of the Navy and also a Georgetown shipping baron, stands at 3400 Prospect. Unfortunately, since you're standing at the back of the house which like its neighbor, was built facing out over the port, you won't see the splendid gardens which reportedly were designed by L'Enfant himself.

And to get a good idea of Colonial living that continues amid the bustle of modern Washington, stroll down to the corner of Prospect and Potomac Streets for a look at the trim white Federal gem with black shutters at 3260 Prospect. The building's clasped hands fire mark is dated 1794.

Returning to 34th Street, backtrack to take a walk along O Street, a leafy (and bumpy—the residents like it that way) cobblestone street where you'll see the peculiar tracks of Georgetown's long-vanished cable-powered streetcar system. O Street is also lined with fine homes, each of which, in a place as old as Georgetown, has a past.

The gaudiest history, however, may belong to the **Bodisco House** at 3322 O, named for Baron Alexander de Bodisco, Russian ambassador to the United States from 1837 until 1854. Bodisco was probably a terrific diplomat and surely a credit to the czar, but is remembered today for his remarkable marriage to Washingtonian Harriet Williams. The wedding took place in this house in June 1839, when Bodisco was sixty-three ("short and stout with . . . a shining brown wig") and Harriet was lovely and sixteen. More than a few eyebrows were raised, but that didn't keep the ceremony from being a high point of the Georgetown social season, with Washington glitterati like President Van Buren, Henry Clay, and the entire diplomatic corps in attendance, proving once again that official and social Washington will turn out for almost anything. Defying all bets and leers, this April-December couple, delicately referred to at the time as "Beauty and the Beast," apparently got along very well, producing six children. The Bodisco house became a Washington social center famous for its lavish and frequent entertaining. When the baron died in 1854, he was buried in Georgetown's Oak Hill cemetery under an obelisk proclaiming his full titles. As for Harriet, she married the British military attaché, presumably another beauty, and lived happily ever after (again). Unfortunately, the Bodisco House is not open to the public.

Thomas Jefferson contributed $50 to the cost of building **St. John's Episcopal Church,** at 3240 O Street, a quintessential colonial church in the Federal style. Dolley Madison was a regular at St. John's, as was Francis Scott Key. The church building was started in 1796 and opened in 1804. Since then, the church and its adjoining parish house have undergone a few modifications, but retain their clean, classic lines and the original "pepper pot" belfry. Inside this classic, spare, high-ceilinged church are fine stained glass windows and, unexpectedly, a mosaic floor that will remind you more of Rome than of Washington. The door to the church's rustic Chapel of the Carpenter is around the corner on Potomac Street. Ring for admission.

From Potomac Street, walk down to N Street and some superb Federalstyle homes, which have remained practically unchanged since the time they were built between 1815 and 1818. As you walk past **Smith Row,** from number 3255 to 3267, and **Cox's Row,** from 3327 to 3339 in the next block, take a look at the wonderful details in these elegant homes—the handsome doorways and fanlights, the dormers, and the recessed swags on each facade. John

Cox, the Mayor of Georgetown who built Cox's Row, turned 3337 over to the Marquis de Lafayette during the 1824 visit when Lafayette Square was named for him. Between the two rows, at 3307 N, stands the Marbury House, where John F. Kennedy lived when he was elected president.

The Capital's first public market was built at 3276 M Street in 1795, then replaced in 1865 by the current historic landmark. The building's original fishmongers, butchers, and produce sellers have long since taken their wares to the Big Market in the Sky, but their much more genteel successors, *Dean and Deluca,* carry on in a market sure to remind you of those great European food halls and their enticing pyramids of lovely fruit and carefully arranged fish and meat. Just don't expect those 1795 prices or the veal deal that Thomas Jefferson got when he shopped here in 1806. Although he may have been a tired shopper, Jefferson didn't get to order a gourmet sandwich at the indoor/outdoor cafe, but you can. Open daily 10:00 A.M. to 8:00 P.M.; 342–2500.

Just beyond Dean and Deluca, at 3282 M Street, you'll find *Pizzeria Paradiso* (337–1245), which serves up some of the best pizza in town. Your margherita, fra diavolo, and maybe even the bottarga, made of fish roe and egg, will arrive fresh from the wood-fired oven on thin, crisp crusts. And the Paradiso always uses fresh ingredients such as real mozzarella and genuine Parma ham, not the ersatz industrial substitutes found in the usual pizza inferno. There's also a good assortment of great sandwiches and desserts. Beer lovers will want to head for the Paradiso's basement, where the "Birreria" serves up a vast selection of the world's top suds, sixteen on draft and eighty bottles at last count. Here you'll find rare brews like Bear Republic from California and some European greats like Coniston Bitter and a raft of Belgians, along with tasting notes that explain everything. Open Monday through Thursday 11:30 A.M. to 11:00 P.M., Friday and Saturday until midnight, and Sunday noon to 10:00 P.M.; www.eatyourpizza.com.

Back in Georgetown's bad old days, Keady's Alley was one of its worst neighborhoods, a collection of shacks, shanties, and sheds that paralleled the C&O Canal just below M Street. Today this former slum has a spiffy new name, *Cady's Alley,* and it's lined with shops filled with some of the country's outstanding collections of home furnishings and antiques. Enter this cobblestone mews of converted nineteenth-century warehouses with exposed walls and tall ceilings at 3318 M Street NW, and then proceed to places like:

Bo Concept, for dramatic and contemporary furniture by top Danish designers. It's the cutting edge from Copenhagen. Main entrance is at 3342 M Street NW; 333–5656. Open 10:00 A.M. to 7:00 P.M. Monday through Saturday, noon to 5:00 P.M. Sunday.

Gore-Dean is a trove of great antiques with an eclectic collection of nineteenth-century French mirrors, Asian ceramic figures and Chinese lacquer tables. China, crystal, and garden furniture too; 3338 M Street NW (625–9199; www.goredean.com). Open Monday through Friday 9:30 A.M. to 5:00 P.M. and Saturday 11:00 A.M. to 6:00 P.M.

Hollis and Knight, for a massive and eclectic treasury of everything from Tibetan rugs to antique grandfather clocks, exquisite crystal, and highly contemporary furniture. Enter at 3320 M Street NW; 333–6999. Open Tuesday through Saturday 10:00 A.M. to 6:00 P.M. Sunday and Monday noon to 5:00 P.M.; www.hollisandknight.com.

Ligne Roset offers urban dwellers a wide selection of cutting-edge furniture from top European designers, along with lots of lamps and other accessories you'll want to make your own. You'll find them at 3306 M Street; 333–6390. Open 11:00 A.M.to 6:00 P.M. Tuesday through Saturday, noon to 5:00 P.M. Sunday; www.ligne-roset-usa.com.

Thos. Moser, to see what fine American woodworking and design is all about. Hand-crafted furniture in rich woods with simple, classical lines from master cabinet workers. They are located at 3300 M Street; 338–4292; 10:00 A.M. to 6:00 P.M. Monday through Saturday, Sunday noon to 5:00 P.M.).

And there's much more to see. To preview all the Alley shops, visit www.cadysalley.com. One other thing—take money.

If shopping at Cady's Alley makes you hunger for more than fine design, you're in luck. Your first option is ***Leopold's Kafe+Konditorei,*** located in the center of the Alley, a luminous and super-attractive piece of Vienna on the Potomac. At Leopold's you'll find contemporary, slightly lighter versions of familiar Viennese dishes, including rich soups, schnitzels, and bratwurst, not to mention our old friend backhendl. And true to Austrian tradition, the pastries are incomparable, which makes it a good place to stop for that 10:00 A.M. coffee or for a continental *fruhstuck* (I mean breakfast) to start the shopping day. Beautiful room, beautiful people. Leopold's is moderately priced. No reservations. Leopold's, at 3318 M Street NW, is open from 8:00 A.M. to 10:00 P.M. Tuesday through Thursday and until 11:00 P.M. Friday and Saturday. Closed Monday. (965–6005; www.kafeleopolds.com).

Another worthy choice is ***Chez Mama-San,*** in a Georgetown town house at the end of the Alley at 1039 33rd Street NW. Although its name is a bit mixed linguistically, Mama-San's, as the canopy tells you, is the home of "Japanese home-style cuisine." Meaning Yo-shoku dishes: western comfort food that's been modified to suit Japanese tastes, including Mama-San's meatloaf and seafood (with a terrific grilled salmon salad) along with curries and beef croquettes. Not to mention a memorable pork cutlet sandwich. Open for lunch Tuesday through Saturday noon to 2:30 P.M. Dinner is served on Tuesday through Thursday from 6:00 to 10:00 P.M.; Friday through Saturday 6:00 to 11:00 P.M. Sunday 5:30 to 9:30 P.M. (333–3888).

Places to Stay in Georgetown

The Georgetown Inn
1310 Wisconsin Avenue NW
333–8900
www.georgetowninn.com
This Olde Georgetowne inn is colonial only when it comes to the decor in its rooms—four-poster beds, faux Sheraton furniture, and brass lamps—but the amenities and services are pure twenty-first century. Downstairs there's an outpost of the California-based Daily Grill, which means great salads and steaks. The inn is expensive; the Daily Grill isn't.

Georgetown Suites
1111 30th Street NW
298–7800
www.georgetownsuites.com
As its name tells you, this is an all-suite hotel located just off M Street, next to bus lines that will take you everywhere you want to go, including the nearest Metro stop. Also handy to the Canal and Washington Harbour. Suites come with full kitchens, but if you don't feel like making breakfast, go down to the lobby for the complimentary continental breakfast bar. Moderate.

Hotel Monticello
1075 Thomas Jefferson Street NW
337–0900
The Monticello is an intimate boutique inn with forty-seven wonderfully furnished suites and a central location in Georgetown. It won't be cheap, but if you're looking for the convenience of upscale suite hotel living with more than a whiff of a small European hotel, this is a real possibility. Expensive.

The Latham Hotel
3000 M Street NW
726–5000
www.thelatham.com
This small European-style hotel is located right on Georgetown's main drag, but only a few steps from the tranquillity of the C&O Canal. No mistake about it, this is a first-class hotel with first-class service and amenities, and you'll pay accordingly. Not only that, the Latham's in-house restaurant, Citronelle, is among the best in the capital, if not the nation. Much less pricey is the attached La Madeleine restaurant, which is a French-style cafeteria (when was the last time you visited one of those?) and a good one. The Latham is expensive.

Places to Eat in Georgetown

Bangkok Joe's
3000 K Street NW
333–4422
See page 110 for full description.

Bistro Lepic
1736 Wisconsin Avenue
333–0111
It's easy to imagine you're dining on the Left Bank at this small, bright restaurant lined with lively oils and prints. It's a big favorite with locals seeking super French cooking at a reasonable price. My favorite is the loin of lamb with truffles, but you might prefer the salmon in potato crust or the beef medallions with polenta. Good wine list too. Reservations are essential. Open daily 11:30 A.M. to 2:30 P.M., Monday through Thursday 5:00 to 10:00 P.M., until 10:30 P.M. on Friday and Saturday, 9:30 P.M. on Sunday. Moderate.

Chez Mama-San
1039 33rd Street NW
333–3888
See page 124 for full description.

Ching Ching Cha
1063 Wisconsin Avenue NW
333–8288
See page 113 for full
description.

Clyde's
3236 M Street NW
333–9180
www.clydes.com
If there's one Georgetown
restaurant that almost everybody likes it's Clyde's. This
landmark restaurant gets the
Oscar for longevity by staying in business since 1963,
when JFK was president and
nightlife on M Street con-
sisted of a few bars like the
Silver Dollar Cafe. (On ama-
teur night, at the Silver
Dollar, an elderly and none-
too-sober gent in a greasy
Uncle Sam suit frequently
tapdanced on stilts.) Clyde's
is still an outstanding neighborhood saloon that also
attracts a national clientele of
visitors. The reason is the
convivial bar and a consistently first-rate kitchen that
turns out great American
stuff from burgers to crab
cakes and inventive salads
and fish dishes, plus a
notable Sunday brunch. It's a
lively scene, so reserve.

Open Monday through Friday
11:30 A.M. to midnight,
weekends 10:00 A.M. to 1:00
A.M., Sunday 9:00 A.M. to
midnight. Moderate.

La Chaumiere
2813 M Street NW
338–1784
www.lachaumieredc.com
This combination of provin-
cial French bistro and
Georgetown institution has a
corps of high-powered regular diners that could staff an
entire administration. The
price you'd pay, however,
would be traces of *chou-
croute garni* on the treaties,
onion soup stains on the legislation, and the remains of a
memorable crab-filled crepe
on the inaugural speech.
Considering the usual quality
of Washington's legislation
and the exacting standards
of La Chaumiere's kitchen,
this would be an excellent
trade-off indeed. Moderate.
Reservations suggested.
Open Monday through
Friday 11:30 A.M. to 2:30 P.M.
and Monday through
Saturday 5:30 to 10:30 P.M.
Moderate.

La Madeleine
3000 M Street
337–6975
www.lamadeleine.com
A French bakery and cafeteria-
style cafe where lunch might
be a quiche or major-league
Caesar salad preceded by
the restaurant's signature
tomato-basil or onion soups.
At dinnertime La Madeleine
shifts to roast turkey and
chicken, pasta, and a tasty
French version of Beef
Wellington. Open Sunday
through Thursday 7:00 A.M.
to 10:00 P.M., Friday and Saturday 6:30 A.M. to
11:30 P.M. Inexpensive.

La Ruche
1039 31st Street NW
965–2684
www.cafelaruche.com
There's a nice Gallic feel
about this out-of-the-way
and unpretentious "beehive"
near the Potomac's left bank.
You can choose between
hefty salads, rich onion and
other soups, and light fare,
including *croque monsieur*
and grilled chicken. The
desserts are ethereal. Open
Monday through Friday
11:30 A.M. to 11:00 P.M., Saturday and Sunday 10:00 A.M.

AUTHOR'S FAVORITE PLACES TO EAT IN GEORGETOWN

Bistro Lepic	Pizzeria Paradiso
Clyde's	Ching Ching Cha
Martin's Tavern	Sequoia
Paolo's	La Chaumiere

to 11:30 P.M. Brunch is served Saturday and Sunday from 10:00 A.M. to 3:00 P.M. Inexpensive.

Leopold's Kafe+Konditorei
3318 M Street NW
965–6005
www.kafeleopolds.com
See page 124 for full description.

Martin's Tavern
1264 Wisconsin Avenue NW
333–7370
See page 114 for full description.

Mendocino Grille and Wine Bar
2917 M Street NW
333–2912
www.mendocinodc.com
It's hard to imagine a more cozy and chic restaurant than the Mendocino Grille, where the stylish blond wood decor and the menu justify its "California cuisine" theme. Lunch emphasizes entree salads, inventive sandwiches, pastas, and grilled fish. Seafood also predominates on a dinner menu that often includes grilled mussels and salmon, fish chowder, oyster stew, and glazed quail. As its name suggests, the wine list is also impressive, with mainly California vintages. Open for lunch Monday through Saturday from 11:30 A.M. to 3:00 P.M. and for dinner Sunday through Thursday 5:30 to 10:00 P.M. and on Friday and Saturday until 11:00 P.M. Reservations are a good idea. Expensive.

Old Glory
3139 M Street
337–3406
www.oldglorybbq.com
You'll think you've been teleported to Memphis at Old Glory, a.k.a. Georgetown's barbecue central, where cook-off winning chefs prepare award-winning ribs and pork. Check out the pulled pork or chicken and the smoky spareribs, topped by one of Old Glory's six homemade sauces. Also nice salads and desserts (non-barbecued). The ornately carved bar, which saw a lot of action at the Rendezvous Barbeque in Memphis over its 110-year life, feels right at home in D.C., especially on the weekends. Monday through Thursday 11:30 A.M. to 2:00 A.M., Friday and Saturday until 3:00 A.M., Sunday 11:00 A.M. to 2:00 A.M. Inexpensive.

Paolo's
1303 Wisconsin Avenue
333–7353
www.paolosristorante.com
The food at this trendy trattoria is billed as California-Italian. Lots of good and original pastas, including shellfish over black pepper linguine, and imaginative salads, many of them featuring seafood and roast chicken. Paolo's wood-oven produces original pizzas such as duck confit and pesto with goat cheese. Main courses also include grilled veal chops and shrimp

scampi. Paolo's also has an outside terrace for watching the Georgetown scene, but the evening scene inside is pretty lively as well. Sunday through Thursday 11:30 A.M. to 11:30 P.M., Friday and Saturday open until 12:30 A.M. Moderate.

Patisserie Poupon
1645 Wisconsin Avenue
342–3248
See page 118 for full description.

Pizzeria Paradiso
3282 M Street
337–1245
See page 123 for full description.

Sequoia
3000 K Street NW
944–4200
See page 110 for full description.

Tony and Joe's
3000 K Street NW
944–4545
See page 110 for full description.

Vietnam Georgetown
2934 M Street
337–4536
This modest establishment always ends up on everyone's list of favorite restaurants and keeps winning local awards for food and value. Try the lemon chicken and grilled salmon. Great pho hoa too. Open daily 11:00 A.M. to midnight. Inexpensive.

Upper Northwest

The Upper Northwest covers a lot of territory, extending in a broad outer arc that starts along the Potomac just north of Georgetown and swings around above Dupont Circle, Adams Morgan, and Shaw, and ends at North Capitol Street, which divides Northwest from Northeast. Along the way it encompasses many of residential Washington's most agreeable neighborhoods, including Shepherd Park, the leafy area between 16th Street and Georgia Avenue, and Palisades, whose main street, MacArthur Boulevard, parallels the Potomac River. In Cleveland Park, an early twentieth-century enclave near the cathedral, media figures, senators, and lawyers live in spacious Victorian houses; their cars sport bumper stickers urging SAVE THE WHALES or even (says a reliable Washington source) DUKAKIS FOR PRESIDENT.

Upper Northwest is also home to off-the-beaten-path treasures like Rock Creek Park, the U.S. Soldiers and Airmen's Home, and the Kreeger Museum. Since this sprawling area is not all that well served by Metrorail, you'll need to take the city's Metrobus system to some of the places you want to go. In view of the distances involved, taxis or your own car are good alternatives for getting around.

The ***Washington National Cathedral*** or, more formally, The Cathedral Church of St. Peter and St. Paul, 3101 Wisconsin Avenue NW, is far from being an off-the-beaten-path location. Every year 800,000 visitors go to Washington's highest point to explore one of America's great churches, a magnificent fourteenth-century-style cathedral begun when Teddy Roosevelt laid the cornerstone in 1907; it was completed in 1990. It would take a book like this just to adequately cover the cathedral's architectural detail and its highlights, including the exquisite stone carvings. For information about joining one of the regularly scheduled tours or attending any of the cathedral's vast array of musical events, special programs, and observances, call 537–6200 or visit www .cathedral.org. The cathedral is best reached by bus, using one of the "30" series lines north from Georgetown and downtown or by taking the Metro to the Tenleytown station (red line) and taking one of the 30 buses south about 1½ miles to the cathedral.

While you're on the cathedral's sprawling fifty-seven-acre close, there are several eminently visitable places that are definitely off the beaten path and are not to be missed. To see them, walk down South Road, to the right of the main doors, and walk down to the ***Herb Cottage.*** The cottage was once the cathedral baptistry, but today it's one of Washington's top gift shops, with a nice selection of decorative china and porcelain, colorful trays and teapots, and nifty flowerpots, along with the obligatory jams and scents. There's a great selection of herbs too. The cottage is open daily 10:00 A.M. to 5:00 P.M. Call 537–8982.

Farther down South Road, an elaborately carved arch leads to the ***Bishop's Garden,*** which was conceived as a medieval walled garden of natural and ageless beauty to accompany a great Gothic cathedral. And that's exactly what it is. The garden is a collection of plants from historic gardens owned by

Herb Cottage, Washington National Cathedral

TOP ATTRACTIONS IN UPPER NORTHWEST

National Cathedral	Kreeger Museum
Rock Creek Park	U.S. Soldiers and Airmen's Home
Hillwood Museum	Naval Observatory

Washington and Jefferson, while the "Hortulus" or "little garden" is planted with herbs found on a plant list created by Charlemagne in 815. The garden also includes ancient boxwoods, beds of fragrant herbs, and colorful seasonal blooms (hint: if it's tulips you're after, try April or May; roses appear in June). The garden's "Shadow House," a gazebo-like stone structure, makes a perfect spot to rest and reflect. During the growing season (April 1 to October 31—no tours in August) guided tours of the garden leave from the Herb Cottage every Wednesday at 10:30 A.M. Reservations essential. Group tours can also be arranged by calling (301) 986–1290.

Below the Bishop's Garden, behind the equestrian statue of Washington, is *Olmsted Woods,* five acres of peaceful urban forest with footpaths great for taking a quiet walk among the black squirrels and songbirds. The woods are an ongoing effort by the Cathedral's All Hallows Guild to restore this oak and beech woodlands to its original pristine condition. The statue of Washington is more than just decoration; in the late eighteenth century these forests are where the first president used to ride horseback. Guided walks in the woods and bird walks are given regularly and leave from the Washington statue. Call 537–2319 or check out www.allhallowsguild.com/woodwalk to get the exact dates.

Refreshed and back on South Road, you're perfectly positioned for a shopping excursion in the cathedral's *Museum Store,* a cavernous and eclectic collection of everything from books and CDs with religious and secular themes to guidebooks and reproductions of the cathedral's gargoyles, grotesques, and other carvings. Definitely off-the-beaten-path is the store's stealth snack bar; it's along the shop's south wall. Open daily 9:30 A.M. to 5:00 P.M. Call 537–6267.

Farther down South Road are the *Cathedral Greenhouses,* which grow and sell hundreds of varieties of herbs, annuals, and perennials. Even if you're not buying, it's fun to walk around, see the plants, and chat up the young employees who obviously love their work and the flowers. The greenhouse also has occasional special programs, including workshops, lectures, and children's events. For more information about them, call 537–6263. Open Monday through Saturday 9:30 A.M. to 5:00 P.M., Sunday 10:00 A.M. to 5:00 P.M.

Church Suppers

Because the Washington National Cathedral is in Cleveland Park, an overwhelmingly residential neighborhood, the selection of nearby restaurants is not large. However, the shopping area 2 blocks to the right as you exit the cathedral has three good choices:

Cafe Deluxe
3228 Wisconsin Avenue NW
686–2233
www.cafedeluxe.com
Every neighborhood should have a restaurant this good. The Deluxe will remind you of a bright and bustling French cafe, but the food is largely American: burgers, great sandwiches, and the zenith of American comfort food, a top-notch meat loaf. Other favorites include pastas, grilled fish, and excellent desserts. There's also sidewalk dining in good weather, but the restaurant takes no reservations. Open Monday through Thursday 11:30 A.M. to 10:30 P.M., Friday and Saturday 11:30 A.M. to 11:30 P.M., Sunday 11:00 A.M. to 10:00 P.M. Moderate.

2 Amys Neapolitan Pizzeria
3715 Macomb Street NW
885–5700
http://2amyspizza.com
One of the city's top pizzerias is owned by Peter Pastan, the owner of Dupont Circle's Obelisk, one of D.C.'s best Italian restaurants. The 2 Amys will remind you of your last visit to Naples, and by that I don't mean everything's drenched in heavy-duty red sauce. This is where pizzas are fresh, slim, and perfectly cooked in a huge, oak-fueled oven. Everyone likes the vongole pizza with clams in the shell, anchovies, and hot peppers and the puttanesca, with anchovies, garlic, and black olives. For traditionalists there's also a classic margherita with tomatoes and mozzarella. And amid all this pizza perfection don't overlook the antipasti, least of all the deep-fried rice balls that the Italians call *suppli a telefono* because of the "cords" of hot, melted cheese that hang down from the center of the rice. Open Monday through Saturday from 11:00 A.M. to 11:00 P.M. Sunday noon to 10:00 P.M. Inexpensive.

Cactus Cantina
3300 Wisconsin Avenue NW
686–7222
www.cactuscantina.com
The *Washingtonian's* estimable food critics called the Cactus Cantina one of the best restaurants in Upper Northwest, and they're absolutely right. This is the place to go for high quality Tex-Mex, especially the fajitas, grilled shrimp, and fat tamales. Believe it or not, the Cantina also has a "Cowboy and Indian Museum." So if you happen across a collection of cowboy hats, a Sioux "puberty bag," a figure of Chief Split Horn, and other Western curiosities, you'll know that it's not those eight or ten margaritas you ran through before dinner. Open Sunday through Thursday 11:00 A.M. to 11:00 P.M., Friday and Saturday 11:00 A.M. to midnight. Sunday brunch is served from 10:30 A.M. to 3:00 P.M. Inexpensive.

The upper level of the Cathedral tower and walls are rimmed with 1,354 curious limestone carvings, known as "gargoyles" and "grotesques," which are mainly decorative. Both the gargoyles and the grotesques have been donated to the Cathedral by individuals and can be pretty fanciful, portraying a few things they never thought of in the Middle Ages, including a bird watcher with binoculars, a unicorn, and a dentist drilling a walrus tusk. There's also a dog named Kiddo and Darth Vader, done by a Nebraska student as part of a national competition. And what's the difference between a gargoyle and a grotesque? The gargoyles are working carvings with pipes in their mouths that allow rainwater to drain through them, while the grotesques are merely decorative.

The Cathedral offers **Gargoyle Tours** of these fanciful carvings at 2:00 P.M. on the fourth Sunday of the month between April and October at 2 P.M.; from May to July they are given on the fourth Thursday of the month at 6:30 P.M. The tour costs $5.00 per person. Reservations not needed. If you can't make the tour, you can get a self-guided tour folder at the docent desk or online at www.cathedral.org/cathedral/visit/self. But since Darth, Kiddo, and the dentist are pretty far up there, try to take along your own binoculars.

One of the city's least known treats for children is the Cathedral's hands-on **Gargoyle's Den,** where they don aprons and gather around work benches to engage in supervised crafts like making their very own gargoyles to take home, learning about stained glass windows, and the construction of the Cathedral. The Den, which is held in the crypt's classroom on Saturdays from 10:00 A.M. to 2:00 P.M., is for kids ages six to twelve. Admission is $5.00 for a group of up to four and $1.00 for each extra person.

Most people are so charmed by the cathedral and the lovely enclave that surrounds it that they'd like to stay on. With a little luck, that just might be possible. The **College of Preachers,** on the grounds at the rear of the cathedral, mainly offers rooms and conference space to church leaders and other individuals attending retreats, meetings, and other events at the cathedral, but opens its rooms to the public on a "space available" basis. It's a lovely experience. The college's Tudor-era building makes every visit feel something like a stay with Henry VIII, especially in the refectory, where the long tables, beamed walls and ceilings, and fabulous stained glass windows would make His Majesty (or Charles Laughton) feel right at home. Nearby there's a quiet, book-filled library and a cloistered garden with fountain. The rooms, most with shared bath, are bright and comfortable. The College of Preachers is located at 3510 Woodley Road NW. Call 537–6380, fax 537–5650, or e-mail kgilliam@cathedral.org; www.cathedralcollege.org.

As you exit the Cathedral grounds on Woodley Road you'll be stepping into *Cleveland Park,* one of Washington's most distinctive and distinguished neighborhoods.

Although many think of Georgetown as D.C.'s "village within a city," they're overlooking a small, early twentieth-century town hidden within the nation's capital. Connoisseurs of American residential architecture always find Nirvana in Cleveland Park, a leafy hamlet replete with late Victorian frame houses with turrets, towers, and deep, wraparound porches.

In the late nineteenth century Cleveland Park was a neighborhood of great estates, one of which was the summer home of President Grover Cleveland, who gave this area its name. Cleveland Park remained ultra-exclusive until 1892, when an extension of the city's streetcar system from downtown, following what had been remote stretches of Connecticut Avenue, brought the city to Cleveland Park's doorstep, after which noted architects arrived to design homes for some of Washington's best families. The result is a village of distinguished homes, grassy lawns, imposing gardens, and splendid architecture, an urban Brigadoon where Victoria still reigns.

A visit to Cleveland Park, which is literally wall to wall with grand houses, both great and small, is well worth a leisurely stroll. Here are a few choice homes to start you off:

Begin your tour at the corner of Highland Place and 34th Street NW and wander over to 3225 Highland Place, an 1898 beauty with an imposing Ionic-columned porch, followed by the formal and elegant brick home at 3209, a perfect example of another architectural style popular in the early twentieth century, the Georgian Revival. Next door at 3207 you'll spot a grand frame mansion set in its own park. Cleveland Park is noted for its architectural eclecticism; you'll see why as you cross the street for a look at the three Japanese-influenced, pagoda-roofed homes at 3154, 3140, and 3138 Highland, where Hokkaido meets Cape Cod.

At Newark Street a left turn leads to the turreted Queen Anne mansion at 3035 Newark, built in 1898 and always one of Washington's most impressive homes. While you're on Newark Street, don't miss the charming and romantic English country cottage, complete with contoured roof, at 3145 and the smashing Tudor Revival at 3149. For more architectural delights, just cross 34th Street and continue your walk along Newark Street.

Not far from the back of the cathedral grounds is the *Vice President's House.* The best way to see what the Secret Service will allow is to stand at the corner of Massachusetts Avenue and 34th Street. Here you can gaze upon the massive white 1893 Queen Anne mansion that was once the home of the superintendent of the Naval Observatory, located next door, and, after that, "Quarters A," the residence of the Chief of Naval Operations, the Navy's top officer. But since 1974 this has been the official residence of the vice president. If you're not invited in, rest assured that it's spacious, comfortable, and just the place you'd want to live when *you* become vice president. Until then, keep standing on that corner.

One of the most fascinating but least known off-the-beaten-path excursions in Washington is the nighttime tour of the ***U.S. Naval Observatory,*** which is strictly off-limits to the public except on Monday evenings, when it opens its gates to outsiders. The observatory is the nation's main celestial tracker, supplier of astronomical data, and keeper of the United States Master Clock. The observatory's sensitive data is essential for accurate navigation and support of communications on earth and in space, so don't touch anything on your tour!

The tour includes a show-and-tell about the Master Clock and discussions with staff astronomers. Best of all, you'll be able to gaze skyward through the great 26-inch telescope that was used in the discovery in 1877 of the two moons of Mars. If the night sky is clear, you'll be invited to look through the historic 12-inch refracting telescope built in 1892. You will not, however, be invited to turn those lenses on the vice president and his family, who live in the big house next door.

The U.S. Naval Observatory is at Massachusetts Avenue at 34th Street NW; 762–1467; www.usno.navy.mil/tour_info. Tours are intermittently on Monday evenings from 8:30 to 10:00 P.M. You must reserve well in advance for these tours, either online or by fax at 762–1489. And you'll have to check in at the tour's departure point at the Observatory's South Gate (on Observatory Circle opposite the New Zealand Embassy) by 8:00 P.M., armed with photo ID. Since you'll be walking outside at night, and sometimes over rough ground, consider bringing along a small flashlight and walking shoes. Cameras are permitted. No Metro.

AUTHOR'S FAVORITES IN UPPER NORTHWEST

Bishop's Garden	Kreeger Museum
Hillwood	2 Amys Neapolitan Pizzeria
Cafe Deluxe	

A River Runs Through It

The *Italian Chancery,* at 3000 Whitehaven Street NW, pays tribute to two world cities, Florence and Washington.

As you can see when you view the building's Massachusetts Avenue facade, the chancery, made of 42,000 pieces of Italian red stone, is a modern and highly dramatic version of a renaissance-era Florentine palazzo. But there's more. If you could see the building from the air you'd find that it is square, reflecting the shape of the original 100-square-mile plot of Washington before the Virginia part was returned to that state. That four-story glass atrium that bisects the chancery represents the Potomac River, which cuts through the building exactly the same way it divided Washington's original layout.

You'll find more on this along with a photo at www.ambwashingtondc.esteri.it.

You'll find one of the District's newest museums on the campus of American University. The **American University Museum,** located in the dramatic and modern Katzen Arts Center at 4400 Massachusetts Avenue NW, brings together a collection of contemporary and imaginative art and sculpture created by mainly Washington and Baltimore artists. One highlight is "Climate of Light," a sculpture of colorful balloons hanging in the Museum's main stairwell. Open Tuesday through Thursday noon to 5:00 P.M., Friday and Saturday noon to 7:00 P.M. Admission free. For more information on the Museum, call 885–1300 or visit www.american.edu/katzen. The N3, N4, N6, and N8 buses will get you there from downtown. Nearest Metro? The Tenleytown–AU stop on the red line is a twenty-minute walk away.

Glover Archbold Park, a slender, 3-mile-long, 183-acre park runs through some of northwest Washington's best neighborhoods and most secluded woodlands. Although it is less well known and smaller than Rock Creek Park, it also makes a great place for an urban ramble or jog.

To reach Glover Archbold, take the Metro's red line to Tenleytown, then walk south several blocks on Wisconsin Avenue to Van Ness Street. A right turn will take you 1 block to a grassy park on the left where a sign marks the northern end of the park. The trail ends at a stone tunnel under the C&O Canal (one of the canal's original structures), which opens on to the canal towpath about a ten-minute walk from Georgetown.

The little red schoolhouse on MacArthur Boulevard, not far from the Potomac, was built in 1864, making it the oldest one-room schoolhouse in the District. Now it's the home of **Discovery Creek,** a children's museum and activity center designed to help kids, especially ages four to eleven, experience and respect the natural environment. The museum is lined with terraria containing lizards and reptiles, plus other exhibits where kids can learn about wildlife and nature. Using the school as a base, Discovery Creek sponsors an extensive year-round program of outdoor adventures and other science- or nature-oriented programs either in the schoolhouse or at other area locations. The school is located on the edge of Palisades Park, which makes nature hikes and other big-league explorations a breeze. Discovery Creek, the Children's Museum of Washington, is at 4954 MacArthur Boulevard NW. Call 337–5111, fax 337–5344, or visit www.discoverycreek.org. Open Saturday and Sunday 10:00 A.M. to 3:00 P.M. Children's groups can be booked by calling 337–5111. Admission for nonmembers is $5.00.

A short walk from Discovery Creek, just up Chain Bridge Road from the intersection with MacArthur Boulevard, you'll find one of the District's least known and most touching places, *The Union Burial Society of Georgetown Cemetery,* a two-acre burial ground for former slaves and their descendants at 2616 Chain Bridge Road. Except for the community's former schoolhouse, which still stands at 2820 Chain Bridge Road (not open to the public), this 200-year-old cemetery is almost the last vestige of a small black settlement that inhabited the residential area now known as the Palisades. It is well cared for by a descendant of one of the families buried there. The cemetery is usually open during the day, but has no fixed hours.

Although this part of the District is not exactly brimming over with restaurants, it boasts one of Washington's favorite neighborhood hangouts, the *Starland Cafe,* at 5125 Macarthur Boulevard NW. The food at Starland is New American Casual, with a menu of big salads, blackened and grilled fish, and top-notch burgers. Since it's co-owned by Grammy-winning songwriter and performer Bill Danoff of the Starland Vocal Band, music is important at Starland. Every Friday at 9:00 P.M. there's live jazz featuring prominent local groups; no cover charge; call 244–9396; www.starlandcafe.com. Lunch Monday through Friday 11:30 A.M. to 3:00 P.M., Sunday 11:00 A.M. to 3:00 P.M. Dinner Sunday through Thursday from 5:30 to 9:30 P.M., Friday and Saturday 5:30 to 10:00 P.M. Moderate.

Another Palisades option is *Bambu,* a sleek and attractive pan-Asian (Thai-Japanese-Chinese) restaurant at 5101 Macarthur Boulevard NW. At lunchtime order one of Bambu's bargain bento boxes, which pair sushi with Thai or Chinese dishes. Seafood and shellfish are always good options at Bambu; try the standout scallops or fried oysters any time. Pad Thai and soups with noodles and fish are other specialties; 364–3088; www.bambudc.com. Hours are Sunday through Thursday 11:00 A.M. to 10:00 P.M., Friday and Saturday 11:00 A.M. to 10:30 P.M. Inexpensive.

And if you're touring the upper reaches of the Palisades near Sibley Hospital, it's good to know about **DC Boat House,** where you'll find a lunch menu focused on sandwiches, salads, and great soups (be sure to try the minestrone). At dinnertime some good choices include crab cakes and ribs. DC Boat House, at 5441 Macarthur Boulevard (362–2628) is open Monday through Thursday 11:00 A.M. to 10:00 P.M. and Friday and Saturday until 11:00 P.M. Inexpensive.

Despite its current tranquillity and affluence, Chain Bridge Road was, in the eighteenth and nineteenth centuries, a busy and much traveled highway leading to Chain Bridge, one of the earliest (and still standing) bridges across the Potomac. If you go a little farther up this sunken road you'll arrive at **Battery Kemble Fort,** very agreeable for walks and picnics. Although it is now a totally suburbanized city park, Battery Kemble was once a keystone of the "circle of forts" that defended the District during the Civil War. You'll also gaze upon the houses of the rich and famous that line Chain Bridge Road, which is now one of Washington's very best addresses.

The **Kreeger Museum** displays the art and sculpture collection of David Lloyd Kreeger, insurance mogul, philanthropist, and art collector extraordinaire, in an intimate atmosphere. In fact, just a glance at the museum itself, a 1967 design by famed architect Philip Johnson, tells visitors that they have arrived at a special place. To get the idea, imagine an architectural wedding of classical and Renaissance—a sprawling Roman villa in white travertine with soaring neo-Palladian windows that expose its exhibit walls to warmth and sunlight. A trip to this small, private museum is like visiting the home of a wealthy friend blessed with exquisite tastes in both art and architecture.

The two-story atrium of the museum's Great Hall showcases impressionist masterpieces including Picassos and van Goghs, while the Kreeger's former dining room now serves up a feast of Monets. Across the atrium, Mondrian's *Mill on the River* presides over a teak-lined library.

The Kreeger's downstairs rooms lack the spacious feel of the Great Hall, but compensate with more Picassos, Miro etchings, a Frank Stella, and works by other abstract expressionists. Somewhat incongruously, there's also a fascinating collection of African wood carvings and tribal masks. The Kreeger Museum is at 2401 Foxhall Road; 337–3050, fax 337–3051. The Kreeger hosts conducted, ninety-minute tours twice a day, at 10:30 A.M. and 1:30 P.M. Tuesday through Friday, for which reservations are required. However, you will not need reservations for tours given during the Kreeger's Saturday afternoon Open Hours, which run from 10:00 A.M. to 4:00 P.M. The museum is closed the month of August. Children under twelve not admitted. Reservations are essential and should be obtained well in advance by phoning 338–3552; www.kreeger museum.com. Suggested donation is $8.00 for adults, $5.00 for seniors and students. Since the Kreeger is far from public transportation, a personal vehicle or taxi is best; free parking on the grounds.

If, after visiting the Kreeger, you're hungering for more than art, one of Washington's best sandwich shops, *Jettie's,* at 1609 Foxhall Road NW, is close at hand. Aside from thick sandwiches, Jettie's also makes formidable salads and soups. And you can sit outside in good weather. Jettie's is open Monday through Friday from 11:00 A.M. to 8:00 P.M., Saturday 10:00 A.M. to 6:00 P.M. and on Sunday 10:00 A.M. to 8:00 P.M. (965–3663; www.jettiesdc.com).

As Truman Capote said about Venice, a visit to **Hillwood** is a great treat, "like eating an entire box of chocolate liqueurs all at one go." This forty-room mansion of cereal heiress Marjorie Merriweather Post is one superlative after another, especially when describing its wealth of Russian decorative art, a collection that began when one of Mrs. Post's four husbands, Joseph E. Davies,

What's New at the Zoo

Although the *National Zoo* is a well-known destination, you might not know that, aside from its famous pandas and cheetahs, it also offers *Kid's Farm,* a great opportunity for children from three to eight to hang out, schmooze with, and pet the animals, and I don't mean the cheetahs. The Farm is a red barn and barnyard stocked with less predatory beasts like goats, donkeys, and cows. Kids won't be able to feed the animals, but petting is encouraged as is the supervised grooming and brushing the donkeys and goats in the Caring Corral. Zoo staff gives talks on the animals and their habits.

Nearby the farm also offers a—get this—giant, 22-foot pizza that's used as an interactive exhibit where children play with oversize toppings and learn about how the tomatoes, cheese, olives, and other ingredients are grown or made. As someone once said about Wagner's music, it's better than it sounds.

You also should know that the Zoo sponsors free concerts every summer from the end of June to early August. *Sunset Serenades* are held every Thursday evening from 6:30 to 8:00 P.M. The musical setting is the Zoo's Lion/Tiger Hill, which presumably soothes the savage beasts, but still doesn't keep them from chiming in occasionally. Picnics are possible, but you can also pick up burgers and hot dogs at the Mane Restaurant.

The National Zoo, at 3001 Connecticut Avenue NW, is served by two red line stations: Woodley Park-Zoo or Cleveland Park. From April 2 to November 1, the Zoo's buildings are open daily from 10:00 A.M. to 6:00 P.M. and the Zoo grounds are open from 6:00 A.M. to 8:00 P.M.; the rest of the year the buildings are open from 10:00 A.M. to 4:30 P.M. and the Zoo's grounds are open from 6:00 A.M. to 6:00 P.M. Sessions at Kid's Farm usually occur twice a day but can vary, so check the Zoo Web site http://nationalzoo.si.edu/Animals/KidsFarm/visit.cfm for the latest.

served as the American ambassador to Moscow in the late '30s. Among Hillwood's riches, the high point is the Icon Room, which gleams with enamel and gold Fabergé eggs and clocks, a dazzling diamond tiara worn by the last empress, and masses of jewel-encrusted gold and silver chalices. The Russian porcelain room is special too, chiefly for the four dinner services that once belonged to Catherine the Great and some pieces from the personal dinner service of Empress Elizabeth I made in the late 1750s.

Hillwood's Russian art is rivaled only by its array of French antiques. A portrait of Empress Eugenie and hangings of Gobelin tapestries look down on Hillwood's French drawing room, where the wood paneling comes from a French château and the rolltop Roentgen desk is a marvel of marquetry. In the dining room Mrs. Post's guests banqueted by the light of Russian Imperial candlesticks on Russian Imperial porcelain; the room's Aubusson carpet once belonged to the Emperor Maximilian. After exploring Hillwood, don't forget to saunter through the estate's glorious formal gardens and look in on the *dacha,* a modest one-room Russian log cabin, which is is now used for small exhibitions of Russian art.

Docent-led and audio-guided tours of Hillwood Museum, at 4155 Linnean Avenue NW, are given regularly Tuesday through Saturday between 10:00 A.M. and 5:00 P.M. Closed in February. Hillwood's Web site is www.hillwood museum.org. Since Hillwood admits a maximum of 250 visitors per day, reservations are required. Call 686–5807 or (877) 445–5966 to get them. Suggested donation: $12.00 for adults, $10.00 for seniors and $5.00 for children six to eighteen. Hillwood's Cafe is open for lunch and afternoon tea from 11:00 A.M. to 4:30 P.M.; reserve for lunch by phoning 243–3920. The Museum Shop, located in the visitor center, will sell you handsome books, gifts, and other mementos of this Washington treasure. Hillwood is about a twenty-minute walk from the Van Ness Metro station (red line) and from all Connecticut Avenue bus routes.

Rock Creek Park is one of America's oldest, largest, and most beautiful urban parks and one of Washington's great treasures. This wedge-shaped, 2,800-acre wilderness follows Rock Creek, a rushing rural stream, for 6 often secluded miles right through the heart of a busy city, starting at the Kennedy Center and ending at the District's border with Maryland, passing the National Zoo as it winds along. And unlike New York's Central Park, Rock Creek is hilly, a gorge with ravines and hidden pockets of heavily wooded forests and running brooks. It's so nice that, after the Civil War, a commission formed to find a "healthier situation" for a new Executive Mansion to replace the White House gave this in-town oasis serious consideration.

Rock Creek was made a national park in 1890 when Congress set it aside as "a pleasuring place for the enjoyment of the people of the United States";

capitalquote

"Rock Creek has an abundance of all the elements that make up not only pleasing, but wild and rugged scenery. There is, perhaps, not another city in the Union that has on its very threshold so much natural beauty and grandeur."

—Naturalist and author John Burroughs

ever since, Washingtonians have happily headed there to bicycle, walk its 29 miles of foot trails, ride the 13 miles of bridle paths, and even play golf. Picnicking too—within this city forest there are dozens of clearings with picnic tables that during the spring and summer are the scenes of family gatherings and softball games. Picnicking in some areas requires permission; call 673–7646 about permits. Presidents also have been big Rock Creek fans, including Teddy Roosevelt, who loved the park and hiked there often, and Ronald Reagan, who rode at the stables. The Park Service Web site for Rock Creek is www.nps.gov/rocr.

The park remains a hidden corner for many visitors without their own automobiles, in part because there are no Metro stations in the park and no buses roll along Rock Creek Parkway and Beach Drive, its two main thoroughfares. Nevertheless, it's not all that difficult to enjoy the park and its excellent facilities.

One way is to start at the corner of Rock Creek Parkway and Virginia Avenue NW across from the Watergate and simply follow the path next to the parkway back into the park. Along the way you'll pass under Embassy Row and behind the zoo before you reach Tilden Street, where the park's most scenic area begins with Peirce Mill.

Another way of getting to Peirce Mill involves taking the Metro's red line to the Cleveland Park station, then walking up Connecticut Avenue 2 blocks north to Rodman Street; at the corner you'll see an inviting little woods with

Peirce Mill, Rock Creek Park

French Bench

Jules Jusserand may not be a household name today, but if you'd lived in Washington any time between 1902 and 1925, when Jusserand was the French ambassador to the United States, you'd certainly have heard about him.

One reason Monsieur Jusserand stayed in Washington for twenty-three years was his ability to befriend every U.S. president he ever met, from Teddy Roosevelt to Warren Harding; he was influential in persuading Woodrow Wilson that the United States should join the Allied side in World War I. What's more, Jusserand was also a noted scholar; his book, *With Americans of Past and Present Days,* won the 1917 Pulitzer Prize for U.S. history.

Jusserand and Teddy Roosevelt were great bird-watchers and frequently went birding together in Rock Creek Park. Jusserand is remembered today with a stone bench in the park, in the woods across Rock Creek from Peirce Mill.

signs directing you down the Melvin Hazen Trail. The trail leads a short distance down to Rock Creek where a left (north) turn on West Ridge Trail takes you, after a few minutes, to the mill.

Peirce Mill, named for the family that built and ran the mill in the early nineteenth century, was one of eight mills that lined Rock Creek in the 1820s and used its waterpower to grind corn and wheat into flour. The mill outlived its economic usefulness and was closed in 1897. But today thanks to the National Park Service, this lovely stone building, with its wooden waterwheel, is once again a functioning flour mill with antique millstones and hoppers that give visitors a fascinating view of a functioning nineteenth-century flour and cornmeal mill. Peirce Mill, at the intersection of Beach Drive and Tilden Street NW, is open Wednesday through Sunday noon to 5:00 P.M. A repair program is in progress, so call 895–6070 to make sure the interior of the mill is visitable or check out www.nps.gov. Contributions are welcome.

Next door to the mill is the trim little "Peirce Barn," built in 1820 as the Peirce family's carriage house. The barn, at 2401 Tilden Street, now hosts the Park Service Visitor Center and serves as a center for ranger-led walks and hikes. The barn also has a small bookstore, exhibits of local history, and games for the kids. Regular hours are Saturday and Sunday noon to 4:00 P.M., but it's best to phone ahead to 895–6070 to make sure the barn is open.

If you're on foot, at Peirce Mill you have the option of following markers along West Ridge Trail 1½ miles south to the National Zoo and its Metro stop on the red line or 2 miles north to the Park's *Nature Center.* The Web site is www.nps.gov/rocr/naturecenter/index.html.

Feeding Time near the Zoo

The National Zoo, in the 3000 block of Connecticut Avenue NW, is very much on the beaten path and is well covered in the usual guidebooks. However, if hunger strikes while you're there you'll find, close by, four restaurants they won't tell you about:

Oxford Tavern
(better known as the "Zoo Bar")
3000 Connecticut Avenue NW
232–4225
www.zoobardc.com
A long menu of pizzas, burgers, sandwiches, and salads, plus a kids' menu. For grownups there's also a lively bar and even livelier music from 10:00 A.M. to 2:00 A.M. Sunday through Thursday and until 3:00 A.M. on Friday and Saturday. Metro: Woodley Park-Zoo (red line).

Lebanese Taverna
2641 Connecticut Avenue NW
265–8681
www.lebanesetaverna.com
A great place to try meze, the Lebanese equivalent of tapas, or the flavorful kebabs and broiled chicken. Open daily 11:00 A.M. to 11:00 P.M. Across from Woodley Park-Zoo Metro station (red line).

Lavandou
3321 Connecticut Avenue NW
966–3002
www.lavandourestaurant.net
If you dine here, you'll be joining the locals in one of their favorite places— one they'd just as soon keep to themselves. Too bad for them, the word is out about Lavandou's pork tenderloin, sea scallops in red wine sauce, and carbonnade, which are among the house specialties. Afterward, call for the dessert cart and forget the calories. Lavandou is a 3-block walk from the zoo gate; Metro: Cleveland Park (red line).

Firehook Bakery and Coffee House
3411 Connecticut Avenue NW
362–2253
www.firehook.com
The Firehook, which has several outlets in the city, specializes in wonderful breads, with dozens of varieties ranging from designer to peasant. Your zoo break can also include a long list of coffees and scrumptious cakes and a tasty Danish to go with them. Definitely not on the Atkins-friendly list. If it's lunch you're after, the Firehook also sells French cheeses, prepared salads, and sandwiches. Open Monday through Thursday 7:00 A.M. to 8:00 P.M., Friday until 9:00 P.M., Saturday 8:00 A.M. to 9:00 P.M. and Sunday from 8:00 A.M. to 7:00 P.M. Metro: Cleveland Park (red line).

The nature center is the hub of Park Service programs and activities in the park, and there are a lot of them. To get an idea of the range of flora and fauna that live here in the middle of a large city, wander through the displays, photographs, and explanatory data in the center's large exhibit area. The center also has a bevy of children's programs, including a special "discovery room" for those under eight. As the park's "information central," the center can supply checklists of birds to watch for, a road map of the bike and other trails that crisscross the park, and instructions on a self-guided walk along the Nature Center Trail, where you can see firsthand most of the plants, birds, and animals you saw mounted back at the center. The center also offers guided nature walks and a small bookshop with a well-chosen selection of publications on natural history.

Perhaps the most remarkable section of the center is its seventy-five-seat planetarium, the only one in the Park Service system, which offers regularly scheduled events that acquaint children with the elements of astronomy and relate ancient yarns about the influence of the stars and moon. Planetarium shows are given on Wednesday at 4:00 P.M. and on Saturday and Sunday at 1:00 and 4:00 P.M. The Nature Center, 5200 Glover Road NW (895–6070), is open Wednesday through Sunday 9:00 A.M. to 5:00 P.M. You can either drive to the center by following the directional signs from nearby Military Road or take the Metro to the Friendship Heights station (red line) then transfer to an E2 or E3 bus to the corner of Oregon Avenue and Military Road, at which point you're a short walk from the center. If you decide to drive, keep in mind that Beach Drive is closed to auto traffic from 7:00 A.M. Saturday to 7:00 P.M. Sunday.

Golfing the District

If you're in town and just can't stay away from the greens, Washington has three golf courses where you can show your stuff. These courses will also rent you clubs at the rate of $7.50 for nine holes and $10.40 for eighteen. Greens fees are $21.50 on weekdays and $26.50 on weekends. And they're all open dawn to dusk year-round. The Web site for all these courses is www.golfdc.com.

East Potomac Park Golf Club
Hains Point and Ohio Drive
(near FDR Memorial)
554–7660
One 18-hole championship course and two 9-hole courses. Snack bar, pro shop, and practice facility.

Langston Golf Course
26th Street and Benning Road NE
(near RFK Stadium)
397–8638
Regulation 18-hole, par 72 championship course. Also lighted driving range, pro shop, snack bar.

Rock Creek Park Golf Club
16th and Rittenhouse Streets NW
882–7332
A hilly 18-hole, par 65 course. Pro shop, 150-yard practice hole, and snack bar.

The **Rock Creek Park Horse Center,** run by a concessionaire, is a short walk from the Nature Center. This is where you can either visit the horses or arrange to ride one and become a true urban cowboy. The horse center has large indoor and outdoor rings and offers a variety of riding programs, including pony rides on weekends by appointment for $20 for fifteen minutes. If you're interested in trail rides, one-hour rides are given Tuesday, Wednesday, and Thursday at 1:30 P.M. and Saturday and Sunday at noon, 1:30, and 3:00 P.M. at a cost of $30, reserve in advance. The horse center's office is open Tuesday through Friday noon to 6:00 P.M. and Saturday and Sunday 9:00 A.M. to 5:00 P.M. The center is closed in winter. Call 362–0117 or visit www.rockcreekhorsecenter.com.

Not far from the horse center, at the corner of Military Road and Oregon Avenue NW, a footpath leads to the well-preserved gun emplacements, earthworks, and moats of a Civil War fortification, **Fort DeRussey,** once a crucial point in the defense of Washington during the Civil War, but now abandoned and silent in the woods of Rock Creek Park.

Despite its daytime glories, you'd be well advised not to walk in this park after nightfall.

If, after your visit to Rock Creek Park, the idea of hiking some of Washington's other trails is appealing, you've got some great walks in store. For an excellent map and overview of what else is available in the District, visit www.washdc.org/trail.html.

Not far from the nature center, you'll see the place where, in July 1864, Confederate forces led by General Jubal Early made their first and last attempt to seize Washington with a bold attack on the Union defenses that surrounded the capital. Early's 20,000 troops launched their assault by marching down the Seventh Street Road, today's Georgia Avenue, from Silver Spring, Maryland, now a Washington suburb. The Confederate forces were met and repelled at **Fort Stevens,** another one of the "circle of forts" that protected the capital in

The Club Bus

The Metro folks have added a new bus service that will help you get from Upper Northwest into the nightlife in other neighborhoods. Route 98, the Adams Morgan–U Street Link, runs between the Woodley Park Zoo/Adams Morgan Metro station and 18th Street, the heart of Adams Morgan; it then continues on to Shaw's U Street/Cardozo Metro station. The service runs every fifteen minutes between 6:00 P.M. and midnight Sunday through Thursday, 6:00 P.M. to 1:00 A.M. on Friday, and 10:00 A.M. to 1:00 A.M. on Saturday. Fare is $1.10, but with a transfer ticket from Metrorail, it's only a quarter.

History Cop

On your wanderings through Washington's historic neighborhoods you might see a young African-American woman with an investigator's badge, a digital camera, and a sheaf of day-glo stickers with "Stop Work" written in big letters. You've just run into Toni Cherry, the District's "history cop," out on her rounds. Ms. Cherry, who works for D.C.'s Historic Preservation Office, is charged with seeing that Washington's officially designated historic properties are protected from illegal or historically incompatible alterations or additions. Since there are 23,500 historic buildings to protect and only one of her, Ms. Cherry gets pretty busy, so when you see her, don't slow her down—just say "thanks" and move on.

wartime, whose commander, Gen. Lew Wallace, would go on to make Charlton Heston famous by writing *Ben Hur.*

Abraham Lincoln visited Fort Stevens during the fighting and even mounted the ramparts to check out the action, exposing his lanky figure to enemy fire. When a young Union officer, said to be future Chief Justice Oliver Wendell Holmes, spotted a tall civilian peering over at the rebel forces, he shouted, "Get down, you damned fool!" Lincoln complied. The spot is marked by a boulder and plaque. You can easily visit Fort Stevens (www.nps.gov/cwdw/stevens), now a grassy park at the corner of 13th Street and Quackenbos Road NW, just off Georgia Avenue; the fort has been partially reconstructed, with its original earthworks and cannon standing ready in their emplacements and pointing north toward the Confederate lines. To reach the fort, take the Metro to Silver Spring (red line), then the 70 or 71 bus to Quackenbos Street.

Nearby, at 6625 Georgia Avenue NW, is **Battleground National Cemetery** (www.nps.gov/batt), where forty-one of the soldiers killed in the defense of Fort Stevens are buried. This poignant, rarely visited plot is the nation's smallest national cemetery. The cannon at the entrance gate are from Fort Stevens and were used in the Civil War battle. Inside, monuments commemorate the fallen of the 122nd New York Volunteers and other regiments; in the rear a flagpole is surrounded by a circle of headstones. Open dawn to dusk. You can visit the cemetery by taking the Metro red line to Silver Spring, then transferring to the 70 or 71 bus line and getting off at Aspen Street.

The **National Museum of Health and Medicine** charts the progress of medicine over the centuries, and many of its exhibits focus on pathology, the history of disease, and the development of human life. The museum also has the world's largest collection of microscopes and an internationally renowned neuroanatomical collection (read brain specimens).

The museum's visual centerpieces, however, are the exhibits of U.S. military medicine in wartime. The most extensive and interesting of these are those covering Civil War medicine, which contain some very graphic photos and wax reproductions of grievous wounds and smashed bones. Another set of models and photographs shows the reconstructive surgery used at the time to repair shattered faces and limbs and the techniques battlefield doctors used for amputations and in dealing with trauma. The museum also has casts of Lincoln's face and hands and the actual bullet that killed the president at Ford's Theatre.

After the Civil War, it's on to a medical tour of Korea's MASH units and World War II, which includes an unforgettable display of the Army's fight against VD, with some photos of afflicted GIs that will definitely make you think more than twice before ever fooling around.

In the "medical nostalgia" category you'll find more historic equipment including a 1954 iron lung and one of those klunky fluoroscopes where shoe shoppers wiggled their toes as they peered down at an X-ray view of their foot bones nestled in their new shoes. There's also a collection of the ivory-handled dental tools used by Paul Revere from 1768–75 when (who knew?) he practiced pre-ride dentistry in Boston. And keep an eye out for the museum's special exhibits, which in the past have included stunning images of the cardiovascular system, using the latest medical imaging technology.

Before you leave, pay a house call at the gift shop, which is just as eclectic as the museum itself. You'll find Sickles' leg depicted on bar coasters (and rightly so, the General was also an enthusiastic drinker) and, on a more serious note, microscope sets and an assortment of children's and adult books on medical topics. This is also the place to snap up nifty silk ties with medical motifs; surgeons will want to take an incisive look at a "sharp tie" with a scalpel pattern that is, you might say, definitely cutting edge.

The National Museum of Health and Medicine is located in building 54 on the campus of Walter Reed Hospital at 6900 Georgia Avenue NW; 782–2200, http://nmhm.washingtondc.museum. Open daily 10:00 A.M. to 5:30 P.M. Reservations required two days in advance. Take the 70 or 71 bus south from the Silver Spring Metro station (red line).

Faced with the blazing heat and swampy moisture of a nonair-conditioned Washington summer, Abraham and Mary Lincoln would drive out Seventh Street NW to stay in the cool and spacious grounds of the **U.S. Soldiers' and Airmen's Home** in the rural expanses of northwest Washington, making the home the first presidential Camp David.

The home was established for aging and ailing soldiers in 1851 and it is still a retirement home for 1,100 soldiers and airmen. One of its main buildings, **Lincoln Cottage,** a fourteen-room Victorian Gothic house, was originally built as a summer retreat by a wealthy banker, then made available to presidents when it was no longer needed for veterans.

Historians estimate that Lincoln spent about one-fourth of his administration living in the cottage (earlier called Anderson Cottage). It was there that he signed the Emancipation Proclamation, conferred with his generals, and spent time with his family, especially young Tad, with whom he often climbed the sprawling 300-year-old copper beech tree that once stood next to the cottage. Lincoln last visited the cottage on April 13, 1865, the day before he was assassinated, to make sure it was ready for his family's next summer visit.

Although the Soldier's and Airmen's Home grounds were an inviting refuge from tropical Washington, Lincoln Cottage has long attracted the attention of Lincoln scholars and historians. The house is still attractive, intact, and structurally sound—in many ways a time capsule where you can walk the porch where Lincoln reflected and peer through the windows at the rooms and fireplace he knew well.

In mid-2000 this little-known but historically significant house was placed at the top of the National Trust for Historic Preservation's list of endangered places needing urgent attention, which in the case of Lincoln means arresting water seepage and deteriorating woodwork. According to the trust's president, "it's probably the country's most significant Lincoln site because it is the only one associated with his presidency, and the only major Lincoln site that has not been restored." One possible use being discussed for a restored cottage is as a study center for Lincoln scholars. Just for the record, the cottage was used by three other presidents as their summer White House: Lincoln's predecessor, James Buchanan, then Rutherford B. Hayes (1877–80) and Chester Alan Arthur (1882–84).

The U.S. Soldier's and Airmen's Home, at Rock Creek Church Road and Upshur Street NW and at 3700 North Capitol Street NW (www.afrh.gov), was, as of mid-2006, closed to the public. However tour groups will be admitted to the grounds beginning in the fall of 2007, when renovation and restoration of the Lincoln Cottage by the National Trust is completed. To find out if the home is open during your visit, call 730–3043 or e-mail publicaffairs@dc.afrh.gov. There is no direct Metro service, but the 60 bus from the Ft. Totten Metro station (red and green lines) will take you to the Upshur Street gate. Best of all: Drive or cab it.

If you have time, visit the nearby *Soldier's Home National Cemetery,* the entrance of which is at the corner of Rock Creek Church Road and Harewood Road. It was among the first to be established to hold the remains of Civil War dead and pre-dates Arlington National Cemetery, which was created, in part, because this cemetery was filled.

Grief at Rock Creek Cemetery

Rock Creek Cemetery, at Rock Creek Church Road and Webster Street NW, is one of the city's oldest burial grounds. Upon entering you'll see St. Paul's Church, which was built well before Washington was a city; it was restored after a 1921 fire, but the walls are originals that date back to 1775.

Since burials began here in 1719, Rock Creek has seen a lot of big-time funerals of leading citizens, but its most visited grave is that of Clover Adams, the wife of writer-historian Henry Adams, who committed suicide in 1885. Her memorial is Grief (1891), a deeply moving statue by noted sculptor Augustus Saint-Gaudens showing a shrouded figure, neither male nor female, its face obscured by shadows. During World War II Eleanor Roosevelt reportedly drove out here frequently to sit and meditate at this powerful memorial. Pick up a map from the box outside the office and take your own self-guided tour. The **Adams memorial** is located in section E to the right of the church. While you're at Rock Creek, take time to look at two other memorable statues. Mary Magdalene as she first recognizes the arisen Christ is the theme of the dramatic **Ffoulke Memorial** (also called **Rabboni,** or Master), located in section B. Sculptor Gutzon Borglum (who later carved Mt. Rushmore) pulled out all the stops in this monument to a Washington merchant.

The haunting **Kauffmann Memorial (1912),** also located in section B, reflects the union of sculpture and landscape that evolved after the ground-breaking Adams Memorial. A melancholy female sits on a large curved bench near a mourning urn in William Ordway's tribute to the owner of the also defunct Washington Evening Star.

The cemetery is open from 7:30 A.M. to dusk, while the office is open from 9:00 A.M. to 5:00 P.M. Monday through Friday and 9:00 A.M. to 1:00 P.M. on Saturday; 829–0585; www.rockcreekparish.org. No Metro.

If you go to the Soldier's Home you'll have both the pleasure of visiting the Lincoln Cottage, one of America's seldom visited historical treasures, and dining at the down-home **Hitching Post,** another off-the-beaten-path find that is also unknown even to Washingtonians. Located just opposite the Soldier's Home's gate on Rock Creek Church Road, the Hitching Post is the quintessential neighborhood restaurant, where you'll either perch on stools at the Formica counter or settle into one of four fuchsia-colored Naugahyde booths to enjoy terrific southern cooking. From their tiny kitchen, Adrienne and Alvin Carter will fix you the best southern fried chicken you've ever had, or enormous crab cakes, arguably the best in town, packed with moist crab meat, along with a side of great slaw. The menu also lists baked ham and lamb chops, which I'm saving for my next visit. The Hitching Post, 200 Upshur Street NW (726–1511), is open Tuesday through Saturday noon to midnight. Inexpensive to moderate.

Places to Stay in Upper Northwest

The Kalorama Guest House
2700 Cathedral Avenue NW
328–0860
www.kalormaguesthouse.com
This urban bed-and-breakfast consists of two handsome 1910–12 town houses with nineteen agreeable rooms, seven of which involve shared bathrooms. And there's no beating the location, a nice residential neighborhood around the corner from the National Zoo and 2 blocks from the Metro. Inexpensive.

Omni Shoreham
2500 Calvert Street NW
234–0700
www.omnishorehamhotel.com
For over seventy-five years this Washington tradition with 812 rooms is hardly a cozy hideaway, but it sure offers a great travel experience, with top-drawer service and a historic feel. The Shoreham is like a small, self-contained city, with restaurants, shops, and a health club. Many rooms have superb views of Rock Creek Park. The Shoreham is also handy to the Metro and the Zoo, and is only a short cab ride from Adams Morgan's lively restaurant scene. Expensive.

Savoy Suites
2505 Wisconsin Avenue NW
337–9700 or
(800) 944–5377
www.savoysuites.com
This large (150-unit) suite hotel calls itself a Georgetown hotel, but it is in fact located close to the National Cathedral in Upper Northwest, a fifteen-minute walk from Georgetown. Some of its 150 comfortable suites have kitchens and many come with Jacuzzi tubs. The Savoy also has Lillie's, a bistro serving traditional Italian favorites. Moderate. No Metro, but on the route of the "30" buses.

Woodley Park Guest House
2647 Woodley Road NW
866–667–0218; 667–0218
www.woodleyparkguest house.com
Formerly known as the Connecticut-Woodley Guest House, this seventeen-room bed-and-breakfast has been both renamed and refreshed by a recent redecoration. Its moderate rates include a large continental breakfast and, at no extra charge, a great location. Although it sits in a quiet residential neighborhood, the Woodley Park is not only close to the Woodley Park–National Zoo Metro station; it's also about a block away from a major restaurant row, an easy walk from the zoo, and a ten-minute stroll to swinging Adams Morgan.

Places to Eat in Upper Northwest

Bambu
5101 Macarthur
Boulevard NW
364–3088
See page 138 for full description.

Blacksalt Restaurant and Fish Market
4883 MacArthur
Boulevard NW
342–9101
www.blacksaltrestaurant.com
The "fish market" part comes first as you enter this snazzy fish house in the Palisades, until recently a restaurant-free zone. As you enter window cases display gleaming shrimp, octopus, rockfish, and other fish fresh from the ocean or the Chesapeake. But if you're dining at Blacksalt and not at home, head for the lively dining scene in the back and a menu packed with exceptional seafood possibilities such as a dense zarzuela fish stew, mussels flown in from Maine, and wild Alaskan halibut; also look for outstanding clam chowder and fried clams. If you're still undecided, just ask for the tasting menu. Blacksalt also offers a thoughtful and reasonably priced wine list. Moderate to expensive. Open for lunch and dinner Tuesday through Sunday. No Metro.

Buck's Fishing and Camping
5031 Connecticut
Avenue NW
364–0777
Despite its name, Buck's doesn't serve up campfire specials, so don't worry about hunkering down here in the wilds of upper Connecticut Avenue for dinners of greasy fish and boiled coffee. The decor may be Early Boathouse, with a canoe hanging from the rafters, hurricane lamps, and rough-hewn wooden tables, but the food is anything but rustic. This is where you'll find

noted chef Carole Greenwood serving up unique prepared dishes such as pan-roasted mussels, grilled sea bass, and an ambrosial duck pot roast. To maintain the fishing camp atmosphere, Buck's also offers a terrific fish fry, along with wood-grilled steaks and lobsters. This high-energy restaurant also has a short but good wine list with reasonable prices. No reservations. Open for dinner Tuesday through Sunday from 5:00 to 11:00 P.M. Expensive.

Cactus Cantina
3300 Wisconsin Avenue NW
686–7222
See page 133 for full description.

Cafe Deluxe
3228 Wisconsin Avenue NW
686–2233
See page 133 for full description.

Chef Geoff's
3201 New Mexico Avenue NW; 237–7800
www.chefgeoff.com
This great American bistro is located in a tony neighborhood that needs all the restaurant help it can get. But Geoff would do well anywhere in the city with his "stone pies" (a.k.a. pizza), crab cakes, and grilled or seared fish entrees. The service is friendly, laid-back, and professional, and the wine list is both well chosen and well priced. Open daily 11:30 A.M. to 10:00 P.M. Sunday brunch starts at 11:00 A.M. Moderate.

Colorado Kitchen
5515 Colorado Avenue NW
545–8280
A lot of D.C. foodies are trekking out to this cheerful storefront restaurant in the city's well-off-the-beaten-path Brightwood neighborhood. The reason is imaginatively prepared comfort food by one of Washington's top young chefs. Don't be fooled—this is "home cooking" of a kind you may never see at home. On the menu you might find "firsts" of shrimp bisque, leek and potato soup, or onion and gorgonzola turnovers followed by "big food" such as meat loaf in black currant gravy, roast monkfish, or a "napoleon" made from ham and Gruyère. The relaxed quality is enhanced by the Formica tables, vinyl chairs, and a counter with stools all against a background of '40s music. Colorado Kitchen keeps quirky hours: open for memorable breakfasts Wednesday through Friday 7:00 to 11:00 A.M., lunch 11:30 A.M. to 2:30 P.M. Wednesday through Friday, and dinner Wednesday through Sunday from 5:00 to 10:00 P.M., brunch on Saturday and Sunday from 11:00 A.M. to 3:00 P.M. Closed Monday and Tuesday. Moderate.

DC Boat House
5441 Macarthur Boulevard
362–2628
See page 139 for full description.

Dino
3425 Connecticut Avenue NW
686–2966
http://dino-dc.com

This lively, relaxed trattoria, a huge favorite among its Cleveland Park neighbors, is owned by Dean (a.k.a. Dino) Gold, a longtime American resident of Italy with a discerning palate who clearly learned a lot about Italian cooking and wine during his stay in Venice and Tuscany. Start off with a plate of artisan Italian cheeses, a plate of exceptional antipasti, or pasta (especially the pappardelle with boar sauce), then move on to grilled fish or meat prepared *alla Italiana*. Along the way you'll enjoy Dino's thoughtful and reasonably priced wine list. Reservations are a good idea. Moderate. Open for dinner 5:30 to 10:30 P.M. Monday through Friday, 5:00 P.M. Saturday and Sunday. Last seating (and they mean it!) at 10:30 P.M. Friday and Saturday, 9:30 P.M. Sunday through Thursday. Brunch/Lunch on Saturday and Sunday 11:30 A.M. to 2:30 P.M. Metro: Cleveland Park (red line).

Firehook Bakery and Coffee House
3411 Connecticut Avenue NW
362–2253
www.firehook.com
See page 144 for full description.

Hitching Post
200 Upshur Street NW
726–1511
See page 150 for full description.

Kotobuki Japanese Cuisine
4822 MacArthur Boulevard NW
625–9080
Wandering sushi fans will definitely want to join knowl-

edgeable Washingtonians in this modest walk-up where top-quality rolls cost about $1.00 each. Kotobuki's orders are locally renowned for their fresh fish ingredients, including nigiri, ozhizushi, sea urchin, and marbled tuna. Open for lunch Tuesday through Saturday and dinner Tuesday through Sunday. Inexpensive.

Lavandou
3321 Connecticut
Avenue NW
966–3002
www.lavandourestaurant.net
See page 144 for full description.

Lebanese Taverna
2641 Connecticut Avenue
NW
265–8681
www.lebanesetaverna.com
See page 144 for full description.

Le Chat Noir
4907 Wisconsin Avenue NW
244–2044
A local food writer called this nifty little bistro "the La Coupole of Tenleytown." Well, maybe that's a stretch, but there's no denying that

neighbors flock here for the great crepes, well-crafted salads, including an excellent Niçoise, and a variety of robust chicken and fish dishes, including a terrific *poulet basquaise.* You can either sit on pews in the back or enjoy the passing parade from tables set up out front. Moderate. Hours are Sunday through Thursday 11:30 A.M. to 10:00 P.M. Fridays and Saturday until 11:00 P.M. Metro: Tenleytown/American University (red line).

Morty's Delicatessen
4620 Wisconsin Avenue NW
686–1989
Manhattan may have lots of local Jewish delis where the neighborhood congregates, but unfortunately they're rare in Washington. Morty's, located in Tenleytown, once a farm town within the District and now one of Washington's oldest localities, has that lower East Side feel, with the bowls of dill pickles (imported from Brooklyn) on the table and waitresses bearing platters loaded with overstuffed sandwiches,

corned beef, chopped liver, and matzo balls. Open 8:00 A.M. to 10:00 P.M. daily. Inexpensive. Metro: American University (red line).

Old Europe
2434 Wisconsin Avenue NW
333–7600
www.old-europe.com
The Old Europe, located about a mile above Georgetown, is both a decades-old veteran of the Washington restaurant scene and one of the District's only German restaurants. So prepare yourself for wonderful sauerbraten, Kassler Rippchen, and great sausages. Of course you'll also find the best bratwurst and sauerkraut this side of Munich, along with wild game and a vast assortment of German and Austrian wines and beers. And every Oktober there's a fest, *naturlich.* Open for lunch Sunday, 12:30 to 3:30 P.M. and Tuesday through Saturday 11:30 A.M. to 2:30 P.M. Dinner: Sunday 4:00 to 8:00 P.M. Tuesday through Thursday 5:00 to 9:00 P.M. and Friday and Saturday from 5:00 to 10:00 P.M. Closed Monday. Moderate.

AUTHOR'S FAVORITE PLACES TO EAT IN UPPER NORTHWEST

Lavandou	Buck's Fishing and Camping
Chef Geoff's	Le Chat Noir
Cafe Deluxe	Colorado Kitchen
2 Amys Neopolitan Pizza	DC Boat House
Dino	

Oxford Tavern

3000 Connecticut
Avenue NW
232–4225
www.zoobardc.com
See page 144 for full
description.

Rocklands Barbecue and Grilling Company

2418 Wisconsin
Avenue NW
333–2558
www.rocklands.com
You'll get probably the best
barbecue in the District in
this modest storefront with a
giant wood grill. Rocklands
has a few stools for sit-down
diners, but you can either eat
your pork ribs or chicken
standing in the corner next to
the world-class collection of
120 spicy sauces and condiments or take them along on
your walk through nearby
Glover Archbold Park. You
can make a virtual visit at
www.rocklands.com, but you
won't get the great smell of
that wood grill. Open Monday through Friday 11:00
A.M. to 10:00 P.M., Saturday
11:00 A.M. to 10:00 P.M., and
Sunday 11:00 A.M. to 9:00
P.M. Inexpensive.

Starland Cafe

5125 Macarthur Boulevard
NW
244–9396
See page 138 for full
description.

Tesoro

4400 Connecticut Avenue
NW; 363–6766
This northwest trattoria does
a good job on the usual Italian fare, including the better-
known pastas and veal
dishes. But Tesoro's menu
includes some less frequently
seen offerings, such as lamb
shanks with vegetables and
a tasty blackened salmon
with pesto risotto. Inexpensive, romantic, and a nice,
reasonably priced wine list—
isn't that what life's really all
about? Metro: Van
Ness–UDC (red line).

2 Amys Neopolitan Pizzeria

3715 Macomb Street NW;
885–5700
See page 133 for full
description.

W Domku Bar and Cafe

821 Upshur Street, NW
722–7475
This neighborhood favorite is
the quintessential off-the-
beaten-path restaurant with
a mega-eclectic menu that
features—get this!—Scandinavian and Slavic specialties.
Here's the place to combine
smorrebrod, open-face
Scandinavian sandwiches,
and gravlax with kielbasa,
dumplings, pierogis, and
kraut. Domku pulls this culinary schizophrenia off with
great aplomb and skill, leading one local restaurant critic
to praise its "good food and
friendly service." Eclectic also
describes the decor. At
Domku you'll dine in splendor on thrift-shop tables,
chairs, and sofas. A large bar
offers aquavit, eastern European booze, and cool music
while the back room pool
table is also a big favorite.
Live music and local talent
on Wednesday nights. Open
Tuesday through Saturday
for lunch and dinner, and for
breakfast Thursday through
Sunday. Moderate. The nearest Metro is Petworth on the
green line, but cabbing it is a
better idea.

Dupont Circle

Dupont Circle is probably Washington's liveliest neighborhood, with a raffish street life and an intellectual reputation fueled by plenty of first-rate bookstores and cafes, several of them catering to the area's large gay community. The Circle offers visitors an abundance of house museums, art galleries, and restaurants along with a laid-back lifestyle that makes casual strolling a joy. Although the present, in itself, would make Dupont Circle an agreeable place to hang out, this neighborhood's past gives it an extra dimension that enriches any visit.

At the beginning of the twentieth century, Dupont Circle was called "Washington's Newport," one of America's most fashionable districts, where the nation's lumber barons, steel kings, and other merchant moguls built the hundreds of grand winter homes and town houses that continue to grace the area. Nowadays this neighborhood and its brownstone town houses, red-brick turrets, and Beaux Arts palaces includes the Massachusetts Avenue corridor called Embassy Row, which bristles with the flags of many nations not even dreamed of during its Victorian heyday. Behind the opulent mansions that line Massachusetts Avenue, quiet streets filter back into Kalorama, a residential neighborhood that has known elegant living in three centuries.

DUPONT CIRCLE

The Dupont Circle stop on the Metro's red line serves most of the sites in this chapter. Dupont Circle itself is named not for a member of the great chemical family, but after Samuel Francis Dupont, an admiral in the Union Navy. A large fountain commemorating his exploits sits in the center of the Circle, which is actually a small oasis at the intersection of three main streets: New Hampshire, Massachusetts, and Connecticut Avenues. Despite the constant traffic, the Circle has a small-town feel, with plenty of benches for checkers and conversation.

Before you leave the Circle, stop to admire three distinguished palaces that, unfortunately, cannot be visited but exemplify this historic neighborhood's elegant pedigree. That ornate white palazzo at 15 Dupont Circle is the **Patterson House,** built by renowned architect Stanford White in 1903 for the publisher of the *Chicago Tribune.* During the Coolidge administration, it served briefly as the interim White House while the real thing was being refurbished. It is now a private women's club. Around the corner, at 1801 Massachusetts Avenue, you'll find the stately **Wadsworth House,** which dates from 1900, making it one of Washington's first Beaux Arts mansions. It is now the home of the Sulgrave Club. Across 18th Street stands the **McCormick apartment building,** built in 1915 as one of the city's first luxury apartments. The Mellens, Phillips, and other magnates lived in the building's 11,000-square-foot apartments. In 1977 the building became the headquarters of the National Trust for Historic Preservation.

In 1892, when millionaire brewer Christian Heurich (pronounced *hy-rick*) built his thirty-one-room dream castle on New Hampshire Avenue just off the Circle, many of the other mansions that ringed Dupont Circle were built by newly minted industrial titans eager to forget their humble or distant origins. Not Heurich, who wanted his home to celebrate his German ancestry. The result is an unlikely marriage of Queen Victoria and Count von Bismarck, a ponderous brownstone home in Romanesque Revival style (or as one observer put it, "beer barrel baronial") with high-ceilinged rooms where William McKinley would feel right at home.

TOP ATTRACTIONS IN DUPONT CIRCLE

Phillips Collection	The Textile Museum
Anderson House	The Woodrow Wilson House
The Heurich House Museum	The Lindens

Embassy Cultural Events

Most visitors don't know it, but many of Washington's foreign embassies offer rich cultural programs showcasing artists and performers from their home countries. Many of these programs take place in the embassy itself or in local theaters and galleries. Among the embassies with active programs are:

Austria
895–6714
www.austria.org./culture

France
944–6091
www.la-maison-francaise.org

Brazil
362–8334
www.bacidc.org

Italy
223–9800
www.italcultusa.org

Canada
682–1740
www.canadianembassy.org

Mexico
252–0012
http://portal.sre.gob.mx/imw/

At the *Heurich House Museum,* you'll see the meaning of ornate, from the parlor brimming with objets d'art, to the music room with its musician's gallery, to the majestic dining room in carved walnut, with a table elaborately set for eighteen. Amid all this Gilded Age splendor you'll find German mythological scenes elaborately carved by craftsmen on the furniture, wainscoting, and the house's seventeen marble fireplaces. If the public rooms become a little too formal, lighten up by heading downstairs to the basement breakfast room, which doubled as the family *bierstube.* Here the Heurichs gathered for family meals and steins of the family product surrounded by mottoes (in German, of course) celebrating the pleasures of the glass. Since Heurich lived to be 102, maybe the suggestion that "A good drink rejuvenates" isn't such bad advice. The mansion is now the headquarters of the Historical Society of Washington, which maintains a reference library and museum shop there. The handsome little garden behind the house is perfect for a picnic or a rest. The Heurich House Museum, 1307 New Hampshire Avenue NW (429–1894; www .heurichhouse.org) is open for walk-in tours on Wednesday, Thursday, and Friday at 11:30 A.M. and 1:00 P.M., Saturdays tours are given at 11:30 A.M., 1:00, and 2:30 P.M. Sunday it's 1:00 and 2:30 P.M. Group tours are possible, and if you're in D.C. on the first Friday of any month, Candlelight Tours are given at 5:30 and 8:30 P.M. Admission: $5.00 per person.

You always knew that Washington is crammed with historic buildings, but you probably never imagined that one of them would be the historic service station located at 22nd and P. In fact the prestigious National Register of Historic

Places includes this former Gulf (now Mobil) station on its list of protected historic structures. According the Trust, this 1936 beauty was designed as part of a Gulf initiative to make their gas stations just as architecturally and esthetically distinguished as other community structures such as banks and libraries. And it's still just that—a reminder of the days when service stations really provided automobile service and not just self-service pumps, candy, and groceries.

Across the street, at 1417 22nd Street NW, try to spend a few minutes and a few bucks at **Books For America,** Steve Hersey's nonprofit bookshop crammed with lightly used, bargain-priced books on every imaginable subject. The store's profits support literacy programs in the District, and you'll be especially welcome if, along with your buying spree, you can donate a few books to this worthy cause. Open 10:00 A.M. to 6:00 P.M. Monday through Saturday; 10:00 A.M. to 4:00 P.M. Sunday (www.booksforamerica.org).

A few steps away on 22nd Street you'll find the **Brickskeller,** where you can get terrific burgers and good buffalo steaks from the Dakotas, not to mention some nice rainbow trout. But the big attraction is the Brickskeller's world-class collection of beers, totaling more than 900 brands at last count (that is, if you're sober enough to count). There are a lot of saloons in this country that make a big deal of their collection of microbrews and exotic foreign labels, but nobody, repeat nobody, beats the Brickskeller. For proof, just check out the house collection of empties that lines the walls of this restaurant, elegantly decorated in Early American Fraternity House style. No wine list to worry about here. To spare yourself the embarrassment of ordering the wrong beer with pierogies or other menu choices, just ask your knowledgeable sommelier of suds to bring over the Brickskeller's book of brews for a consultation. (Hint: A young, presumptuous, and slightly spritzy San Miguel—a late harvest '97— would be perfect). The Brickskeller is located at 1523 22nd Street NW (293–1885; www.thebrickskeller.com). Open Monday through Friday 11:30 A.M. to 2:00 A.M., Saturday 6:00 P.M. to 3:00 A.M., and Sunday 6:00 P.M. to 2:00 A.M. Inexpensive—if you stop after only one beer.

AUTHOR'S FAVORITES IN DUPONT CIRCLE

Phillips Collection	Adams Morgan
Second Story Books	Kalorama Walk
Kramerbooks and Afterwords Cafe and Grill	Embassy Row

P.S. If you've ever wanted to live over a major-league beer hall and all the bar food you could possibly handle, you'll be interested to know that the top three floors of the Brickskeller's building are taken up by **The Brickskeller Inn,** a small hotel with over 40 smallish and spartan rooms.

None of Massachusetts Avenue's great mansions reflects power and wealth more than **Anderson House,** whose massive facade fairly oozes authority. Now the headquarters of the Society of the Cincinnati, a venerable organization of Revolutionary War descendants, Anderson House was for many years the home of wealthy career diplomat Larz Anderson. In keeping with the "Washington's Newport" reputation of this neighborhood, the Andersons used this colossal house for only a few months every year.

Keep in mind that Anderson House suffers from a touch of schizophrenia. You'll start off on the ground floor with the Society's impressive collections of Revolutionary War memorabilia and paintings by John Trumbull, Gilbert Stuart, and other early American artists. But on the second floor, the Anderson House suddenly becomes a treasure trove of eclectic antiquities and furnishings that largely reflect Anderson's years in Europe and Asia as the American ambassador to Japan and Belgium. Several rooms hold rare Japanese and Chinese carvings and lacquers acquired during Anderson's years in Asia, while others are strictly European, including the highly traditional English parlor with Hepplewhite chairs and portraits by Reynolds and Hoppner.

What makes the very rich different from you and me becomes obvious in the Anderson's sumptuous dining room. You know you're not back home in your cozy breakfast nook when you see how the Andersons, even *à deux*, dined at a table for twenty-eight in a room graced with Carrara marble floors, seventeenth-century Belgian tapestries, and priceless Japanese screens. After dinner the ambassador and his wife led their guests downstairs to their vast ballroom, which conjures up visions of black-tie evenings in a long-vanished Washington. Outside the ballroom there's the garden and, in the center, a grand seventeenth-century Buddha. Amid this elegance and ostentation you'll find indications that this regal couple also had a nice sense

capitalquote

"Massachusetts Avenue runs the whole length of the city, and is inserted on the maps as a full-blown street, about four miles in length. Go there, and you will find yourself not only out of town, away among the fields, but you will find yourself beyond the fields, in an uncultivated, undrained wilderness. Tucking your trowsers up to your knees you will wade through the bogs, you will lose yourself among rude hillocks, you will be out of the reach of humanity."

Anthony Trollope
in *North America* (1862)

of humor; in the solarium you'll see the amusing cartoon of the Andersons tooting along in their open touring car and a map tracing their favorite drives around Washington. Anderson House, at 2118 Massachusetts Avenue NW (785–2040), is open for one-hour guided tours Tuesday through Saturday 1:00 to 4:00 P.M. Tours start at 1:15, 2:15, and 3:15 P.M.

diplomatic niceties

To avoid making a diplomatic gaffe that would embarrass your country, you should know that an embassy is where the ambassador lives. The building where he and his exalted flunkies have their offices is called the chancery.

In the Phillips Mansion at Massachusetts Avenue and 21st Street, you'll find one of America's finest collections of modern art. Private at first, the **Phillips Collection** went public in 1921, when wealthy collector Duncan Phillips opened a few rooms of the family home to art lovers. The collection has since expanded to occupy the entire mansion and a recent annex.

The collection reflects Phillips's refined and diverse tastes, especially his love for the French Impressionists. Here, in an intimate and charming setting, you'll find Renoir's *Luncheon of the Boating Party* and other treasures such as Degas' *Dancers at the Bar* and masterpieces by Bonnard, Cézanne, Matisse, and Daumier. There are also important works by neoclassicists and realists such as Corot and Courbet along with American modernists Georgia O'Keeffe and Edward Hopper. As you wander through this explosion of great art, you'll also be able to inspect the public rooms of the Phillips mansion, including the grandiose Music Room, with its intricate Italianate ceiling. The Music Room is also the site of the collection's Sunday afternoon concerts, which are held at 5:00 P.M. September through May. The concerts are free with museum admission, but it's a good idea to arrive early. The Phillips Collection, 1600 21st Street NW (387–2151; www.phillipscollection.org), is open Tuesday, through Saturday

The Beat Goes On

Not far from Dupont Circle, where 20th and O Streets join New Hampshire Avenue, you can wander into tiny **Sonny Bono Park,** a grassy triangle that memorializes the pop star turned politician who died in a 1998 skiing accident. The park, with benches, flowers, and, from an anonymous donor, a TV plaque dedicated to the former congressman, is small but agreeable, which is why on sunny days you're likely to find a few locals reading or dining in this little oasis.

10:00 A.M. to 5:00 P.M., Sunday noon to 7:00 P.M.; closed Monday. On Thursday, when there's an "Artful Evenings" program of live jazz, lectures, and a cash bar, the hours are 10:00 A.M. to 8:30 P.M. Sunday concerts are held in the Music Room at 5:00 P.M. from October through May. Regular admission is $8.00, but free if you're under eighteen; the charge for Artful Evenings is $8.00.

The Phillips also has an excellent gift shop open Tuesday through Saturday from 10:00 A.M. to 5:00 P.M. and Sunday from noon to 5:00 P.M. Closed Monday. Next to the gift shop, the Phillips Cafe serves coffee, light lunches, and soups Tuesday through Saturday 10:45 A.M. to 4:30 P.M. and on Sunday from noon to 4:30 P.M.

Back on 21st Street, a left turn leads to R Street and a handsome block lined with century-old brownstones. Franklin and Eleanor Roosevelt raised their burgeoning family in the town house at 2131 R from 1916 to 1920, when FDR was the dashing young assistant secretary of the Navy. The house is now the residence of the ambassador of Mali and cannot be visited. The flower-banked marble steps near the corner of 22nd and Decatur Street have been dubbed "The Spanish Steps," even though they bear not the slightest resemblance to the original staircase in Rome. Anyway, they are all that remains of Kalorama (Greek for "beautiful view"), the eighteenth-century manor house that gave this neighborhood its name.

Before ascending the Steps, check out the rehabbed police callbox at the corner of 22nd and Bancroft, which contains a sculpture of an 1890s police officer phoning his precinct from a box just like the one in front of you.

At the top of the Spanish Steps you'll find "Freedom Place," so named because it was once a stop on the Underground Railroad, which spirited slaves out of the south and into freedom in the north. It is now a lovely Mediterranean mansion of yellow stucco fronted by a pair of Chinese lions flanking the front door and, seated in the front yard, a large panda, also yellow. The house also boasts an immaculate garden and, on the S Street wall, a trompe l'oeil mural that includes its name.

Across from the Irish Embassy, in the 2200 block of S Street, stands Mitchell Park, which looks like your average urban park, with one exception—there's a dog buried in the sandbox. Back in 1918 Morton and Elizabeth Mitchell donated this choice real estate to the city with the proviso that the grave of Bock, their much-loved poodle, be maintained in perpetuity. And that's why you'll find that Bock still lies there under the tree in the center of the recreation area.

A left turn on S Street leads past the Irish Embassy, with a harp over the entrance, to the **Textile Museum,** which just might be the best-kept secret in

Gallery Scene

It's only natural that the Phillips would become the hub of a thriving gallery community in its neighborhood. Here are a few to start you out:

In Hillyer Court, a tiny mews that cuts through the two wings of the Phillips, you'll discover the *Foundry Gallery,* a cooperative with nonstop shows by thirty artists, including local printmakers, painters, and photographers. Not only that, you'll be able to schmooze with Washington artists like Peter Robinson, then wonder about why, after all those art appreciation classes you still can't paint like that. Open Wednesday through Sunday noon to 6:00 P.M. (387–0203; www.foundry-gallery.org).

R Street, between Connecticut and Florida Avenues, is the real heart of this art neighborhood. Galleryland starts at 2114 R Street with the *Burdick Gallery,* dedicated to the carvings, sculptures, and prints of the Inuit people of the Canadian Arctic. Open Tuesday through Saturday from 11:00 A.M. to 5:00 P.M. (986–5682; www.burdickgallery.com).

At the *Fondo del Sol Visual Arts Center* you won't need a passport to explore the vibrant art and cultural heritage of the Americas. Exhibitions here run the gamut from pre-Columbian art down to the most contemporary paintings out of Brazil. The center also sponsors a wide-ranging program of lectures, concerts, and other educational events, plus an annual summer festival of Caribbean music. The center, at 2112 R Street NW (483–2777), is open Wednesday through Saturday 1:00 to 6:30 P.M. Contributions appreciated, amigo.

Two galleries occupy the 1872 town house at 2106 R Street NW. Upstairs, you'll find the *Alex Gallery,* a well-established commercial gallery that features contemporary European and American artists. Its downstairs sibling, *Gallery A,* features young and emerging artists. 667–2599; www.alexgalleries.com. Both are open Tuesday through Saturday from 11:00 A.M. to 5:00 P.M.

At the *Robert Brown Gallery,* the focus is on international artists, most of them contemporary, but you might also find art by Giacometti and Henry Moore in this eclectic space. Even more eclectic, ask to see Brown's fascinating collection of Chinese advertising posters from the '20s and '30s. Robert Brown Gallery, 2030 R Street NW, 484–4383; www.robertbrowngallery.com. Open Tuesday through Saturday noon to 6:00 P.M.

The *Marsha Mateyka Gallery,* just off Connecticut Avenue at 2012 R Street, presents a broad array of contemporary styles. This top gallery is located in an 1886 townhouse that has been brought back from the brink and made into a wonderful exhibit space. The building may be Victorian, but this gallery is the place to come for contemporary sculpture, paintings, and works on paper by leading American and European artists. 328–0088; www.marshamateykagallery.com. Open Wednesday through Saturday 11:00 A.M. to 5:00 P.M.

a city notorious for its leaks and indiscretions. The museum is the creation of George Hewitt Myers (as in Bristol-Myers), whose lifelong love of the textile arts began with an Oriental rug in his dorm room at Yale. Seven decades later, Myers's undergraduate hobby has become a world-class collection of more than 14,000 textiles and 1,400 carpets that are housed in the elegant rooms of his former town home and the mansion next door. The museum's regular holdings include every conceivable example of the textile arts throughout the ages, from fifth-century Coptic and Islamic textiles and pre-Columbian textiles from Peru down to twentieth-century native weavings from Central America and New Mexico, all splendidly displayed under brilliant spotlights that accentuate their dazzling colors and intricate designs. The museum also hosts visiting collections, often with original themes, including the recent pairing of subtly patterned Amish quilts with boldly colored nineteenth-century Caucasian rugs.

capitalquote

"It is sometimes called the City of Magnificent Distances, but it might with greater propriety be termed the City of Magnificent Intentions. . . . Spacious avenues that begin in nothing and lead no where; streets, mile long, that only want houses, roads and inhabitants; public buildings that need but a public to be complete."

—Charles Dickens, *American Notes*, 1842

And the gift shop is not to be missed. Just like the visual excitement of the museum's exhibits, its shop, located in the Myerses' former library, is one of the most colorful, attractive—and jumbled—you'll find anywhere; aside from reproductions of classic textiles in various forms, it also offers a fine selection of books on the textile arts. The Textile Museum, 2320 S Street NW (667–0441; www.textilemuseum.org), is open Monday through Saturday 10:00 A.M. to 5:00 P.M., Sunday 1:00 to 5:00 P.M. Docent-led tours can be reserved two weeks in advance. Suggested admission contribution of $5.00.

These days, presidents usually hotfoot it out of town the minute their terms end, but in March 1921, when Woodrow Wilson left office, he actually stayed on in Washington, moving from 1600 Pennsylvania across town to an elegant Georgian Revival home that immediately became nationally known as "the house on S Street." Although the world Wilson helped create at Versailles has changed beyond recognition, his Washington town house has remained much as it was when he died there in 1924. Its combination of personal belongings and White House memorabilia makes **Woodrow Wilson House** both a fascinating presidential museum and a wonderfully preserved upper-class home of the 1920s, from the Wilsons' windup Victrola ready to play a 78 of "Oh You

Beautiful Doll" to the box of Kellogg's "Pep" on the kitchen table. Wandering in this time warp, visitors find it easy to imagine that the Wilsons stepped out only a moment ago for a drive in nearby Rock Creek Park.

Wilson House docents say that for most visitors the real center of the house is Wilson's library, a comfortable and cluttered retreat filled with the personal and official mementos of his presidency. Wilson's cabinet chair is pushed back from a desk covered with personal papers; nearby stands a vintage microphone used for a 1923 broadcast. There's a "Graphoscope" movie projector (a 1913 gift from Douglas Fairbanks), and on the wall hangs a map of the brave but fleeting new Europe created by Wilson at Versailles. The house contains many personal and poignant touches. In the living room his massive Steinway and its period sheet music await the former president; in the upstairs bedroom, where Wilson died, a suit, walking stick, and boater are laid out for the next day's activities. A few steps away, in the nurse's room, we see a crude "shock stimulator" used in treating the paralyzed ex-president in his final months. Woodrow Wilson House, 2340 S Street NW (387–4062; www.woodrowwilson house.org), is open Tuesday through Sunday 10:00 A.M. to 4:00 P.M. Admission is $5.00 for adults; under seven free.

After leaving the Wilson House you'll be *(a)* standing at 24th and S Streets and *(b)* confronted with two choices, both of which represent an embarrassment of riches for a wonderful stroll. Make that decision the Washington way and waffle. Take both and you'll be doing just like the local politicians, who often feel very strongly about something—both ways. So pull up a bench in the little park at 24th and Massachusetts that honors Irish patriot Robert Emmit and ponder your decision. Note that the restored police call box in front of you is not painted in emerald green, but in burgundy and gold, the team colors of the Washington Redskins.

Your first option is to explore **Kalorama,** one of Washington's and the nation's finest residential neighborhoods. To do this, turn right and walk up 24th Street to explore side streets like California Street, Wyoming Avenue, and Tracy Place, which you'll find lined with elegant homes designed for America's super-rich by some of the foremost architects of their time.

One of these homes, the former Walsh-McLean mansion at 1825 Phelps Place NW, is now the **Russian Cultural Centre,** which sponsors musical and other programs that showcase Russian culture. The centre also has a permanent exhibit of icons and paintings, which you can see Monday through Friday from 10:00 A.M. to 6:00 P.M. and on Saturday by appointment. Be advised, however, that you'll be just as impressed by the magnificent rooms and parlors of this knockout mansion as by the art itself. To find out what's showing while you're in town, call 265–3840 or visit www.rcusa.org.

The Islamic Center

Although the Washington skyline bristles with towers and columns, the most distinctive spire of all is the 160-foot minaret of the Islamic Center at 2551 Massachusetts Avenue NW. Dedicated in 1957, the center was funded by contributions and gifts from a number of Islamic governments. The imposing, two-ton bronze chandelier was the gift of Egypt, while the Shah of Iran donated the elegant Persian carpets. The center's interior courtyard gleams with blue and gold mosaics and tiles. Visitors are always welcome but must observe a modest dress code—no bare arms or legs (translation: no shorts) and women must have head coverings. Visiting hours are daily from 10:00 A.M. to 5:00 P.M.; bear in mind, however, that viewing the center's exquisite interior is difficult on Fridays, when mandatory prayers draw thousands of worshipers. 332–8343.

The forest of colorful flags along these streets tells you that most of these homes are now inhabited by foreign ambassadors. One of them is the Tudor mansion at 2221 Kalorama Road, built in 1911 for a mining millionaire, but that is now, as you can see from the mammoth tricolor floating from the facade, the residence of the French ambassador.

Close by, at 2401 Kalorama Road, stands what I think is Washington's most magnificent house, *The Lindens,* a wonderful frame Georgian home with the look of colonial New England. And well it should—The Lindens was actually built in Danvers, Massachusetts, in 1754, but in 1934 was dismantled and moved to Washington in sections. Check out the house's windows, which are originals, and the lovely little park and garden that surrounds it. Georgetown's Stone House is the oldest house *built* in Washington, but The Lindens is Washington's oldest house. Nearby, at the corner of 24th Street and Kalorama Road, you'll find a restored police call box with a drawing depicting the Lindens being reassembled.

Your other possibility is to return to Dupont Circle from 24th and S Streets, strolling past the most splendid palaces of Embassy Row. The opulence starts right away with the Embassy of Cameroon's imposing French château at 2349 Massachusetts, which is one of Washington's premiere Beaux Arts palaces. Architects know this romantic pile as the *Hauge House,* named for the wealthy Norwegian diplomat who built it in 1906. Speaking of Beaux Arts, wandering along Embassy Row you'll see a number of town houses similar to the Croatian Embassy—early twentieth-century buildings with French style that would feel right at home in Paris. The Croatian Embassy at 2343 Massachusetts also offers passersby a fine little statue by sculptor Ivan Mestrovic.

Before reaching Sheridan Circle you also pass the magnificent Embassy of Haiti at 2311 and (ho-hum) yet another French château at 2315 that is now the Pakistani Embassy.

At Sheridan Circle, where General Phil Sheridan is spending his eternity directing traffic on horseback, look for the Spanish Mission–style stucco house at 2306 Massachusetts. This was the home of Alice Pike Barney, who from 1902 to 1924 used the house as her studio and made it Washington's most dazzling artistic and literary salon. Lucky Washingtonians remember that until a few years ago Ms. Barney's flamboyant house and its paintings were open to the public. Not any more. The Barney House is now the Embassy of Latvia.

On Sheridan Circle, between 23rd Street and Massachusetts Avenue, a small granite and bronze monument marks one of Washington's few successful acts of political terrorism. On this spot on September 21, 1976, a car bomb explosion killed former Chilean Ambassador Orlando Letelier and his American associate Roni Moffit. Chilean agents working for Gen. Augusto Pinochet were charged and convicted of this heinous crime.

One block away, on the corner where 22nd Street joins Massachusetts Avenue, you'll arrive at *Argyle House,* a massive Victorian pile. As the date high on the imposing facade at 2201 22nd Street tells you, this mansion was built in 1900, and its owner was Captain Frederick Miller, who was both a senior naval officer and a big time cat fancier. You can see his love for felines when you look up high on Argyle House's roof line and find a large stone cat perched, quietly watching the traffic zoom along Massachusetts Avenue. But

Kalorama Triangle

If you follow Kalorama Road across Connecticut Avenue you'll enter the historic district known as *"Kalorama Triangle,"* which extends as far as Columbia Road, the main street of Adams Morgan. On early maps of the District, this appears as a hilly woodland cut by ravines—once part of the rural estate of poet-diplomat Joel Barlow—but later developed as one of D.C.'s "streetcar suburbs" that sprung up with the construction of the now-vanished Connecticut Avenue trolley line in 1897. If you wander at random along the streets of Kalorama Triangle you'll be repaid with a look at some of the city's finest residential architecture, including the grand apartment houses at 2029 and 2101 Connecticut Avenue and handsome turn-of-the-twentieth-century row houses in the 2300 block of 19th Street. Although many of the former palaces of the Gilded Age's golden people have disappeared, just like their owners, the Triangle still boasts one of Washington's grandest homes, the Beaux Arts Lothrop mansion at 2101 Connecticut. It is not open to visitors.

Top-Secret Touring

Curious about what actually goes on inside those sumptuous embassies? If your CIA friend told you, he'd have to kill you, but there's an easier way to get that intelligence. In fact there are two tours that will let you crash those formidable gates.

The **Kalorama House and Embassy Tour** takes place on the second Sunday in September from noon to 5:00 P.M. These self-guided walking tours start at the Wilson House, which sponsors this annual event, and visit both distinguished private homes and embassies all over Kalorama. Tickets cost $22 when purchased in advance or $25 at the Wilson House on the day of the tour. For more details or to order tickets, call 387–4062, ext. 18.

The Dupont Circle House Tour. This October event can take you to homes, apartments, artists' studios, and other historic buildings in the Dupont Circle neighborhood. Tickets $25 in advance or $30 on tour day (265–3222; www.dupont circle.com/housetour).

tabby isn't the only cat prowling Argyle House; take a look at the fierce lions that support the stone bench in Captain Miller's front garden.

Across Florida Avenue stands one of Washington's great Gilded Age mansions. The **Townsend House,** at 2121 Massachusetts Avenue, was built in 1904 as an eighteenth-century French château by Richard Townsend, a railroad magnate, and his wife, heir to another rail fortune. The Townsends spared no expense in creating this grand home. In fact Frederick Law Olmsted, the designer of Central Park, was their landscape architect. Later the house belonged to Sumner Welles, FDR's Undersecretary of State. It is now the home of the **Cosmos Club,** a private club of achievers in the arts, science, and politics, whose lucky members get to read, dine, and dance in vast and sumptuous rooms once frequented by the super-rich of early twentieth-century Washington.

Your walk to the Circle will take you past the Anderson House and then Washington's most overwhelming building, the **Walsh-McLean House** at 2020 Massachusetts. The house was built in 1903 by Thomas Walsh, a fabulously wealthy gold miner whose daughter, Evalyn Walsh McLean, went on to own the Hope diamond. Stupendous doesn't begin to describe this house, which boasts a grand stairwell copied from a *Titanic*–era ocean liner that Walsh took a shine to. The building is now the Embassy of Indonesia. Walk-in visits are not possible, but individual and group tours of the mansion's palatial music and ballrooms can be requested by faxing the Embassy's Information Division at 775–5365 or phoning 775–5295 and stating your preferred dates and number of visitors. For more on this grand building, visit www.embassyofindonesia.org.

One of the pleasures of wandering in this raffish area is poking through the lively shops and cafes that make the Circle a favorite of window shoppers and serious buyers. Dupont Circle is also a center for Washington's specialty book sellers, so bibliophiles, buyers, and browsers have a field day cruising the neighborhood. But don't forget to look up every now and then or you'll miss seeing that most of Connecticut Avenue's shops and cafes are lodged in what were once some of the city's grandest town houses.

Start your shopping at **Second Story Books,** at 20th and P Streets, a few steps from the Circle. Second Story gets its name from its first location as a small used book store over an Asian restaurant in northwest Washington. It is now one of the largest used and rare book stores in the world, with three outlets in the Washington area. The browsing is intense at Second Story, which is floor-to-ceiling, wall-to-wall books—a paradise for bibliophiles looking for rarities or anyone searching for that out-of-print book that was lent out but never seen again. In good weather the store sets up an outside remnants table with a well-earned reputation as a bargain-hunter's delight. Used CDs too. Second Story Books, 2000 P Street NW (659–8884; www.secondstorybooks.com), is open daily 10:00 A.M. to 10:00 P.M.

capital quote

"Washington was the one city in the east where any woman with money and talent could set up housekeeping and become an important hostess."

—Alice Hoge, writing in
Cissy Patterson

St. Francis of Kalorama

Look carefully across the street from the French residence and you'll spy an antique, robin's egg blue police call box that has been turned into a tiny shrine with a ceramic tile of St. Francis of Assisi. Francis, who is surrounded by friendly birds and carries a red flower, is flanked by colored eggs and a bud vase that often sports spring flowers. This delightful little vignette is part of a D.C. Heritage "Art on Call" program (see page xvii).

At the intersection of Florida and Massachusetts Avenues you'll spot another former police call box, this one trimmed in crimson and gold. The box honors George Washington with a portrait of the future President as a young surveyor riding on horseback through D.C. The call box plaque speculates that this painting could show Washington riding nearby, along Florida Avenue, which in Colonial days would have been the natural route for Washington to follow as he rode from the then-Capital, Philadelphia, back home to Mt. Vernon.

If you've been thinking that vinyl records are totally extinct, just stick your head into **DJ Hut,** for a look at one of the last outposts of the LP disk. This second-floor shop is always crowded with Washington-area DJs looking for new sounds for their clubs. Since we're not talking Vivaldi or Mantovani here, the audition process can be a trifle noisy, as the jocks check out records by the Dungeon Family or Dilated Peoples on professional turntables. Lots of fun, especially if you're into hip-hop. DJ Hut, on the second floor at 2010 P Street NW (659–2010); www.djhut.com, is open Monday through Thursday noon to 9:00 P.M., Friday noon to 10:00 P.M., Saturday noon to 9:00 P.M., and Sunday 1:00 to 6:00 P.M.

If you're a musician, and especially if you're fond of the guitar, you shouldn't pass up a visit to **The Guitar Shop** while you're in town. This national Mecca for guitar-lovers, which is located upstairs at 1216 Connecticut, is wall to wall, floor to ceiling with over 2,000 guitars, mandolins, and banjos, some of them new, some collectable, and several quite rare (331–7333; www.theguitar shop.us). Open noon to 7:00 P.M. Monday through Friday, 11:00 A.M. to 6:00 P.M. Saturday; closed Sunday.

At 1517 Connecticut Avenue you'll find the Circle's most concentrated shopping, beginning with **Kramerbooks,** one of Washington's top booksellers and one of a dwindling number of its independents. Kramerbooks' knowledgeable staff, personalized service, and impeccably selected inventory make this the perfect place to track down that special request or find the right book on everything from poetry to appreciating architecture to tips on souping up your sex life. Speaking of which, at the height of the Lewinsky scandal, Kramerbooks did all of us a favor by tearing up the special prosecutor's subpoena for its records of Monica's purchase of a book for President Clinton (since you asked, it was *Vox* by Nicholson Baker; if you read it you'll understand why it was a thoughtful gift). To read more about Kramer's principled (and costly) rejection of the Starr subpoena, check out the store's Web site at www.kramers.com.

Kramerbooks is also important if you're hungering for more than knowledge. Its **Afterwords Cafe and Grill** may be in the rear of the store, but it's

Florida Bound

Florida Avenue, the western boundary of the Dupont Circle area was, in Colonial times, the main highway between the port of Georgetown and New York and New England; George Washington traveled it frequently. Known as Boundary Road in the nineteenth century, it was just that—the District's outer limit.

Hidden Treasure

At first blush, O Street between 20th and 21st Streets is merely a leafy and refined block of elegant brownstone town houses dating from the close of the nineteenth century. However, behind the brass plaque and imposing door of 2020 you'll find something totally unexpected—*The Mansion on O Street,* one of America's most eclectic and imaginative hotels—a small inn created by linking four 1892 town houses to form a luxurious complex containing a grand ballroom, seven dining rooms, twelve conference rooms, eighteen guestrooms, and sixteen fireplaces.

From the entryway you spot a typical Victorian parlor, except that this one holds vintage leather barber chairs and an 1800s pool table. Stairs lead past a cat puppet to an upstairs series of wildly and whimsically decorated theme rooms, including the two-story Log Cabin Suite, complete with a simulated rain forest, and the art deco Penthouse Suite with its private elevator, full kitchen, and aquarium above the bed. If you've been missing work, ask for the Corporate Suite, decorated like an office where the bed is headboarded with filing cabinets. And there's much more, including great antiques and a collection of art that ranges from Remington bronzes to rare oils and maps; the mansion also hosts periodic traveling art exhibits. The library has over 1,000 volumes. Luxury touches include a chef, stereo systems, scores of TV sets, and enough soaking tubs, Jacuzzis, and spa showers to bathe some countries. Everything you see in the mansion is for sale, including the shower made from an English telephone booth (if you can wrestle it out to your car). You can arrange to tour the mansion by appointment by calling 496–2020; a charitable donation of $5.00 is expected.

If instead you decide to stay at the mansion, you'll be joining a celebrity-laden guest list that includes Sylvester Stallone, Kim Basinger, and Hillary Clinton. Reservations by e-mail (hotel@mansion.com) and fax (659–0547) only. And, yes, it's expensive. The Mansion on O Street, 2020 O Street NW (496–2000; www.omansion.com).

a real restaurant and a good one, nothing like the little add-on cafes you'll find in many other bookstores. Breakfasts are notable and inexpensive; the rest of the day you can order entree salads and sandwiches, while dinners can run the gamut from jumbo crab cakes to grilled fish and pastas. On Saturday and Sunday the Dupont literati gather here over brunch for profound, cholesterol-laden discussions of big topics. Kramerbooks and Afterwords Cafe, at 1517 Connecticut Avenue NW (387–1400), are both open Sunday through Thursday 7:30 A.M. to 1:00 A.M. and twenty-four hours Friday and Saturday.

In addition to being a social hub and information center for Dupont Circle's gay community, *Lambda Rising,* at 1625 Connecticut, is one of the most comprehensive gay/lesbian bookstores in the country. In fact, it was the original shop for what is now a national chain of bookstores for gay men and

Down on the Dupont Farm

It's a bit incongruous, but this highly sophisticated and hip neighborhood, better known for art than asparagus, has its own farmers' market. Every Sunday from 9:00 A.M. to 1:00 P.M. vendors congregate behind the Riggs Bank just off the Circle at the corner of Massachusetts and 20th Street to sell organic vegetables trucked in from neighboring states. You'll also find a good selection of flowers, exotic fruits, and even handwoven sweaters from Ecuador (www.freshfarmmarket.org).

women. Lambda Rising is open Friday and Saturday 10:00 A.M. to midnight; the rest of the week it's 10:00 A.M. to 10:00 P.M. (462–6969; www.lambdarising.com).

Best Cellars is probably the most dramatic wine store in the country. No jumble of dusty bottles, hastily scrawled price tags, or underlit shelves here; just a starkly attractive and beautifully illuminated display of top wines. Furthermore, Best Cellars arranges their wines unconventionally, by taste categories such as "fruity," "crisp," and "bold," making it easier for you to match wine with food. Best Cellars, 1643 Connecticut Avenue (387–3146; www.best cellars.com), is open Monday through Thursday 10:00 A.M. to 9:00 P.M., Friday and Saturday until 10:00 P.M.

Upon entering *Secondi,* it's hard to believe that you're in a consignment clothing store and not a trendy, definitely upscale boutique. There are serious bargains here, from recycled dinner gowns to barely worn designer dresses with labels that even some men will recognize. Alas, there's a touch of sexism here: All of this secondhand chic is only for women; no men's clothing sold. Secondi, upstairs at 1702 Connecticut Avenue NW, is open Monday, Tuesday, and Saturday 11:00 A.M. to 6:00 P.M., Wednesday through Friday 11:00 A.M. to 7:00 P.M., and Sunday 1:00 to 5:00 P.M. Call 667–1122 or check out www.secondi.com.

To dine in an equally chic restaurant, walk across Connecticut Avenue to *La Tomate.* With its stark white walls, splashy paintings, and sunny Mediterranean look, La Tomate might just have floated in from southern Europe. Those impressions are soon confirmed by a menu that is strong on pastas based on shellfish and vegetables, and second courses like spezzatino di pollo and veal Milanese. As a bonus, this "Italian bistro" has large sidewalk windows perfect for the people-watching that comes with the Dupont Circle territory. La Tomate, 1701 Connecticut Avenue NW, is open Monday through Thursday 11:30 A.M. to 10:30 P.M., Friday and Saturday 11:30 A.M. to 11:30 P.M., and Sunday 11:30 A.M. to 10:00 P.M. It's a good idea to reserve by calling 667–5505 or visiting www.latomatebistro.com.

Ginza specializes in things Japanese, so you'll find a nice selection of Asian items there for your home, office, and garden, including samurai dolls, tea sets, lacquered boxes, and many books on Japan and its art. And if you really must have a samurai T-shirt, this is the place to get it. Ginza, 1721 Connecticut Avenue NW, is open Monday through Saturday 11:00 A.M. to 7:00 P.M., Sunday noon to 6:00 P.M. (331–7991; www.ginzaonline.com).

If you're from out of town or another country and can't wait to find out what's going on back home, head for *The Newsroom,* which carries magazines and newspapers from practically everywhere. There's also a large selection of language teaching manuals and materials. The Newsroom, at 1803 Connecticut Avenue (332–1489), is open 7:00 A.M. to 9:00 P.M. every day.

If you've had your fill of shopping, another good walk involves exploring the Dupont Circle neighborhood east of Connecticut Avenue beginning at 18th and Church Streets, where there's a lovely little garden rimmed with daffodils and azaleas that's just perfect for resting or picnicking. This was the site of *St. Thomas Episcopal Church,* a miniature Gothic cathedral where Franklin and Eleanor Roosevelt frequently worshiped. St. Thomas was destroyed by arson in 1970; all that remains of one of Washington's loveliest and most cherished churches is the fire-scorched north altar wall. Although St. Thomas may physically be gone, its sense of tranquillity lingers on in the park, and its parishioners still hold services in the adjoining rectory, which was undamaged by the fire.

Even die-hard Republicans like to take a bipartisan peek at the *Woman's National Democratic Club,* at 1526 New Hampshire Avenue NW, which is located in the delightful Whittemore House, an 1892 charmer built in a freeform, slightly undulating shape with protruding dormer windows and a gorgeous caped roof. Beyond the house's wood paneled entrance hall, a series of spacious and handsomely furnished rooms commemorates Democratic First Ladies—especially Eleanor Roosevelt, a frequent visitor—and leaders of the

Museum Meander

Nine leading museums and arts sites welcome visitors and provide special musical and other programs during the annual *Dupont-Kalorama Museum Walk,* held on the first weekend of June. The Phillips Collection sponsors hands-on art activities for children, the Fondo del Sol Visual Arts Center goes aural with live Latin music, and there's sheepshearing at the Textile Museum. A free shuttle will take you around, stopping at each site on Saturday from 10:00 A.M. to 4:00 P.M., and Sunday 1:00 to 5:00 P.M. Call 387–4062, ext. 12 for full information or visit www.dkmuseums.com.

suffrage movement. The Club's museum also offers special exhibits on democratic politics and political figures along with a collection of campaign and political memorabilia. Tours by appointment only. Call 232–7363 to reserve or, visit www.democraticwoman.org for more about the house and museum.

Further up 18th Street, at the corner of New Hampshire Avenue, you'll see the Beaux Arts prow of one of Washington's most spectacular homes, the fifty-four-room **Belmont Mansion,** which could have floated in from Versailles. The house now belongs to the Order of the Eastern Star, which admits only members of the Eastern Star, Masons, or their guests. If you qualify you can take your chances by turning up at the door during tour times, which are Monday through Friday from 9:00 A.M. to 3:00 P.M., or apply online at www.eastern star.org. Get more information by phoning 667–4737. If you get in, you'll pass through a regal entrance hall, climb a granite double staircase under amethyst chandeliers, and go upstairs to the Belmonts' former parlors with their gold piano and a grand dining room that sports a ceiling from the Doge's Palace in Venice. If you're not cleared, you'll have to settle for standing outside and admiring the magnificent Louis XIV style of the building and its lovely gardens of unclassified tulips and azaleas.

Around the corner on R Street, the **National Museum of American Jewish Military History,** which operates under the auspices of the Jewish War Veterans of the U.S.A., documents the contributions that Jewish men and women have made to American military efforts in every war. The museum's exhibits include medals, weapons, and other military memorabilia, along with photos, diaries, and letters from the museum's large photographic and documentary archive. Recent shows have included *Women in the Military: A Jewish Perspec-*

Exotic Eats

The stretch of 18th Street between R Street and Columbia Road has blossomed into a veritable United Nations of storefront restaurants with exotic cuisines rarely represented on any city's culinary lineup. For a change of pace, try the following:

Caravan Grill
1825 18th Street
518–0444
Persian delights such as yogurt soup or a kebab from the restaurant's long list. Also a large buffet at lunch and dinner.

Adams Morgan

If you're fond of Ethiopian food, you could easily end up spending many evenings in Adams Morgan, which, along with its other multicultural dining possibilities, boasts a disproportionate number of Washington's Ethiopian restaurants. The specialties at each include a wide range of hot or mild chicken, lamb or beef stews, and tasty, subtle vegetable dishes, all accompanied by injera, the spongy pancakes you'll use to mop up your plate. No silverware, grazie. Here are two of the best; both are inexpensive to moderate in price.

Addis Ababa
2106 18th Street, NW
232–6092
Open noon to 12:30 A.M. daily. Live entertainment on the weekend.

Meskerem
2434 18th Street NW
462–4100
http://meskeremonline.com
Open Sunday through Thursday noon to midnight, Friday through Saturday, noon to 1:00 A.M. Live Ethiopian music after 11:30 P.M. on Friday and Saturday.

tive, The Life and Career of Commodore Uriah Phillips Levy, and *Jewish GIs Remember the Concentration Camps.* The museum, at 1811 R Street NW (265–6280; www.nmajmh.org), is open Monday through Friday 9:00 A.M. to 5:00 P.M.; closed Saturday, Sunday, and Jewish holidays. Contributions appreciated.

That residential block of brownstones on S Street between 17th and 18th Streets is a survivor of what Washingtonians call the *"Strivers' Section."* The "Strivers" in question were the cadre of prominent black professionals and intellectuals who, in the 1920s, were fighting for recognition and equality in what was then a thoroughly Southern city. In this block, which is now on the National Register of Historic Places, lived Benjamin Davis, the first African American to become a U.S. general (at 1721 S), poet Langston Hughes (1749 S), and noted jurist Charles Houston (1744 S).

You'll find good eats for your pooch at *Doggie Style Bakery,* where you can buy Fido a personalized birthday cake, cheese balls, and peanut butter rabbits. I (I mean my dog) really liked the personalized bones and doughnuts. Veggie bagels too! Special events include doggie happy hours and a Halloween costume party. Doggie Style Bakery, 1825 18th Street NW; 667–0595. Before visiting give your best friend an advance peek at the menu by visiting www.doggiestylebakery.com. Hours: Monday through Saturday 11:00 A.M. to 8:30 P.M., Sunday 11:00 A.M. to 6:00 P.M.

Now you're nearing the point on 18th Street where Dupont Circle ends and the area known as *Adams Morgan* begins. Adams Morgan (or Madam's

Cool Rules

Finally, if you're looking for a combination of good food and cool sounds, here are two possibilities:

Felix
2406 18th Street
483–3549
www.thefelix.com
Features "imaginative American" cooking, and the martinis are divine, but go easy if you're staying around for Felix's program of live music. On Wednesday the music starts at 8:30 P.M., but on the weekends it runs from 11:00 P.M. to 2:00 A.M. While you're there check out the intimate Spy Lounge next door, where a DJ spins cool jazz on Thursday and the weekend. Moderate.

The Blue Room
2321 18th Street NW
332–0800
www.blueroomdc.com
The food is mainly tapas-style dishes involving fish and pastas, and it's accompanied by ultra-cool music that DJs play here Wednesday through Sunday from 8:00 P.M. until 3:00 A.M. The crowd is definitely urban chic and the music you'll hear may be acid jazz or down tempo, but it will never be the top 40. Closed Sunday through Tuesday. Moderate.

Organ, as it is sometimes called) is one of the District's most tumultuous neighborhoods and a social center of the city's Latino, Caribbean, and African residents. Perfectly routine and quiet by day, Adams Morgan really comes to life at night, when it becomes Washington's liveliest restaurant scene. If you go, keep in mind that Adams Morgan has no Metro station, that the Dupont Circle stop is at least thirty minutes away, and that the parking situation is catastrophic. Take a cab. Here are a few restaurants to think about:

In spite of the pun, the **Grill from Ipanema** is a top Brazilian restaurant, where you can guzzle caipirinhas, made with limes, sugar, and million-proof rum. It's a good idea to have only one before ordering conch chowder, Brazilian grilled meat, or Brazil's national dish, feijoada, a feast of black beans, brined beef, sausage, and cuts of pork. The restaurant is at 1858 Columbia Road NW (986–0757; www.thegrillfromipanema.com). Inexpensive.

Cashion's Eat Place, 1819 Columbia Road NW (797–1819; www.cashions eatplace.com), will remind you of a 1937 Parisian bistro—the intimate atmosphere, the bar with habitués sitting under a painting of a nude, more than a whiff of romance in the air, and cool jazz is playing somewhere, and the food is even better than the setting, an eclectic menu that swings from roast leg of lamb to duck breast with foie gras, or veal cheeks. Call it modern American with a southern accent. Chef-owner Ann Cashion changes the menu daily, but not to worry, you'll be in good hands. Reservations are a must, especially for the yummy Sunday brunch. Open for dinner Tuesday and Sunday 5:30 to 10:00 P.M., until 11:00 P.M. Wednesday through Saturday. Sunday brunch 11:30 A.M. to 2:30 P.M. Moderate.

Places to Stay in Dupont Circle

The Carlyle Suites
1731 New Hampshire Avenue NW
234–3200
fax 387–0085
www.carlylesuites.com
This converted apartment house on one of Dupont Circle's quieter residential streets announces its art deco origins in a lobby covered with louvered sconces and other Chrysler Building touches. The Carlyle, with its 170 comfortable suites with mini-kitchens and dining areas, offers comfort and value, especially for families. The handsome restaurant, Lillie's, open daily 7:00 to 11:00 A.M. and 5:00 to 10:00 P.M., offers mainly light fare such as pastas, soup, and sandwiches, but also grilled steaks and fish. Moderate.

The Churchill
1914 Connecticut Avenue NW; 797–2000
fax 462–0944
www.thechurchillhotel.com
The National Trust for Historic Preservation includes the Churchill on its list of historic North American hotels. This grand old Beaux Arts structure began life in 1906 as a luxury apartment house,

but was later converted into an elegant and equally comfortable hotel with 144 guest rooms and suites. And you can't beat the location right on Connecticut Avenue, Dupont Circle's main stem, and on the edge of Embassy Row. Moderate.

The Dupont at the Circle
1604 19th Street NW
332–5251
(888) 412–1000
www.dupontatthecircle.com
Located just off the Circle, this is one of the District's top bed-and-breakfasts, with seven handsome rooms and suites, each with its private bath. If you stay in the period Lincoln Room, you'll get presidential treatment, including a chance to sleep in a replica of the famous Lincoln Bed (no campaign contribution required). Basically moderately priced, but the larger suites, including the spacious Plum Suite, are expensive.

Hotel Tabard Inn
1739 N Street NW
785–1277
fax 785–6173
www.tabardinn.com
A British writer once described this inn as "the sort of place favored by Englishmen who prefer 'character' to room service and by Americans who want to assert their individuality." That's a pretty good description of this small, laid-back

hotel with a distinctly British feel: big rooms with Victorian decor, occasionally quirky furnishings, and moderate prices. Also notable is the hotel's restaurant, a cozy, casual favorite with the locals. Moderate.

The Inn at Dupont Circle
1312 19th Street NW
467–6777
fax 293–8819
www.theinnatdupontcircle.com
This bed-and-breakfast is located in an 1895 Victorian town house right at the Dupont Circle stop of the shuttle bus service to Georgetown and only steps from the Circle itself. The inn's six Victorian-style rooms boast 12-foot ceilings and most have fireplaces complete with the original tiles. Downstairs in the salon an 1872 rosewood grand piano awaits your delicate touch—anyone choosing to leave the room can flee outside to the inn's charming little patio and garden with a heated solarium. Rates are moderate and include a full buffet breakfast.

Jurys Doyle Washington
1500 New Hampshire Avenue NW
483–6000
www.jurysdoyle.com
Because it's right on the Circle and next to the Metro station, you can't get much more centrally located than this D.C. outpost of Ireland's

largest hotel group. The hotel's 300-plus attractive rooms are often filled with business travelers and foreign officials visiting on State Department grants, so it pays to reserve in advance. The Irish theme carries over into the hotel's atmospheric pub, where Bushmill's is the national pastime, and its restaurant, The Dupont Grille, where, you'll be happy to hear, the cooking is better than in Dublin. Moderate.

Jurys Normandy Inn
2118 Wyoming Avenue NW
483–1350
www.jurysdoyle.com
One of Kalorama's few hotels, Jurys Normandy is a handsome hideaway not far from Dupont Circle and handy to the Connecticut Avenue bus lines. The Normandy is very much like a small European boutique hotel (after all, it's Irish-owned) from the gentlemen's club lobby to the seventy-five well-furnished rooms. Even without its great location, the Normandy is a real find anywhere in the city. Inexpensive to moderate.

The Kalorama Guest House
1854 Mintwood Place
667–6369
The Kalorama is actually a collection of three turn-of-the-century town houses located in the 1800 block of leafy Mintwood Place, one of the quieter streets in sometimes raucous Adams Morgan. The guest house offers thirty rooms and suites, all nicely furnished; breakfast is included. Moderate.

Swann House
1808 New Hampshire Avenue NW
265–4414
www.swannhouse.com
This is one of the District's few bed-and-breakfasts, and it's a good one. This redbrick Victorian mansion, which was built in 1883 by a noted Washington architect and artist, has more than its share of elegant period touches—the crown moldings, 12-foot ceilings, inlaid floors, and other features you'd expect from a Victorian beauty. But more to the point, many of its twelve spacious rooms come with tasteful antiques, working fireplaces, and whopping bathrooms, plus fax machines and dataport phones that make Swann House a business favorite. And, thankfully, not an antimacassar or sherry bottle anywhere in sight. Swann House also has its own swimming pool, which is small, but just what you want during those sizzling Washington summers. Moderate.

Topaz Hotel
1733 N Street NW
393–3000
fax 785–9581
www.topazhotel.com
The theme of this boutique hotel is wellness, but other words that might describe the Topaz are "colorful" and "sophisticated." Colorful starts when you check in with desk clerks wearing iridescent orange and green silk tunics, then drift into the Topaz Bar with its blue pencil lights and settle into a floor to ceiling settee to start your

stay with an energy cocktail. Upstairs, all of the Topaz's ninety-nine rooms are large, comfortable, and handsomely furnished, but several are set aside as special yoga rooms, with meditation space, New Age music, and instructional videos. Following the Topaz's wellness theme, the hotel also offers "energy rooms" with exercise possibilities. The hotel also offers special weekend rates that include aromatherapy sessions and massages. Every night the relentlessly cool Topaz Bar draws crowds of young, with-it professionals, possibly looking for the bar's specialty, the potent "Blue Nirvana" cocktail, emphatically not an herbal potion, but which does deliver a certain feeling of wellness (or is that buzziness?). All of this excitement and a great location between downtown and Dupont Circle. Moderate to expensive.

Windsor Park Hotel
2116 Kalorama Road
(corner of Connecticut Avenue)
483–7700
www.windsorparkhotel.com
If the idea of living in Kalorama appeals to you, if only for a few nights, then check into the Windsor. This clean and comfortable budget find, with its forty nicely furnished rooms, gets a big play from diplomats in town to consult at their Washington embassies and from Americans lured by its strategic location for bus travel all over the city. Moderate.

Places to Eat in Dupont Circle

Addis Ababa
2106 18th Street NW
232–6092
See page 175 for full description.

Afterwords Cafe and Grill
1517 Connecticut Avenue NW
387–1400
See pages 170–71 for full description.

Bistrot Du Coin
1738 Connecticut Avenue NW; 234–6969
fax 234–6965
If you've been pining away for your Paris favorites—the escargots, moules marinières with frites, and all kinds of tartines, leave your passport in the drawer and head for this authentic French bistro that has somehow migrated successfully from the Seine to the Potomac. Lunchtime is pretty restrained, but the noise level and fun build into the evenings, especially on the weekends, where you'll need a reservation to shoehorn in for your onion soup and choucroute garnie. And every Sunday the Bistrot observes the ancient French tradition of *le brunch*. Bonne chance. Open Monday to Wednesday 11:30 A.M. to 11:00 P.M., Thursday through Saturday 11:30 A.M. to 1:00 A.M., and Sunday 11:00 A.M. to 11:00 P.M.

The Blue Room
2321 18th Street NW
332–0800
See page 176 for full description.

Brickskeller
1523 22nd Street NW
293–1885
www.thebrickskeller.com
See pages 159 for full description.

Cashion's Eat Place
1819 Columbia Road NW
797–1819
See page 176 for full description,

Caravan Grill
1825 18th Street NW
518–0444
See page 174 for full description.

City Lights of China
1731 Connecticut Avenue
265–6688
www.citylightsofchina.com
This citywide favorite invariably makes everyone's list of their favorite restaurants. One reason for that is great food, from specialties like the shark's fin soup and crispy noodles with seafood to the usual Chinese fare of Szechuan beef or Kung Pao shrimp. The other is the combination of reasonable prices and excellent service. Open Monday through Friday 11:30 A.M. to 10:30 P.M., Saturday noon to 11:00 P.M., and Sunday noon to 10:30 P.M. Moderate.

Etrusco Trattoria
1606 20th Street NW
667–0047
It's hard to imagine a better dining experience than Etrusco, where you'll swear you're back in Siena as you enjoy outstanding Tuscan dishes like ribollita, papardelle slathered with a rich duck ragu, and grilled sea bass in a wine and rosemary sauce. Owner/chef Francesco Ricchi also makes great osso buco and splen-

AUTHOR'S FAVORITE PLACES TO EAT IN DUPONT CIRCLE

Sette Trattoria

The Obelisk

Hank's Oyster Bar

Etrusco Trattoria

Hotel Tabard Inn

Cashion's Eat Place

Bistrot Du Coin

did, homemade sausages and a robust soup of mussels and clams; for dessert try his chocolate Grandfather's Cake. Just as memorable is the atmosphere of a great Italian restaurant with fresh flowers and attractive decor where the sounds you hear are of happy people having a great time enjoying terrific food. Maybe the exceptional wine list has something to do with that, or perhaps it's the friendly, professional service. Reservations a must. Open for dinner only, Monday through Saturday. Moderate.

Felix
2406 18th Street
483–3549
See page 176 for full description.

Grill from Ipanema
1858 Columbia Road NW
986–0757
See page 176 for full description.

Hank's Oyster Bar
1624 Q Street NW
462–4265
www.hanksdc.com
This immensely popular fish restaurant owes its popularity (and high energy level) to chef Jamie Leeds' pitch-perfect touch with seasonal seafood, including shad roe and soft shell crab. At Hank's you'll find those dense lobster rolls, steamed mussels, and fisherman's platters that are sure to remind you of that summer at the beach in New England. The oyster bar part involves difficult choices from the long list of briny bivalves on the blackboard; if they have it try the "sake oyster shooter." The Saturday and Sunday brunch is

another neighborhood favorite. Sidewalk tables in good weather. No reservations, but if you phone thirty minutes before you arrive, they'll put you on the list. Open Sunday to Tuesday 5:30 to 10:00 P.M., Wednesday through Saturday until 11:00 P.M. Saturday and Sunday Brunch 11:00 A.M. to 3:00 P.M. Moderate.

The Iron Gate Inn
1734 N Street NW
737–1370
If you're thinking about having an intimate tryst at one of Washington's most romantic dining spots, you can't do better than the Iron Gate's vine-covered patio. In cool weather just move inside to a table in one of the restaurant's firelit rooms. The Iron Gate's menu has an eastern Mediterranean accent, with listings for lamb shank with orzo and roast chicken. Open Monday through Friday 11:30 A.M. to 2:30 P.M., Monday through Saturday 5:30 to 10:00 P.M. Moderate.

La Tomate
1701 Connecticut Avenue NW
667–5505
See page 172 for full description.

Meskerem
2434 18th Street NW
462–4100
See page 175 for full description.

Mimi's American Bistro
2120 P Street NW
464–6464
www.mimisdc.com
As Woody Allen once said about something else, Mimi's is "the most fun you can have without laughing."

Mimi's is the only D.C. restaurant where the waitstaff will serenade you during dinner with show tunes, romantic ballads, and jazz favorites. But don't go to Mimi's for a soulful chat, because the effect of all this excitement and talent is a noisy, happy room. And the food is worth a visit on its own, with a bistro menu that's heavy on grilled fish, aged beef, and rack of lamb; there's also a Mediterranean twist with grilled figs, duck in fruit sauce, and couscous. Reservations strongly advised. Moderate.

The Obelisk
2029 P Street
872–1180
Located in a town house, this might be the city's best Italian restaurant. The Obelisk has a short but exquisite fixed-price menu (at this writing $65), that varies nightly. On our latest visit the antipasti choices included peppers prepared with vegetables and cheese or stuffed pig's foot. The first course involved deciding between halibut raviolini and gnocchi with Gorgonzola cheese, while the entree possibilities included veal tenderloin with juniper relish, pan-cooked grouper, and roast squab with mushrooms and polenta. Memorable desserts and wines too. Reservations are essential. Open Tuesday through Saturday 6:00 to 10:00 P.M. Expensive.

Pines of Florence
2100 Connecticut Avenue NW
332–8233
Although Kalorama has many delights, an active restaurant

scene isn't one of them. However, if hunger strikes on your wanderings, this trattoria is a good choice. But with all those southern Italian favorites and the hearty red sauces, shouldn't it be renamed Pines of Palermo? Open Monday through Thursday 11:00 A.M. to 10:30 P.M., Friday until 10:00 P.M., Saturday noon to 11:00 P.M., and Sunday noon to 10:00 P.M. Inexpensive.

Rosemary's Thyme
1801 18th Street NW
332–3200
The food at Rosemary's Thyme is as handsome and lively as the surroundings in this "Mediterranean-Creole bistro," which is saying a lot.

You come here for big salads, shellfish pastas, unbelievable lamb shanks, and a long list of kabobs; wraps of freshly baked *pide,* a Turkish flat bread, are another specialty. The long and fairly priced wine list is a plus. Reservations recommended. Open Monday through Thursday 5:00 to 11:00 P.M., Friday and Saturday 11:00 A.M. to midnight, Sunday 11:00 A.M. to 10:00 P.M. Moderate.

Sette Osteria
1666 Connecticut
Avenue NW
483–3070
www.setteosteria.com
Walking into this sparkling newcomer is about as close

as you'll come to finding Italian summer on a gray day in D.C. Italian wicker chairs with bright fabric cushions, vivid Deruta tiles set in terra-cotta floors, and major ceramics from Orvieto all frame an equally cheery menu. The pizzas and pastas, along with the entrees, are mainly Southern Italian. Aside from some of the southern standards, you'll find seldom-seen dishes such as penne with bacon and pecorino and pizza with escarole, anchovies, and prosciutto. Good salads and antipasti as well. The mainly southern wine list is long, well chosen and fairly priced. The Sette Osteria Web site alone is worth a visit. Moderate.

Shaw and U Street

As soon as you see the stunning mural of Duke Ellington on the wall opposite the Lincoln Theater, you have a pretty good idea of what this neighborhood is all about. Music in general and the Duke in particular are the soul of Shaw, an area that for decades has been Washington's answer to New York's Harlem and Chicago's Bronzeville. Shaw is the traditional center of the city's black cultural, professional, and educational world in what was for many years a strictly segregated national capital. An intellectual hub as well, Shaw is the home of Howard University, founded during Reconstruction in 1867, a magnet for American black leaders and still one of our premier historically black universities.

Unique among Washington's neighborhoods, Shaw has always been black, starting in Civil War days when freed slaves began living modestly in what was then a rural setting within the District. Black professionals erected their own homes in Shaw during Reconstruction, and began to form a cultural and social legacy that made Washington the center of African-American life in the United States. One result has been that this area has some of the city's handsomest Victorian row houses and business buildings, mostly built, financed, and designed by African Americans.

Duke Ellington grew up in Shaw, at 1212 T Street in the years before World War I, when U Street was a musical mecca. During those years the clubs along U Street, Washington's elegant "Black Broadway," made the neighborhood the center of African-American cabaret and social life, especially in the 1920s and 1930s, when ragtime and cakewalk began to morph into "jass." Duke played his first gig ever on the top floor of the True Reformer's Hall at 12th and U, a building now being renovated, after which he advertised in the Washington Yellow Pages that he and his band of "colored syncopaters" were open for business.

Already in decline since the 1950s, U Street was hard hit by the 1968 riots that followed Martin Luther King Jr.'s assassination, after which the area became an urban war zone, where drug markets, crack houses, and vice of every kind flourished. Happily, Shaw is now in the midst of a vigorous recovery. Historic buildings are being restored and the neighborhood is experiencing a minor real estate boom, with new dwellings being built and historic ones being renovated by black upscale professionals, known hereabouts as "buppies." And on 14th Street, once Washington's "automobile row," plays and concerts are drawing theatergoers to a street that is slowly recovering from the trauma of 1968.

Best of all, nightlife is once again flourishing along U Street. The *Washington Post* attributes its recovery to the coming of the Metro in 1991 and a gentrification movement that has affected much of the District. Whatever the reason, U Street is back and, although you'll still want to exercise the usual nighttime caution, it's once again an area where Washingtonians go to enjoy nightlife and have a good time.

Another local community now undergoing revitalization is **Le Droit Park,** an urban enclave with a definite small-town feel and quiet streets with names like Spruce, Elm, and Larch. Its architecture is also small town, mostly 1870 vintage romantic Victorian, with styles like Queen Anne and Gothic cottage. Le Droit Park has traditionally been associated with the intellectual life of its neighbor, Howard University, and has been the home of many black leaders and

TOP ATTRACTIONS IN SHAW AND U STREET

Lincoln Theater	Logan Circle
Busboys and Poets	African-American Civil War Memorial
Mary McLeod Bethune Council House	Ben's Chili Bowl

educators, including the Reverend Jesse Jackson and the Duke himself, who lived at 420 Elm Street NW.

Le Droit Park is also the home of the ***Squished Penny Museum.*** If you're one of the thousands of people who have put pennies on the tracks to have them flattened by a train or squashed Lincoln's profile in those arcade machines all over America, you're really going to appreciate this special museum. Run by internationally renowned squishers Pete and Christine, it features a permanent exhibit of pennies they have been personally flattened at tourist attractions all across the country, including the Circus Museum in Sarasota, Florida, and the Osmond Museum in Branson, Missouri. But that's only part of their 56,000–penny collection, which goes back decades to the hobby's earliest roots. While you're there you'll probably run into one of the many Americans and foreigners who gather in this mecca of squishdom to swap stories or trade coins. You can also squish your own pennies at a machine bought from an arcade in Georgia, buy a T-shirt announcing "I'm on a Squishin' Mission," or pick up a copy of the museum's magazine, which is named, you guessed it, *The Centinel.* Pete and Christine will also make custom pennies with your personal design for use as party favors, weird calling cards, or to commemorate births and weddings. Souvenir pennies with Washington designs are also available.

thehowardtheater

One Shaw musical landmark yet to be restored and saved from decay is the Howard Theater, a sumptuous palace at Seventh and T Streets NW, which opened in 1910. This is where Ellington and other jazz greats like Jelly Roll Morton and Ella Fitzgerald performed regularly. Unfortunately, it is unrestored and falling into decay and is emphatically not open to visitors.

The museum is located at 416 T Street NW, and is open by appointment only. Call 986–5644 or e-mail petey@squished.com. The Web site is www .squished.com.

But we'll start our tour at ***Logan Circle,*** which in its Victorian heyday was one of Washington's prime residential neighborhoods, where the wealthy and famous lived in grand Victorian mansions. When the neighborhood went into a tailspin in the 1950s those ornate buildings became bordellos, crack houses, and boarding houses, but the neighborhood's recent resurgence has returned these McKinley-era beauties to their former grandeur, making Logan Circle the epicenter of some of Washington's most elegant architecture—a treasure trove of grand Victorian town houses. Its ongoing restoration and historic preservation is a classic example of how a neighborhood can be restored and revived through community cooperation. Nevertheless, visitors to this fast-changing, moderately priced, and definitely hip area will find archaeological evidence of the Circle's gritty past on its main stem, 14th Street, once the city's "automobile row," which still has a smattering of seedy liquor stores and, for some dedicated bargain shoppers, pawn shops. For more about this comeback, visit www.logancircle.org.

After taking in the grand homes that ring the Circle, head down Vermont Avenue to the **Mary McLeod Bethune Council House.** At this handsome Victorian town house just off Logan Circle, you'll find the museum and archives that preserve and interpret the life of one of the great figures in African-American history, the remarkable woman who became a friend and valued adviser on minority matters to Eleanor and Franklin Roosevelt. Before coming to Washington to advise the Roosevelts, Bethune was already a prominent political activist for black causes and an educator who founded the school that is today Florida's Bethune-Cookman College.

The ground-level parlor holds mementos of Ms. Bethune, including her grand piano and photographs of her and her colleagues in the black women's movement. In the rear a video traces the history of the movement and the close relationship Ms. Bethune established with both Roosevelts. On the same level you'll see an excellent bookstore and shop with items dedicated to African-American history. Upstairs, in Bethune's bedroom, more pictures and photographs capture the essence of a remarkable life. The house also holds extensive archives of the National Council of Negro Women, which she founded in 1935, and other documents connected with the struggle of African-American women. The Mary McLeod Bethune Council House, 1318 Vermont Avenue NW (673–2402, www.nps.gov/mamc), is open Monday through Saturday 10:00 A.M. to 4:00 P.M. Access to the archives is by appointment only; to get one, call the archivist at 673–2402. Metro: McPherson Square (orange and blue lines).

The food is better than the pun at **Thai Tanic,** where first-rate Thai cooking includes fish cakes and curried duck. The decor is ultrahip, with Formica

AUTHOR'S FAVORITES IN SHAW AND U STREET

African-American Civil War Memorial	Ben's Chili Bowl
Candida's World of Books	U-topia
Logan Circle	Florida Avenue Grill

tables and vinyl chairs straight out of Planet Eisenhower. And not an iceberg in sight. Thai Tanic, 1326 14th Street NW; 588–1795. Open 11:00 A.M. to 10:00 P.M. Monday through Friday, Saturday and Sunday noon to 10:00 P.M. Metro: McPherson Square (blue and orange lines).

At 1337 14th Street NW, **Dakota Cowgirl** is a major local hangout in a large industrial space just off Logan Circle. Big also describes the salads and the burgers, which defy description. Open daily at 11:00 A.M. to 1:00 A.M.; 232–7010. Metro: McPherson Square (blue and orange lines).

Stop by **Reincarnations,** at 1401 14th Street to see a massively eclectic mix of furniture and accessories ranging in style from classic to retro and the highly contemporary pieces from leading European and American designers. Reincarnations also offers colorful painted furniture and decorative tiles. And all at surprisingly reasonable prices. Call 319–1606 or visit www.reincarnations furnishings.com. Open Tuesday through Sunday 11:00 A.M. to 8:00 P.M.

You'll find a wealth of paintings, photographs, and sculpture by local artists at **Plan B,** the chic, spare showcase at 1530 14th Street. Check their Web site, www.planb.com, to get a schedule of their receptions, showings, and other events (234–2711). Open Wednesday through Saturday from noon to 7:00 P.M. and Sunday from 1:00 to 5:00 P.M.

The **Studio Theater,** at 1333 P Street NW, offers three stages of performances of contemporary theater. In its twenty-five years, the studio has earned a national reputation and praise in the national press for innovative, imaginative theater and, along the way, has garnered dozens of national awards. To find what's playing during your visit, call the box office at 332–3300, or drop in between 10:00 A.M. and 6:00 P.M., Monday through Friday. For a virtual visit, it's www.studiotheatre.org. Metro: U Street–Cardozo (green line).

If you're looking for a map to chart your hike across New Guinea, or some ideas for your next safari along Namibia's Skeleton Coast, **Candida's World of Books** is the place to visit—a bookstore offering one of the city's largest collections of travel guides and literature. Aside from its planet-wide selection of books, the store also has language courses, phrase books, dictionaries, and serious study guides for most languages you've ever heard of, from Tagalog to Serbo-Croat. You'll also find guides to art and architecture, international cookbooks, and guides aimed at young travelers. Candida's World of Books, at 1541 14th Street NW, is open Tuesday through Saturday from 10:00 A.M. to 10:00 P.M. and Sunday from noon to 6:00 P.M. Closed Monday (667–4811; www.candidas worldofbooks.com). Metro: U Street–Cardozo (green line).

Rice, a sleek and spare Thai restaurant at 1608 14th Street NW, serves up some of the best and totally authentic Thai dishes in town in Zen-like serenity. Favorites include shrimp dumpling soup, a variety of green and red curries,

Panang chicken, and of course, Pad Thai. All go great with the Singha beer from Bangkok. Open for lunch daily from 11:00 A.M. to 2:30 P.M. Dinners Monday through Thursday from 5:00 to 10:30 P.M.; Rice is open Friday and Saturday from 11:00 A.M. to 11:00 P.M.; 11:00 A.M. to 10:30 P.M. on Sunday. Call 234–2400 or go to www.ricerestaurant.com. Moderate.

Jazz aficionados will definitely want to think about visiting *HR57*, where open mike, straight-ahead jam sessions lure crowds every Wednesday through Saturday night. The sessions here are laid-back and impromptu, and usually feature visiting or local professional musicians. HR57, more formally known as the Center for the Preservation of Jazz and Blues is a nonprofit cultural center that takes its name from the 1987 House Resolution that designated jazz as an American treasure. And you'll hear the best of it here in this storefront jazz mecca. There's also a set dinner each night, usually fried chicken, red beans and rice, and potato salad, not to mention the ambrosial fresh lemonade. The action at HR57, 1610 14th Street NW (667–3700), starts at 8:00 P.M. on Wednesday and Thursday and 9:00 P.M. on Friday and Saturday. Admission is $8.00; the fixed-price dinner will run you another $6.00. Metro: U Street–Cardozo (green line).

For a blast from the past, drop into *Sparky's Espresso Cafe,* at 1720 14th Street NW, a neighborhood diner where you can live (or relive) the 1950s in red plastic booths. Order breakfast, specialty coffees, or sandwiches from the blackboard menu, then join the locals in reading or, in the evening, listening to poetry and, sometimes, live bands. Exhibits by local artists, too. Open Monday through Thursday 7:30 A.M. to 11:00 P.M., Friday and Saturday 7:00 A.M. to midnight and Sunday 9:00 A.M. to 10:00 P.M. Call 332–9334; www.sparkyscafe.com.

You might have a Hallmark store in your hometown, but no matter what they have in stock, it's a far cry from the assortment at *Pulp,* at 1803 14th Street. I won't do any quoting here—let's just say that Pulp is perfect if you're looking for a greeting to mark any and every, repeat every, possible occasion, romantic problem, or embarrassing social situation. In addition you can buy quirky stuff like Nico, the barista action figure, an Elvis lunchbox, Votivo candles in many scents, and dozens of refrigerator magnets, some of them quite naughty. Upstairs there's a Frida Kahlo shrine with night-lights and finger puppets honoring the great Mexican painter. Open Monday through Saturday 11:00 A.M. to 7:00 P.M., Saturday 10:00 A.M. to 7:00 P.M., Sunday 10:00 A.M. to 5:00 P.M. (462–7857; www.pulpdc.com).

The words "cool" and "hardware store" rarely appear in the same sentence, unless the writer is talking about *Home Rule.* This ultratrendy storefront is packed with nifty tools and gear to take home, including retro Italian toasters that Mussolini might have used, jazzy picture frames, and great glassware.

Home Rule, at 1807 14th Street NW, is open Monday through Saturday from 11:00 A.M. to 7:00 P.M. and Sunday noon to 5:00 P.M. (797–5544; www.home rule.com). Metro: U Street–Cardozo (green line).

Go Mama Go!, at 1809 14th Street NW, features a mega-eclectic selection of gifts, furnishings, and artwork, ranging from Tunisian glassware, Moroccan mirrors, and lots of Asian prints. Says the store's Thai-born owner Noi Chudnoff, "If it's beautiful, it belongs here." That's obvious. Don't forget to check out the Asian wrapping paper with architectural drawings by Leonardo da Vinci. Open Monday noon to 7:00 P.M., Tuesday through Saturday 11:00 A.M. to 7:00 P.M., and Sunday noon to 5:00 P.M. Call 299–0850; www.gomamago.com. Metro: U Street–Cardozo (green line).

For a look at the best in custom furniture from cutting-edge designers from California and Brazil, stop off at *Vastu,* 1829 14th Street. According to the owners, Vastu is the name of an ancient Sanskrit design school using Earth elements, colors, and textures. And that's what you'll find in the showroom— furniture and furnishings made from warm and inviting natural materials, especially gleaming woods like rosewood and teak. But Vastu also has its share of more unusual textures such as aluminum and microsuede, along with handcrafted ceramic lamps and vases. And on the walls you'll find a choice selection of art by local artists. Call 234–8344. Open 11:00 A.M. to 7:00 P.M. Tuesday through Saturday and noon to 5:00 P.M. Sunday; www.vastudc.com.

Next door, *Muleh,* at 1831 14th Street, you'll find dining tables, benches, and chairs with classic designs, most of them made from reclaimed teak and mahogany from the Philippines and Indonesia. (Muleh means "welcome" in Javanese) Muleh hours are 11:00 A.M. to 7:00 P.M. Tuesday through Saturday and noon to 5:00 P.M. Sunday (667–3440; www.muleh.com).

For a lot of local residents music and food on 14th Street mean *Cafe Saint-Ex* at number 1847, and it's easy to see why. Upstairs, it's like being back on Paris' Left Bank in a classic, well-visited brasserie of dark wood, mirrors, ceiling fans, and a serious bar. You'll spot the cafe's aviation theme as soon as you see the walls lined with stained glass images of aircraft and vintage posters of old aviation films. Despite the French feel to Cafe Saint-Ex (it's named for French aviator, war hero, and writer Antoine de Saint Exupery), the menu is the best in American bistro, with a long list of salads, chops, and pastas. Then it's back to the Latin Quarter for the wine list, where French vintages prevail, and at reasonable prices. After dinner, head downstairs to "Gate 54," what the French would call a cave—a basement room with a hangar atmosphere, where a DJ spins everything from bossa nova to classic jazz. Lots of fun and good food at moderate prices. Open Sunday 11:00 A.M. to 1:30 A.M. and Monday from

5:00 P.M. to 1:30 A.M. Tuesday through Thursday hours are 11:00 A.M. to 1:30 A.M., while Friday and Saturday Saint-Ex is open 11:00 A.M. to 2:30 A.M. Call 265–7839; http://saint-ex.com.

U street is also the epicenter of a big-time jazz scene that comes alive even on weeknights. Another scene worth exploring is the one at **Busboys and Poets,** a few steps from the intersection at 2021 U, where you'll find a multimedia restaurant set in a rumpus room stuffed with communal tables and couches. At Busboys and Poets, lunches and dinners featuring an ethnic mix of Italian, Middle Eastern, and, yes, even American dishes, including gourmet burgers, catfish with collards, and salads. Busboys and Poets also has a significant bookstore with books by noted African-American authors, including hometown poet Langston Hughes; it's also the site of frequent film screenings. Open Sunday through Thursday from 10:00 A.M. to midnight, Friday and Saturday until 2:00 A.M. (387–7638; www.busboysandpoets.com). Inexpensive.

Continuing down U street you'll wander past **Polly's Cafe,** at 1342 U Street NW (265–8385). This neighborhood favorite is cool and laid-back, with great music to listen to by the fire. The excellent bar food is another reason Polly pulls them in, with a menu that offers top-notch burgers, portobello mushroom steaks, and fried calamari. Open Monday through Friday 6:00 to 11:00 P.M., Saturday and Sunday 10:00 A.M. to 11:00 P.M. Inexpensive to moderate (265–8385; www.pollyscafe.com).

The Whitelaw, at 1839 13th Street NW, is now a sparkling 1919 Beaux Arts apartment house offering affordable housing to local residents. But until 1945 it was the only hotel in Washington open to blacks. Duke Ellington stayed there, as did Cab Calloway, Joe Louis, and many other visiting notables. During its depths in the '50s and '60s the Whitelaw was a notorious drug den and bordello that was finally closed because of its dilapidated condition, not to mention its reputation. Thanks to a combination of local funding and community pride, the Whitelaw has been beautifully restored to its former elegance. Especially striking is the graceful

Polly's Cafe

Tell Them *Off the Beaten Path* Sent You

Going to *Signal 66* is like visiting a 1920s speakeasy—walk down an alley to a nondescript door marked "926 N," where a buzzer will admit you to a former livery stable that is now one of the District's most exciting arts and communications spaces. Entering the high-ceilinged exhibit space, you might find a "warehouse party" in progress, along with shows by local and other artists in the gallery's three studios. There's a lot going on at Signal 66, including musical sessions with top local pop bands. Signal 66 is also the home of a recording studio and Web site operated by its artist-owners. Signal 66, at the rear of 926 N Street NW, is open Saturday from 1:00 to 5:00 P.M., and Friday from 6:30 to 8:30 P.M. Find out what's going on by phoning 607–3228 or going to www.signal66.com. The media production Web site operated at the gallery is www.planetvox.com. Metro: Mt. Vernon Square–Convention Center (yellow line).

dining room, with its original stained glass ceiling. Because people live there, you can't just wander around, but if you ring the bell marked *office* and ask nicely, you just might get in. It's worth it.

No doubt about it, the **Lincoln Theater** is one of Washington's hidden treasures. When it was built in 1922, the Lincoln was where African Americans could watch vaudeville shows and first-run films in a city whose theaters were strictly segregated. Duke Ellington and Count Basie also played there, in a mammoth ballroom that once stood behind the current theater. The Lincoln was for years the heart and soul of black cultural and social life, but during the 1950s it fell on hard times. Restored to its original glory in 1994, today it's one of Washington's great interior spaces, where you walk off a busy street into the gilt, architectural detail, and plush of an elegant theater of the 1920s. Call the box office at 328–6000 for details of the Lincoln's rich cultural programs, which include plays, concerts, and dance and film festivals. The Lincoln Theater, 1215 U Street NW, is across the street from the 13th Street exit of the U Street–Cardozo Metro station on the green line.

If there were a Michelin guide to Washington, you'd find **Ben's Chili Bowl,** at 1213 U, marked with the red symbols that mean "restaurant of habitues," i.e., all the smart locals hang out there because it's so great. Ben's building was once the Minnehaha Theater, in its day one of the best, which advertised "clean vaudeville" acts. But since 1958 Ben's has been a gathering place for everyone in black Washington, from night workers to students at nearby Howard University to Bill Cosby, who's been coming here for years for the chili half smokes. And you might, as I did, spot Michael Jordan folded into one of Ben's booths. Ben's atmosphere probably resembles those places you knew in the '50s—Formica lunch counters with stools, shiny red plastic chairs, and food served right from the grill. Ben's dishes will also take you back to all those pre-cholesterol days, with dishes like half smokes or Kosher hot dogs doused with spicy chili, not to mention breakfasts highlighted by eggs and scrapple or sausages, or hot cakes with grits or home fries. Funky music too. It's wonderful! Be still my heart (note to my cardiologist: just kidding!). Ben's Chili Bowl, 1213 U Street NW (667–0909; www.benschilibowl.com), is open Monday through Thursday 6:00 A.M. to 2:00 A.M., Friday and Saturday 7:00 A.M. to 4:00 A.M., Sunday noon to 8:00 P.M. Reservations—are you kidding? Inexpensive. Metro: Shaw–Howard U (green line).

One of the great finds during the preparation of this guide was *The Islander,* a modest storefront at 1201 U Street specializing in Caribbean cookery, with a friendly atmosphere just as relaxed as the islands themselves. The dishes show the islands' African/East Indian roots. Start off with callaloo (a spinach-okra mix) or plantain, then shift into high gear with the excellent calypso chicken with a mild red sauce, roti, a curried wrap with Indian overtones, or a curried shrimp or goat accompanied by peleau (fried chickpeas and rice) and a bottle of Trinidadian beer. The Islander is open Tuesday through Thursday noon to 11:00 P.M., until midnight. Friday and Saturday, and Sunday 1:00 to 11:00 P.M. Live jazz Saturday and Sunday nights. Metro: U Street–Cardozo (green line). Call 234–4955.

The second floor auditorium in the recently restored *True Reformers Hall* at 1200 U Street is where Duke played some of his earliest gigs. The hall isn't open to the public, but the *African-American Civil War Museum* on the building's ground floor has interesting exhibits of memorabilia, including photographs, maps, and uniforms that show vividly the contributions that African-American troops made to the Union cause. The museum's

African-American Civil War Memorial

founder/director, Frank Smith, will be glad to answer your questions and tell you about special walking tours of this historic neighborhood. Call 667–2667; www.afro amcivilwar.org. Open Monday through Friday 10:00 A.M. to 5:00 P.M. and Saturday 10:00 A.M. to 2:00 P.M. Metro: U Street–Cardozo (green line).

At 1005 U Street you'll find *Oohhs and Aahhs,* arguably D.C.'s top soul kitchen, where the chef-owners serve up the macaroni and cheese, corn bread, and fried chicken you remember from your youth (or wish you did). Open for lunch and dinner Tuesday through Saturday, until 11:00 P.M. on Friday and Saturday; 667–7142. Inexpensive.

At the intersection of U Street and Vermont Avenue, the ***African-American Civil War Memorial,*** one of Washington's newest national memorials, honors the 210,000 black troops who fought with the "U.S. Colored Troops" during the Civil War. The names of those soldiers are inscribed on this open-air memorial's polished metal tablets and are guarded by a statue, *Spirit of Freedom,* depicting a group of African-Americans who fought in the Union Army. The names of the soldiers are listed by regiment, one of which is the famous 53rd Massachusetts, which fought with distinction at the battles of Forts Pillow and Wagner under a white colonel, Robert Shaw (for whom this area is named); their bravery was dramatized in the film *Glory.* The memorial is located at the entrance to the U Street–Cardozo Metro at Tenth and U Streets NW.

The ***Black Fashion Museum*** is dedicated to the contributions that African Americans have made to fashion and design. This century-old row house highlights Elizabeth Keckley, a former slave who designed Mary Lincoln's dresses and was also her personal confidante; a copy of a Keckley design for Mrs. Lincoln is a major attraction. Another important exhibit honors an already famous Ann Lowe, who in 1953 designed Jackie Kennedy's wedding gown. The Black Fashion Museum, 2007 Vermont Avenue NW, is open only by appointment. To get one, call 667–0744 or e-mail bfmdc@aol.com. Web site: www.bfmdc.org. Metro: U Street–Cardozo (green line).

At 14th and U Streets, a left turn will take you to ***Simply Home,*** at 1412 U, where you can combine two of life's greatest pleasures—shopping and dining. The shopping part is a boutique of Thai housewares, handsome furniture, and vibrant silks in rich textures and colors. Next door Simply Home Cuisine offers classic Thai meals that include an assortment of curries, garden and spring rolls, and many tofu-based dishes. The store is open daily from 9:00 A.M. to 11:00 P.M. (986–8607) while from Sunday to Thursday the restaurant hours are 10:30 A.M. to 9:00 P.M. Open until 10:00 P.M. Friday and Saturday (234–8424; www.simplyhomedc.com).

Coppi's, at 1414 U Street NW is just the place for terrific pizza, including some varieties you've probably never seen. Coppi's also features Ligurian spe-

cialties such as pesto with scallops and stuffed sardines. Call 319–7773. Open
Monday through Thursday from 6:00 to 11:00 P.M., Friday and Saturday 5:00 P.M.
to midnight, and Sunday 5:00 to 11:00 P.M. Inexpensive. Metro: U Street–Cardozo
(green line).

The utterly funky **U-topia,** at 1418 U Street, is one of the area's most popular and laid-back restaurants, with a good selection of bar food and light fare
with a Cajun touch. U-topia's Sunday brunch from noon to 4:00 P.M. is, to say
the least, abundant, provided you make it through the potent $1.00 mimosas
and Bloody Marys. No reservations. Open Sunday through Thursday 11:00 A.M.
to 11:30 P.M., Friday and Saturday 11:30 A.M. to 1:00 A.M., and Sunday 11:00 A.M.
to 11:30 P.M. U-topia also offers significant jazz action nightly (483–7669;
www.utopiandc.com). Metro: U Street–Cardozo (green line).

At 1428 U Street you'll find **Good Wood,** which offers an eclectic collection of nineteenth-century American antiques from local auctions, including
stand-up desks, fireplaces, and even a church window or two. Local decora-
tors report terrific finds. Open Thursday 5:00 to 9:00 P.M., Friday and Saturday
11:00 A.M. to 7:00 P.M., and Sunday 11:00 A.M. to 5:00 P.M. Call them at
986–3640 or take a look at www.goodwooddc.com. Metro: U Street–Cardozo
(green line).

If you're following a no-nonsense, high-carbohydrate diet or ready to
indulge your sweet tooth, **Cakelove,** at 1506 U Street NW, is definitely for you.
From the sidewalk you can inhale the chocolate, butter, and sugar aromas (only
1,000 calories per breath), then peer in and watch owner/baker (and former
lawyer) Warren Brown making cakes, cookies, and his terrifyingly rich chocolate cupcake, all from scratch. Call 588–7100; www.cakelove.com. Open Monday through Friday 8:00 A.M. to 7:00 P.M., Saturday 10:00 A.M. to 5:00 P.M., Sunday
11:00 A.M. to 4:00 P.M. Metro: U Street–Cardozo (green line).

Across the street at 1501 U, Warren Brown has opened the **Love Café,**
with a breakfast menu of French toast and frittatas, luncheon sandwiches and
salads, and, of course, great desserts and pastries from Cakelove; 265–9800.
Love Café hours are: Monday through Friday 8:00 A.M. to 11:00 P.M., Saturday
9:00 A.M. to 11:00 P.M., and Sunday 10:00 A.M. to 10:00 P.M..

Although 1600 Pennsylvania is the nation's best-known address, the por-
tion of **16th Street** that transits the Shaw-U Street neighborhood is well worth
a leisurely stroll. Once a premier residential area, 16th Street fell on hard times
and neglect for decades. Now, however, 16th Street is definitely back—once
again a good address, as its historic buildings, superb mansions, and stately
embassies return to their Victorian Age splendor. If you go, the best Metro stations to use are either Dupont Circle, on the red line for the lower stretch of
16th or, as you approach Meridian Hill, U Street/Cardozo on the green line.

Start your walk at the *Jewish Community Center,* at 1529 16th Street NW, one of the District's top, but less well known, cultural assets. The JCC's auditorium is the home of Theater J, one of Washington's most original theater companies, and a showcase for young and talented actors and playwrights. JCC also sponsors a Jewish Music Festival, and programs of book talks and discussions by noted Jewish writers along with occasional art exhibits. For a full picture of the JCC's nonstop activities, check out www.dcjcc.org or phone 518–9400.

The center also operates the *JCC Cafe,* where you'll find homemade soups and a full roster of tasty salads, sandwiches, and entrees. Their phone number is 387–3246; www.jcccafe.com. Open Sunday through Thursday 11:00 A.M. to 8:00 P.M. Reservations essential. Next to the cafe is the JCC's *Judaica Gift and Bookstore,* with jewelry, books, gifts, and toys for the kids. Open Monday through Thursday 1:00 to 5:00 P.M. and 6:00 to 9:00 P.M., Sunday noon to 8:00 P.M. The entrance for both the gift shop and the cafe is around the corner on R Street. Metro: Dupont Circle (red line).

At the end of the nineteenth century a number of religious groups decided to establish their Washington "embassies" by building prestigious "national" churches in the nation's capital, many of them along 16th Street.

The most obvious, in every way, is the staggering *National Temple of the Scottish Rite* at 1733 16th Street NW, which was modeled after the temple of King Mausolos at Halicarnassos, one of the seven wonders of the ancient world. Out in front of this behemoth are two massive sphinxes (one representing "power" and the other "wisdom") that lend an even more pharaonic air to this incredible building. The temple is the headquarters of the Scottish Rite, an ancient order of Freemasonry that stresses education and community service.

You can tour the temple weekdays from 8:00 A.M. to 3:30 P.M. and the first Saturday of every month from 10:30 A.M. to 3:00 P.M. Your tour will take you first through the 200,000 volume library on freemasonry, then to a series of sumptuous meeting rooms and ceremonial chambers, all gleaming with rare woods, intricate mosaics, and marble pillars. You won't forget it. Call 232–3579; www.srmason-sj.org. Metro: Dupont Circle (red line) and take the Q Street exit.

Not far from the temple is a much less imposing national church. The *Church of the Holy City* at 1611 16th Street NW, is the National Swedenborgian church. Peer into this charming English Gothic structure and you'll be rewarded with a wonderful series of stained glass windows illustrating the Bible story (462–6734; www.holycitydc.org). Metro: Dupont Circle (red line).

At the corner of 16th and U Streets, you'll see the grand *Balfour Apartments,* built in 1901 as one of the city's first luxury apartment houses. The style

National Temple of the Scottish Rite

is imposing and typical of the period, from its majestic Beaux Arts exterior to the red and gold stone lobby and a grand staircase. Now a condominium, the Balfour is not open to the public. Metro: Dupont Circle (red line).

Further up 16th Street you'll arrive at *Meridian Hill;* the name comes from the zero meridian of the United States, which Thomas Jefferson placed along 16th Street: A boundary stone to that effect once stood at the corner of Florida and 16th. In the nineteenth century its high ground and panoramic views made Meridian Hill an enclave of the wealthy and helped turn 16th Street into the city's earlier embassy row. A number of embassies remain there, but many more have left because of security concerns. Meridian Hill's decline, however, seems to have halted and in recent years the area has begun to revive and regentrify.

Two of the neighborhood's great homes remain and attract visitors; both are owned by the Meridian International Center, a nonprofit educational and cultural institution that seeks to promote international understanding through exchanges of people, ideas, and the arts. The center also sponsors a wide-ranging program of briefings, lectures, and other programs on global issues.

The thirty-room *Meridian House,* just off 16th Street at 1630 Crescent Place NW, was built in 1920 by steel heir and career diplomat Irwin Laughlin. Shortly after it was completed, the house was called "one of the finest examples of architecture in the French style in America." Meridian House is open to the public, but because of its busy schedule of meetings and other events, it's best to phone ahead to 939–5568 to arrange your visit. If you go, you'll explore the glorious rooms of an urban French château with a dramatic entrance foyer, followed by a dining room with a seventeenth-century tapestry and elegant drawing room and reception gallery. You'll also stroll through French doors into a lovely terraced garden shaded by a grove of linden trees.

Meridian House's next door neighbor, the **White-Meyer House**, was built in 1911 for Henry White, a former Ambassador to France, but was occupied from 1929 until 1971 by Eugene Meyer, the publisher of the *Washington Post*. The grand rooms of the White-Meyer House now host a series of internationally oriented art and cultural exhibits on a rotating basis; check the *Post's* Weekend magazine for the latest schedule. The White-Meyer House, at 1630 Crescent Place NW, is usually open Wednesday through Sunday from 2:00 to 5:00 P.M., but since it hosts a number of special events, it's a good idea to call ahead; the number is 667–6800. The Web site for both Meridian and White-Meyer House is www.meridian.org.

Meridian Hill Park, at 16th and W Streets, across from the two mansions, is both part of the National Park system and a neighborhood park that may remind you of Rome's Borghese Gardens or Villa Medici. Because of its terraces and dramatic water cascade with thirteen pools, experts call this Renaissance villa park a masterpiece of landscape architecture. A walk around the park will reveal some interesting statuary, including the only known statue of, and monument to, President James Buchanan, called by some "America's worst president." Joan of Arc also rides again on Meridian Hill, while another statue depicts Dante, the Italian Renaissance writer, holding his *Divine Comedy*; just the place for reading poetry, if you brought any along. Aside from its unusual collection of statues, Meridian Hill Park is also an agreeable place where local families take their kids during the day, but avoid after sunset. So should you.

Walking uphill along 16th Street from Meridian Hill Park, you'll find gathered the ghosts of embassies past in Washington's former embassy row, the creation of Mary Foote Henderson, the wealthy and influential widow of Senator John B. Henderson of Missouri. In the early twentieth century, Mary, a grande dame of Washington society and certainly no shrinking violet, single-handedly turned this stretch of 16th Street and parts of Meridian Hill into an exclusive neighborhood of mansions, which she built and rented to society figures and foreign governments. The ambitious Mary also wanted a new White House built there, but obviously she failed. She did, however, succeed in getting Congress to designate (briefly) "her" 16th Street as the "Avenue of Presidents." Mary herself lived in Henderson's Castle, a now-demolished redbrick pile at the corner of Florida and 16th, a spot now occupied by the Beekman Place condominiums. However, you can still see the castle's walls and turreted gates.

For some years Mary's mansions had fallen on hard times, but now many are being brought back to life. You'll find one of them at 2600 16th Street, at the four-story Venetian Gothic building known locally as the **Pink Palace**. No doge ever lived here and there aren't many gondoliers paddling outside on

16th Street, but this 1906 palazzo has been home to a series of the rich and/or famous, including Mrs. Marshall Field of Chicago and several cabinet members. It is now the headquarters of the *Inter-American Defense Board.*

For more examples of 16th Street's glory days as Embassy Row, check out the former *Cuban Embassy* at 2630 16th (now part of the Swiss Embassy) the French–influenced *Polish Embassy* (2640 16th) and the charming *Lithuanian Embassy* at 2622 16th, with its elaborate stone doorway and windows. The grand rooms of the Polish Embassy are sometimes opened for cultural events; to find out when they're scheduled go to www.poland embassy.org/culture or phone 234–3800. In a class of its own is the former *Italian Embassy* at 2700 16th, now vacant, but a wonderful example of an Italian Renaissance mansion.

One of the best examples is the *Mexican Cultural Institute* at 2829 16th Street, which was built in 1910 for President Taft's treasury secretary as a surprise gift from his wife. Today, the big surprise in this luxurious mansion is one of Washington's most graceful and dramatic staircases, along which unfurls a vibrant, four-story mural of Mexican history by artist Roberto Cueva del Rio. Once upstairs visitors enter a grand, turn-of-the-century mansion with a sunny, blue-tiled conservatory with a fountain and a delightful music room. The institute is open weekdays from 10:00 A.M. to 6:30 P.M. The institute sponsors a comprehensive program of cultural presentations that showcase Mexican art, music, and, dance. For information about their programs, call 728–1628 or check out www.sre.gob.mx/imw.

Places to Stay in Shaw and U Street

Akwaaba
1708 16th Street NW
332–4100
(866) 466–3855
www.akwaaba.com/
washington_dc
Akwaaba means "welcome" in Ghana, but it also clearly applies to guests of this African-American–themed literary bed-and-breakfast.

Aside from its rooms named for prominent black writers and poets, a visit to Akwaaba, with its original tiled fireplaces, stained glass windows, and spacious, high-ceilinged rooms, will warp you back to Victorian times, when this grand townhouse was built. All of Akwaaba's eight guest rooms are handsomely appointed and well stocked with volumes of African-American history, literature, and poetry. But if you're looking for big, sunny front rooms with bay windows and

Jacuzzi tubs, ask for the Langston Hughes or Zora Neale Hurston suites. Moderate. Metro: Dupont Circle (red line).

The Embassy Inn
1627 16th Street NW
234–7800
www.windsorembassyinns.com
The Embassy is an economical find located near the Dupont Circle and Adams Morgan neighborhoods and an easy walk or bus ride from downtown. This former apartment house has thirty-

eight cheerful rooms and a European feel that includes a continental breakfast to help you start your days out there on the unbeaten path. Metro: Dupont Circle (red line).

Hotel Helix
1430 Rhode Island Avenue NW
462–9001
www. hotelfelix.com
Talk about trendy! This Hollywood-themed boutique hotel fits right in to the resurgent Logan Circle neighborhood. Your stay will begin at one of the "check-in pods," and continue in one of the Helix's 218 ultra-edgy rooms and suites. Later, down in the Helix Lounge, which manages to be both hot and cool, pull up an ottoman, order up a pastel-colored drink, and (if you're very lucky) you'll be able to check out the starlets. Metro: Dupont Circle (red line).

Shipman House Bed and Breakfast
1310 Q Street NW
328–3510
www.aaronshipmanhouse .com
This 1887 Victorian home has been nicely converted into a bed-and-breakfast that

has received national press attention for its restoration and elegant features. The house abounds in period touches like stained glass windows and grand fireplaces, not to mention its luxurious paneled rooms and garden with fountains. The Shipman House has six guest rooms that will take you straight back to those never-to-be-forgotten days of Grover Cleveland and Rutherford B. Hayes. For longer stays there's also a self-contained apartment. Inexpensive. Metro: U Street–Cardozo (green line).

The Windsor Inn
1842 16th Street NW
667–0300
www.windsorembassyinns .com
The Windsor, built in 1913, is now on the National Register of Historic Places, in part because of its art deco lobby with mosaics and tiles from its early days as a luxury apartment house. The Windsor's forty-six rooms are nicely furnished and the rates are reasonable. You'll also like the neighborhood of handsome Victorian town houses and mansions. Metro: Dupont Circle (red line).

Places to Eat in Shaw and U Street

Ben's Chili Bowl
1213 U Street NW
667–0909
See pages 192–93 for full description.

Busboys and Poets
2021 U Street NW
387–7638
www.busboysandpoets.com
See page 191 for full description.

Cafe Saint-Ex
1847 14th Street NW
265–7839
See pages 190–91 for full description.

Coppi's
1414 U Street NW
319–7773
See pages 194–95 for full description.

Dakota Cowgirl
1337 14th Street NW
232–7010
See page 188 for full description.

AUTHOR'S FAVORITE PLACES TO EAT IN SHAW AND U STREET

Rice

Logan Tavern

Ben's Chili Bowl

Coppi's

Cakelove

Cafe Saint-Ex

Florida Avenue Grill
1100 Florida Avenue NW
265–1586
This classic, counter-and-stools (plus a few booths) neighborhood grill is lined with photos of the political and showbiz leaders who have dined in this Washington institution on "Southern-style food." It's easy to see why. Breakfasts are big here, with possibilities that range from hotcakes to omelets and sides of scrapple, spicy half smokes, grits with red-eye gravy, or all of the above. Lunch or dinner might be tasty barbecue, pork chops, or real southern fried chicken like the Colonel doesn't make. Open Tuesday through Friday 8:00 A.M. to 9:00 P.M., Saturday 6:00 A.M. to 9:00 P.M. Inexpensive. Metro: U Street–Cardozo (green line).

JCC Cafe
1529 16th Street NW
387–3246
See page 196 for full description.

Local 16
1602 U Street NW
265–2828
www.localsixteen.com
No, this converted town house isn't a union hall, but takes its name from nearby 16th Street. Local 16 is actually three establishments in one. The pre-dinner drink scene is lively, followed by dinner time and a straightforward menu tat ranges from burgers to nicely done grilled fish and risottos. But well before midnight the bar scene returns with a vengeance in the upstairs lounge and on the outdoor

deck, especially on Friday and Saturday nights, when the bar is open until 3:00 A.M. and DJs hold forth. Dinner is served from 5:30 until 1100 P.M. Moderate. Metro: U Street–Cardozo (green line).

Logan Tavern
1423 P Street
332–3710
www.logantavern.com
This lively bistro just oozes energy and panache. The dining room is open, with a large wooden community table in the center and old photos of the neighborhood on the walls. The food at Logan is mainly of the "American Comfort" variety—pastas, meatloaf, large salads, and grilled fish; judging from the number of locals that flock there, those chefs in the back must know what they're doing. Logan Tavern is open Monday through Thursday from 5:00 to 11:00 P.M., Friday noon to midnight, Saturday 11:00 A.M. to 4:00 P.M. and 5:00 to 11 P.M., Sunday 11:00 A.M. to 11:00 P.M. Brunch served Saturday and Sunday from 11:00 A.M. to 4:00 P.M.

Love Café
1501 U Street NW
265–9800
www.cakelove.com
See page 195 for full description.

Mar de Plata
1410 14th Street NW
234–2679
Hot and cold tapas like seafood salad, grilled sausage, and fried pork with cassava are the specialties in this bright and cheerful

Spanish storefront. You can make a meal of the tapas or forge ahead to second courses like paella, carne guisada (Spanish for a tasty beef stew), and grilled salmon. A good selection of Spanish wines and sherries plus service that makes you feel that *estas en tu casa*. Open Monday through Thursday noon to 3:00 P.M. and 4:00 to 11:00 P.M., and Friday to Sunday noon to 3:00 P.M. and 4:00 P.M. to midnight. Moderate. Metro: U Street–Cardozo (green line).

Oohhs and Aahhs
1005 U Street NW
667–7142
See page 194 for full description.

Polly's Cafe
1342 U Street NW
265–8385
See page 191 for full description.

Rice
1608 14th Street NW
234–1400
See pages 188–89 for full description.

The Saloon
1205 U Street NW
462–2640
Located in a nicely restored 1890s vintage building, the Saloon's menu is strictly all-American, with burgers, sandwiches, and grills, but the beer list is international and includes suds from fifteen countries. The Saloon is open Tuesday through Saturday 5:00 P.M. to 1:00 A.M. Inexpensive. Metro: U Street–Cardozo (green line).

Simply Home
1412 U Sreet NW
234–8424
www.simplyhomedc.com.
See page 194 for full
description.

Sparky's Espresso Cafe
1720 14th Street NW
332–9334
See page 189 for full
description.

Thai Tanic
1326 14th Street NW
588–1795
See pages 187–88 for full
description.

U-topia
1418 U Street NW
483–7669
See page 195 for full
description.

Indexes

Entries for Restaurants, Lodgings, Children's Sites, African-American Sites, Jewish Sites, Lincoln Sites, House Museums, and Sculptures, Statues, and Memorials appear in the special indexes beginning on page 211.

GENERAL INDEX

LODGINGS

CHILDREN'S SITES

SCULPTURE, STATUES, AND MEMORIALS

About the Author

William B. Whitman is a former diplomat who spent most of his career in Yugoslavia and in Italy, where he started writing about travel and food. He now lives in Washington, D.C. and writes for major magazines, including *Capitol File, National Geographic Traveler, Hemispheres,* and *Forbes-FYI.* Bill is the author of *The Quotable Politician,* a choice collection of quotations by famous politicians about politics, foreign affairs, and political life in general, published by Lyons Press. Bill has also written two other books, *Literary Cities of Italy,* which takes readers to the literary landmarks of Rome, Florence, and Venice, and *Wines of Virginia,* a comprehensive guide to Virginia's wines and wineries.